D0773325

DREAM BABIES

◆CHRISTINA◆
HARDYMENT

DREAM BABIES

*Three Centuries
of Good Advice on Child Care*

HARPER & ROW, PUBLISHERS, New York
Cambridge, Philadelphia, San Francisco, London,
Mexico City, São Paulo, Sydney

1817

FIRST U.S. EDITION

Library of Congress Cataloging in Publication Data

Hardyment, Christina.
    Dream babies.

    Bibliography: p.
    Includes index.
    1. Child rearing—History.   I. Title.
HQ769.H2834 1983   649'.1'09   83-47532
ISBN 0-06-015195-1

83 84 85 86 87 10 9 8 7 6 5 4 3 2 1

To Matilda, Daisy, Ellen and Susanna

Contents

Contents

Illustrations

Plates

ix

Illustrations

Figures

Preface

It is common practice today for parents to consult a book when a baby is born. Mothers expect, or get willy-nilly, information from books, magazines, radio and television on how to feed, wash, lull and discipline their children. They rarely trust their own experience, rarely offer their advice to other mothers, and exist in a perpetual state of anxiety as the debate between the experts surges to and fro, overturning 'misconceptions', offering 'new insights' and contradicting everything once sacred to baby's granny.

Much of the information packed into today's manuals is useful, most of the writers are humane, sympathetic people who genuinely believe that they help their readers to bring up better babies, or at least to bring up babies better. They can even see their own flaws:

> Too much is written for the new mother. Most of the literature is aimed at giving her advice. Very little of it offers her support for her own individual reactions and intuitions. Baby books tell her how to become the perfect mother. Eminent authorities intellectualize the process of becoming a mother ... She finds that many of her instinctual reactions are frowned upon by one authority or another. The literature that was designed to support her becomes an undermining influence. (Brazelton, *Infants and Mothers*)

The mother who would prefer to bring up her own children rather than the dream children of the experts has two defences. One is reflected in the newest trend in baby-care books—the collection of shared experiences, such as Ann Oakley's *From Here to Maternity*, or the Boston Women's Collective's *Ourselves and Our Children*. Hearing about other parents' experiences is a comfort, it gives a feeling of togetherness. It has a tyranny of its own, however, since there

xi

are usually very definite, if not explicit, assumptions in such books. To Ann Oakley, hospitals are threats; for the Bostonians, children are sacred cows. Inexorably, one is made part of a self-conscious peer group, a live specimen pinned under the microscope of articulate sociologists, watching oneself being a mother.

The second defence, and the aim of this book, is to counter the barrage of information with information of a different kind. If we can understand why baby-care manuals were first written, and how they came to exceed their original brief, then we can confine them to their proper province. If it can be made clear that, while babies and mothers remain constants, advice on the former to the latter veers with the winds of social, philosophical and psychological change, then we can see the advice in the books we use today as a temporary crutch, not eternal verity. Moreover, a little history reveals how misconceptions of Freud, and maxims from Truby King, still nag at us through the muddled memories of our mothers, and it enables us to put grandmother's advice into a much-needed perspective. The history of baby-care books is no substitute for a modern book of baby-care—but it is an essential antidote.

Defensiveness is not the only function of this book. It also has the straight historical purpose of describing how people thought babies should be brought up, from the eighteenth century to the present day. I don't claim that this is how people actually brought up their children: a comparison of the Newsoms' *Infant Care in an Urban Community* with the current edition of Spock would be enough to discourage one from any such assumption. Again, in the historical context, this book aims to be an antidote, rather than a substitute. Too much reliance seems to me to have been put on the extreme and the extraordinary in our picture of past parenthood. Eccentric upper-class Englishmen or fanatical Massachusetts Puritans dominate the scene. It is at least possible that many parents practised what popular theorists of their day preached.

I found that the pattern which emerged from the manuals was surprising, not at all consistent with the images of heavy father/remote and neglectful mother so often vaguely projected over eighteenth- and nineteenth-century nurseries. Mrs Gaskell's contemporaries could hardly have been more maternally attentive. The Child Study Movement at the turn of this century showed that permissiveness and baby worship were not late twentieth-century prerogatives. The 1920s were officially more repressive than any nineteenth-century decade. To some extent it seemed possible to argue that a strictly brought-up generation turned to its children with determined gentleness, and conversely the indulged child grew up to berate its offspring into submission. But generally wider swings in mood—new philosophies, economic depression or imperial affluence, the threat of war—had the most profound effects.

It seemed right to take up the thread of advice on baby-care in the middle of the eighteenth century, because it was then that medical and philosophical events led a significant number of people to write books on the subject. Earlier manuals survive, usually in Latin, and intended for doctors rather than mothers to refer to. The significance of the eighteenth century was that books began to be addressed to 'intelligent Parents as well as the medical World' (Underwood, *Treatise on Diseases of Children*, 1789), and to be written in English. To set the scene the manuals sought to change, a sketch is given of how the early eighteenth-century baby was cared for. Although on crucial matters like feeding, a continuous story can be followed, it would have been tedious to detail at every point how babies were to be dressed, or dosed. Sometimes it was interesting, sometimes it wasn't—so I have concentrated on such issues when they mattered most.

I wrote that babies and mothers remained constants. There isn't space in this book to give the evidence for this—the voices of the mothers revealing their hopes and doubts, and the children reminiscing about their childhoods. Hester Thrale, Elizabeth Gaskell, Millicent Shinn, Rosalie Watson and many others, have left minutely detailed accounts of their babies' lives which make it clear that there are as many ways of bringing up children at any one time as there are mothers and babies. Some are blindly loving, and criticized by their contemporaries for it, equally others are censured for their unnecessary severity. Child-care experts show the same variety of personality. Regardless of the time at which they are writing, they can be classified as cuddly or astringent—lap theorists or iron men (or maidens). The latter claim that things are now disgracefully lax, the former that fifty years ago child-care was appallingly strict. In this sense, Penelope Leach has more in common with Lydia Sigourney, 'sweet singer of Hertford' in the 1830s, than with her contemporaries, Ronald and Cynthia Illingworth. Hugh Jolly should look to Samuel Smiles for a kindred spirit rather than to Benjamin Spock. Knowing that personal opinion affects interpretation in baby-care books is an important defence for parents. They have less need to be anxious about their own views if the 'experts' are recognized to be subjective.

What right men have to talk about bringing up babies at all is a question which feminists have asked, and it arises from the moment that the first of the experts, William Cadogan, crowed the triumph of 'Men of Sense' over ignorant women. Men dominated the medical profession, and intruded into midwifery; the composed advice of seventeenth-century midwives had no eighteenth-century parallel. Locke and Rousseau felt that their voices should be heard on practical matters like breast-feeding, as well as on the moral side of management. They were healthily balanced by writers like Hannah More, Mrs Trimmer and Maria Edgeworth. In the nineteenth century, women writers continued to hold their own, confident in their experience and common sense, although they had to bow to male medical expertise. The scientific approach at the end of the nineteenth century was dominated by men, who pushed women into a subservient place, describing them as fitted to do no more than record incidents in their child's life which the father, the 'scientific educator', could analyse. Ellen Key's trumpet call for a 'Renaissance of Motherhood' died away in face of the implacable masculinity of Truby King's 'mothercraft'. But women kept writing—Mrs Frankenburg, Selma Fraiberg and Penelope Leach maintained the relevance of their own maternal experience allied to physical and psychological science.

Although the relative influence of men and women as baby-care experts has a superficial interest, I didn't find that it was as important as the wider issues which governed thinking, or as critical as the personality type of the writer, regardless of his or her sex. I would far rather read Brazelton than Edith Buxbaum; femininity is no guarantee of maternal tenderness. Babies have fathers as well as mothers; perhaps some of the most satisfying and well-balanced books have been written by husband/wife partnerships.

Inevitably the baby-care manuals, particularly pre-1950s manuals, show considerable upper- and middle-class bias. They were written by and for the comfortably off, for people who could afford to sit back and consider how their children ought to grow up. Manuals written for the working class often revealed, as I show, an insufferably superior attitude, telling them to bring up their children along rather different lines to those felt suitable for 'intelligent parents'. Nevertheless, the ideas put forward by the baby-care experts were inescapably the common intellectual currency of their day, and interesting for all their limitations. What is perhaps most startling to the modern reader of these neglected authorities is how often they anticipate or improve upon the most modern thinkers. Harriet Martineau could have told John Bowlby about attachment and loss; Andrew Combe was as conscious of early influences as Benjamin Spock. The old approaches can even suggest some new possibilities—I have tried some of them out on my own four small daughters, and they work. We still read Jane Austen or Henry James with profit. Baby-care manuals by their contemporaries—James Nelson or Marion Harland, for example—retain a wit and immediacy which the modern parent can enjoy. Reading about the vintage volumes of baby-care will, I hope, encourage parents to approach modern books in the spirit of connoisseurs, to sample them and select what they feel fits in with their own feelings towards their children. We need information, not prescriptions, from the professionals. Telling mothers and fathers how to bring up their children in books is arguably as silly as sending false teeth through the post and hoping that they will fit.

July 1982   C.H.

Acknowledgments

Working at home in the gaps left by children and housework is a problem all mothers are familiar with. My first debts are to the libraries which have generous borrowing regulations, Cambridge University Library and the London Library. The British Library is a splendid final arbiter, and the staff in all three have been most helpful as they blew the dust from hundreds of unopened volumes of outdated baby-care. I would also like to thank the friends who read and offered useful criticism of the book in all its forms: Pat Cutforth, Elizabeth Crawford, Gillian Crampton Smith, Phil Tabor and Helen Sanford. Dr Anne M. Young shared her specialized knowledge of domestic medicine chests. Liz Calder and Liz Cowen at Jonathan Cape, and Gill Coleridge at Anthony Sheil, shepherded me into professionalism in the nicest possible way, and Nicola Beauman gave the whole project a decisive first push. Barbara Collins has helped me to look after our four children for more than five years now, and without her infallible and good-natured support I could never have extracted three 'writing mornings' a week from the muddle of family life. Tom Griffith has advised, reassured, and supported me more than I believed a husband could.

Credits

For permission to reproduce photographs the author and publishers are grateful to the following: George Allen & Unwin for the second table on p. 185 from *Infant Care in an Urban Community* by J. and E. Newsom, 1963; Appleton-Century-Crofts for the opening to Chapter 4 from *Growing Super Children* by I. Newton Kugelmass, 1935; BBC Hulton Picture Library for nos 8, 11, 18 and 24; Bettmann Archive, New York, for the opening to Chapter 1; Jonathan Cape for no. 36 from *Teach Your Baby Maths* by Glenn Doman, 1979; Dr Peter Carter's private collection for no. 7; Churchill Livingstone for no. 31 from *Care of Young Babies* by John Gibbens, 1940 and Figure 1 from *Mothercraft Manual* by Mabel Liddiard, 1924; Mary Evans Picture Library for nos 1, 2, 6, 10, 12 and 21; Faber & Faber Ltd for nos 27 and 28 from *Enjoy Your Baby* by E. Elias, 1934; Harper & Row for no. 35 from *Infancy: World of the Newborn* by Martin Richards, 1980; Posy Simmonds for the opening to Chapter 5; Sotheby's for nos 14 and 16; Victoria and Albert Museum for no. 15; John R. Young, B.A., Vet. M.B. for no. 5.

The other pictures in the book are from the following sources: no. 9 from *American Advertising Posters of the Nineteenth Century* by Mary Black, Dover Publications, 1977; no. 22 and the opening to Chapter 3 from 'Imperialism and Motherhood', *History Workshop*, 5, by Anna Davin, Spring 1978; no. 20 from 'American Feeding Bottles' by T. G. Drake, *Journal of the History of Medicine*, 1948; no. 13 from *My Little Boy* by Carl Ewald, Methuen, 1908; no. 3 from *Female Instructor and Young Wife's Companion*, Fisher, 1811; no. 33 from *Good Housekeeping's Mothercraft*, Waverley, 1959; no. 30 from *Prams, Mailcarts and Bassinets* by Jack Hampshire, Midas, 1980; no. 25 from *Natural Feeding of Infants* by F. Truby King, 1918; no. 32 from *Mothercraft* by Mary Truby King, Whitcombe and Tombs, 1934; Figure 2 from *Hygiene of Women and Children* by Janet E. Lane-Clayson, Oxford Medical Publications, 1929; no. 23 from *The Montessori Method* by Maria Montessori, Stokes, 1912; no. 26 from *The Motherhood Book*, Amalgamated Press, 1934; no. 17 from *Practical Guide to the English Kindergarten* by Johann and Bertha Ronge, Swann-Sonnenschein, 1873; no. 4 from *Infant Feeding by Artificial Means*, by S. H. Sadler, Scientific Press, 1896; no. 29 from *The Family Book* by Gwen St Aubyn, Barker, 1935; no. 34 and Figure 3 from *Commonsense book of Baby and Child Care* by Dr Benjamin Spock, Duell Sloan, 1946. No. 19 and the opening to Chapter 2 are from the author's own collection.

1
Nature and Reason
1750–1820

The Unenlightened Baby

At the beginning of the eighteenth century, the typical baby was helped into the world by a self-taught midwife, licked with the 'basting tongue', or scoured with salt to remove the 'slippery glue' from its skin, and tightly swaddled on to a board. Its head was wrapped in 'compresses three, four, or five times doubled', pinned to a cap, and further braced by a tight neck stay. Swaddling was thought to prevent it distorting its supposedly fragile bones by kicking about too much. It also kept babies warm in a draughty age, and was a convenience. While the half-strangled baby hung from a nail, its minder could get on with other tasks. Swaddling slowed down a baby's heartbeat, and encouraged extreme passivity— more sleep, less crying; a swaddled baby made no demands on the adult world around it. The bulk of the bandages meant that the 'stinks and sournesses' of babyhood could be largely ignored. This was not altogether due to inertia. 'There is an odd Notion enough entertained about change,' wrote one puzzled eighteenth-century doctor. 'Some imagine that clean Linnen and fresh cloths draw and rob them of their nourishing Juices' (Cadogan, *Essay on Nursing*).

The baby would not be put to the breast until the mother's milk was seen to come in, perhaps on the second or third day. Meanwhile, purges were applied 'to cleanse the child of its long-hoarded Excrement'. Oil of almonds, syrup of roses and chicory with rhubarb were accepted recipes. Continental practice, then as now, was more extreme—senna, rochelle salts, castor oil or an enema. A strengthening glass of wine (oatmeal and whisky in Scotland) was often given, and sometimes more positive nourishment too: 'oil, panada, caudle, or some such unwholesome mess'. Meanwhile, the mother's breast might be drawn by the nurse, or by an older baby, to prevent the discomfort of full breasts before baby and breast struck up their balance of demand and supply. If the baby had difficulty sucking, the midwife would nick through the thin filament of skin beneath the tongue with a fingernail kept long and sharp for the purpose. Any sign of milk in the baby's own nipples led to their being vigorously squeezed, a practice which could have caused permanent damage to the breasts.

Failure to breast-feed generally led to the adoption of a wet-nurse. Animal milks were distrusted, and bringing up by hand on pap or panada was 'a lottery in which there are a hundred blanks for one prize'. Ettmuller described the flour and water mixture often given as 'a viscous and crude paste more proper to binders to bind their books than for the nourishment of infants'. Was it convenience or incapacity that led many upper- and middle-class women to send their children 'out to nurse'? Tight corseting cannot have encouraged healthy breasts, and a Parisian surgeon declared to Benjamin Franklin a little later in the century that 'the women of Paris could not give suck: "Car", dit-il, "elles n'ont point de tétons." He assured me that it was a fact, and bade me look at them and observe how flat they were on the Breast; they have nothing more there, said he, than I have on the back of my hand.' Frequent pregnancies left many mothers physically feeble, and complications following child-birth affected their ability to nurse. They had an alternative in wet-nursing which poorer classes did not have, and which saved the lives of babies who would otherwise have died.

Nevertheless, sheer self-interest was quoted by many authorities as the reason for sending babies out of the house. *Paedotrophia*, a didactic poem on infant management (written in Latin by Scevole de Sainte Marthe in 1585) hinted at this.

> But you, perhaps, by other cares beguiled,
> Wish, to the nurse's home to move the child;
> Because by his continued cries at home,
> Your sleeps are broken and your joys o'ercome.

This French attitude was echoed by Aphra Behn a hundred years later. In *Ten Pleasures of Marriage* she satirized the parent who handed a child over to a wet-nurse so that 'both you and your wife are freed from tossing and tumbling with it in the night'. Galen's belief that 'carnal copulation troubleth the blood, and so by consequence the milk' may have encouraged husbands to post off their newborns (maybe this is what Laius had in mind when he ditched Oedipus). Even in 1792, when maternal nursing had come back into fashion, Mary Wollstonecraft could write: 'There are many husbands so devoid of sense and parental affection that, during the first effervescence of voluptuous fondness, they refuse to let their wives suckle their children.'

That fashion or incapacity, rather than lack of affection for the child, led to wet-nursing is suggested by the care taken in selecting a nurse. Sainte Marthe's advice summons up a vision of delight:

> Chuse one of middle age, nor old nor young,
> Nor plump nor slim her make, but firm and strong,
> Upon her cheek let health refulgent glow
> In vivid colours, that good humour show;
> Long be her arms, and broad her ample chest;
> Her neck be finely turned and full her breast:
> Let the twin hills be white as mountain snow,
> Their swelling veins with circling juices flow;
> Each in a well-projecting nipple end,
> And milk in copious streams from these descend:
> This the delighted babe will instant chuse,
> And he knows best what quantity to use.

Care was the more necessary since it was believed that with its milk the child drank in its foster-nurse's characteristics. James I's wife, Queen Anne, asked rhetorically: 'Would I let my child, the child of a king, suck the milk of a servant, and mingle the royal blood with the blood of a servant?' The *Nurse's Guide* put down Caligula's drunkenness and Tiberius's cruelty to vices drawn from their wet-nurses. Thomas Muffet's *Health's Improvement* (1584) found conclusive proof of the theory in the effect of different nurses' temperaments on the senile Dr Caius: 'What made Dr Caius in his last sickness so peevish and so full of frets at Cambridge, when he suck't one woman (whom I spare the name) froward of conditions and bad of diet, and contrariwise so quiet and well when he suckt another of contrary dispositions?' Quillet's *Callipaediae* exhorted mothers to breast-feed their own children, warning them in heroic couplets of the dangers of promiscuous nurses: 'Who draws the flaggy breasts of wanton Dames/Shall base Desires imbibe, and burn with guilty Flames.' There may have been practical truth in this, since syphilis was rife—transferred by handling and cleaning, however, rather than imbibed from the nipple. Certainly an epidemic of syphilis among wet-nurses in St Malo later in the century led local mothers to feed their own children.

Feeding was the most critical concern in infant care. One doctor estimated that nine out of ten infant deaths were due to the mismanagement of feeding. Although this must have been an exaggeration at a time when smallpox, whooping cough and viral fevers took a substantial toll, it reflected the fact that something had gone seriously wrong with feeding techniques. From the number of recipes for milkless, starch-based paps and panadas offered by seventeenth- and early eighteenth-century doctors, and the savage criticism of these foods by later writers, it seems possible that too much confidence was being placed in such mixtures as alternatives, rather than merely as supplements to breast-milk. Certainly not enough fruit and vegetables were given to small children—such food was regarded as acid and indigestible. The many deaths ascribed to teething were more probably caused by vitamin C deficiency leading to infantile scurvy. Scurvy has all the symptoms popularly ascribed to teething by early eighteenth-century doctors such as Arbuthnot, 'irritation of the tender nervous parts of the jaw, occasioning inflammation, fevers, convulsions, gangrene, etc.'.

Babies were clearly so uncomfortable that nothing short of constant motion could keep them quiet. Well-to-do families had an under-nurse simply called the Rocker. Brouzet's 1755 manual offered four pages of advice on cradle rocking. However, there were few other material accessories for babies, a reflection of the way they were hurried into adulthood.

Swaddling clothes were succeeded by cumbersome minia-ture versions of adult dress, under which savagely constricting stays were worn. Crawling was disapproved of, partly because of the filth liable to be found on floors, partly because it hinted at the baser, animal side of man's nature. Go-carts were used: little frames in which children half-stood, half-sat, sometimes with wheels like modern baby-walkers. Little Gerard Anne Evans was painted by Hogarth holding a doll set in a toy version.

Just as the eighteenth-century baby had a stomach stoked with unsuitable food, so its head was stuffed with unsuitable knowledge. The attainments of a prodigy like Queenie Thrale at two years old were remarkable.

> She repeats the Pater Noster, the three Christian virtues, and the signs of the Zodiac in Watts' verses; she likewise knows them on the globe perfectly well . . . She knows her nine figures and the simplest combinations of them; but none beyond a hundred; she knows all the Heathen Deities by their Attributes and counts to 20 without missing one. (Hester Thrale, *Family Book*, 1764)

Or do we underestimate our two year olds?

There was no children's literature until the middle years of the century, when Jack of Newbury's bright little woodcut books began to appear. Letters would be learnt by rote from a hornbook, and words picked out from the family Bible. The child would then move on to a book like Comenius's *Orbis Sensualium Pictus*, first published in 1658, and still in use in schools in 1845. As books go, it was an excellent one, depicting everything under the sun, and keying Latin and French vocabulary to every object illustrated. It introduced the child to the adult world, but made no concessions to the under-fives. Babies were sent to school, but to be minded by a dame rather than taught.

Most advice on disciplining small children before the eighteenth century was written by Puritans, which has led to a misleading emphasis on their theories by modern historians. The most important fact to be borne in mind about infancy at this time is that nearly half the babies born died before they were five years old, most of them before their first birthday. This led to a mood of resignation among parents, which

7

should not be misread as uncaringness. In 1594 Sainte Marthe wrote:

> Of all the misfortunes incident to humanity, none is so distressing to a feeling mind as the death of children. It is an affliction which preys upon the mind and increases with time. The longer time the sufferer has to reflect upon his loss, the more he thinks what his son, or daughter, might have been . . . It is the only evil in life for which nature has not provided a remedy.

Unless the family was a Puritan one, the reaction to the appallingly high infant mortality rate was as likely to be an indulgent attitude to small children as a repressive one. The Puritans were clearly arguing against such indulgence in their tracts, pleading for a rapid saving of a potentially damned soul before the child died. Earle's *Micro-cosmographie* (1628) and Locke's *Essay Concerning Human Understanding* (1690) disagreed with Pechey's Puritan assumption that 'Iniquity is co-natural to infants.' Instead they saw the infant mind as a blank tablet upon which the parents could inscribe what they willed. But only when enough small children survived to make early education worthwhile would parents take up this idea with enthusiasm. Until then, the Puritans made themselves most loudly heard, because to them it was essential that sin should be eradicated as soon after birth as possible. Crying was an expression of anger, and to 'nip this animosity in the bud' required the discipline of the rod. 'Break their will betimes,' commanded the terrifying John Hersey, a New England minister.

> Begin the work before they can run, before they can speak plainly or speak at all. Whatever pains it costs, conquer their stubbornness; break their wills if you will not damn the child. Therefore let a child from a year old be taught to fear the rod and cry softly. Make him do as he is bid if you whip him ten times running to do it; let none persuade you that it is cruel to do this. (Quoted by de Mause.)

I don't think it makes sense to take passages like this, ally them with cases of pigs gorging themselves on swaddled babies in provincial France, and conclude, as some historians do, that the general approach of parents to children in the bad old days was an infanticidal one. Many of the instances that are accepted as evidence of general practice were only recorded because they were exceptional cases—it is as if one used the records of today's NSPCC as evidence of modern child-care practice. The countless records of loving parents from Genesis onwards are ignored in favour of the sensational. Moreover, if Puritans were more extreme disciplinarians than their contemporaries, they were in general more careful of their babies over such matters as breast-feeding and maternal care. Wet-nurses were disapproved of, and the importance of breast-feeding was reflected when John Cotton used it as an analogy to imbibing the Scriptures in *Spiritual Milk for Boston Babies in either England, Drawn out of the Breasts of both Testaments for their Souls' Nourishment* (1646). The real grief felt by a parent who lost thirteen of his fifteen children is evident if one reads Cotton Mather's diary, as well as his Puritan tracts. In an epidemic of measles, he lost his wife, a maid and two daughters with agonizing resignation, but the death of a third, little Jerusha, was almost too much to bear:

> Betwixt 9h and 10h at Night, my lovely Jerusha Expired. She was two years and about seven months old . . . I begg'd, I begg'd, that such a bitter Cup, as the Death of that lovely child, might pass from me . . .
>
> Just before she died, she asked me to pray with her; which I did with distressed, but resigning Soul; and I gave her up unto the Lord. The Minute she died, she said, That she would go to Jesus Christ . . . Lord I am oppressed; undertake for me. (Quoted by Wisley.)

It was clearly a great comfort to Mather that a $2\frac{1}{2}$-year-old child could pray with him on her deathbed. The Puritans valued their children more rather than less highly than their contemporaries—their attentions, if severe by the standards of the Spock age, were essentially loving.

Foundling Fathers

Today's baby-care manuals are the unrecognizably swollen descendants of terse little booklets written by enlightened doctors for the use of nurses in foundling hospitals. Their original brief was the fundamental one of the infant's physical survival. 'It is with great Pleasure I see at last the Preservation of Children become the Care of Men of Sense. In my opinion, this Business has been too long fatally left to the management of Women, who cannot be supposed to have a proper Knowledge to fit them for the Task, notwithstanding they look upon it to be their own Province.' The opening words of William Cadogan's *Essay on Nursing* (1748) placed him firmly in the line of men who felt they knew more about babies than women. The line, although occasionally weakening, stretches unbroken to the present day, when one can read that it is 'taken for granted' that the new mother 'will have the advice of experts, and will not have to rely on the advice of her own mother. The previous generation of mothers may not be the best advisers of the present generation'. Here Dr Jolly is merely echoing Hugh Downman:

> Hence, ye doating train
> Of Midwives and of Nurses ignorant!
> Old Beldames grey, in error positive
> And stiff in prejudice. (*Infancy*)

William Cadogan was a new-style doctor. His generation had broken away from the old humoural medicine with its seasoning of astrology. Harvey's work on the circulation of the blood, the use of the microscope, morbid anatomy, and diagnosis based on observation—clinical medicine—were all elements of what amounted to a medical revolution in the seventeenth and eighteenth centuries. Doctors were beginning to understand life, although they could not necessarily save it. Paediatrics, a notoriously difficult branch of medicine, limped along in the shadow of obstetrics until improvements in delivery techniques provoked new interest in the product. Cadogan qualified in 1737, became an army physician for a while, and then settled in private practice in Bristol. His own

10

inclination, helped by the birth of a daughter in 1746, led him into paediatrics, because he was asked to contribute an essay for the use of nurses in the London Foundling Hospital.

The foundling hospital movement was the first large-scale practical attempt to do something about the appalling infant mortality rate of the mid-eighteenth century. The first hospital was opened by Thomas Coram in 1741, in response to the infant corpses and deserted babies that littered the streets of London. By 1753 over a hundred infants a day were being offered to the hospital, and there was some criticism of the encouragement it gave to 'the progress of vulgar Amours/The breeding of Rogues and th'increasing of Whores' (Pelagius). Nevertheless, the government supported the movement with funds in 1756. Initially, gathering babies into hospitals decreased, rather than increased, their chances of survival. Some two-thirds of the 15,000 babies brought to Coram's hospital between 1756 and 1761 died, due to 'the profuse waste and imperfect workmanship of nature' (Cadogan).

This defeatist attitude rapidly went out of fashion. The opportunity for mass observation of children which the foundling hospitals provided encouraged doctors to experiment with food, clothes, and daily management. The conclusions which they wrote down for the benefit of their staff were quickly recognized as of general interest, and published for the family market. Yorkshireman William Buchan gained enough experience at Ackworth Foundling Hospital to write *Domestic Medicine*, published at six shillings in 1769. It was an immediate success, running through eighteen editions in the author's lifetime. It was published all over Europe, in America, and was even translated into Russian. The Empress Catherine sent Buchan a gold medal and a commendatory letter, which might have done a little to console him for having sold the original copyright outright to the publishers. Buchan wrote two briefer books later on, *Offices and Duties of a Mother* (1800) and *Advice to Mothers* (1803). They were chattier and more avuncular in tone, with less fact and more opinion: a step towards the popularizing manuals which had to be written as medical practice went beyond the understanding of the lay mind.

11

The rise of foundling hospitals increased interest in the provision made for babies left to the care of the parish. Parish overseers were supposed to track down the fathers of foundlings and fine them ten pounds. Even if they succeeded, only a fraction of this money ever reached the foster-nurse, who therefore had little incentive to keep the child alive. 'Excellent killing nurses' were noted in one particularly parsimonious parish's records. In *Earnest Appeal for Mercy to the Children of the Poor*, Jonas Hanway estimated that only one in seventy of such children survived. Shocking exposures such as Hanway's were reinforced by the enormous public concern at the publication of the London Bills of Mortality. Cadogan wrote an essay in the *Gentleman's Magazine* in 1765 on causes of mortality in the under-twos, 'in answer to Queries in the Public Press concerning the causes of the Great Mortality of Infants in this metropolis'. The Bills revealed that 60 per cent of children baptized died before they were two. Nor was it a prerogative of the poor to die young. Doctors claimed that middle- and upper-class urban families were just as likely to lose children. Cities were becoming less and less suitable places to bring children up in. The more houses, the worse the quality of fresh food, water and milk. An Act of Parliament in 1767 even attempted to evacuate the infant poor to the country.

Improved obstetrics must have reduced perinatal mortality considerably. Male midwives (midhusbands?) like Michael Underwood extended their concern for the well-being of babies to the management of their infancy. Underwood was attached to the British Lying-in Hospital in London, where he attended the Princess of Wales at the birth of Princess Charlotte, Prinny's only legitimate child. His *Treatise on the Diseases of Children* (1789) was a more general work than the title suggested. It had three volumes, one on diseases, one on surgery and one on the general management of infants. By 1848 there had been ten English editions, four American, one French and one German. Significantly, it was addressed to 'intelligent Parents, as well as the medical world', and its aim was to get rid of the 'wild prejudices and anile prescriptions of the old writers' by returning 'to the simplicity of nature and the result of dispassionate observation'. Less brisk and more discursive than Cadogan or Buchan, Underwood always had time to consider the baby's own feelings. Approaching infant care through midwifery may have created profounder sympathies than general medicine supplied.

Apothecaries also had their contribution to make to theories about rearing children. They formed a cheap alternative to more professional medicine, but were increasingly criticized by doctors proper. Undoubtedly many were unscrupulous in their prescription of quack potions, but James Nelson was one of the exceptions. The father of seven children, he practised in London's Red Lion Square, and defended his profession with some fervour. Since apothecaries were cheaper to consult than physicians, he pointed out that they were more likely to see patients before their symptoms became too acute, and so often had a better chance of curing them. Nelson's *Essay on the Government of Children* (1753) was the first all-round book on the subject, dealing with health, manners and education of children from birth to about the age of twenty, and all 420 pages are gripping reading. 'The Love of our Children is a great ruling Principle in Human Nature,' he declared. Unfortunately, parental ignorance too often left children inadequately guided in the earliest years, and they became 'unruly to a Degree of Pity . . . Slaves to themselves and Plagues to all about them'. His theme was that strict discipline in later childhood would be unnecessary if the first years were properly managed by 'rational and natural methods'.

Another apothecary, George Armstrong, had a more practical approach to baby-care, although he did write a brief and useful *Account of the Diseases most Incident to Children* (1767), for parents as well as doctors. He disliked the idea of taking children away from their parents, and hoped to make it unnecessary by opening a dispensary for the children of the infant poor, defraying most of its expenses from his own pocket. He treated 35,000 children there, so that they had no need to go to the children's hospitals. 'If you take a sick Child from its Parent or Nurse, you break its Heart immediately,' he warned, anticipating Bowlby's *Child Care and the Growth of Love* by two hundred years. He lost his battle. The dispensary was closed down after twelve years for lack of funds, and sick children were again committed to the isolation of hospitals.

The medical men began to feel that simplification and lightness of touch were appropriate to the books they hoped mothers and nurses rather than their colleagues would read. William Moss, another obstetric surgeon, designed his *Essay on the Management of Children* (1781) 'for domestic use, purposely adapted for Female Comprehension, in a manner perfectly consistent with the Delicacy of the Sex'. He added technical footnotes in small print for 'medical readers'. Hugh Smith was positively flirtatious in his *Letters to Married Women* (6th edn, 1792), and made it clear that he felt their fluffy little heads would be unable to take much serious detail. 'Believe it not,' he wheedled, 'when it is insinuated that your bosoms are less charming for having a dear little cherub at your breast.'

Improving the infant's chance of survival was only half of the eighteenth-century story. The philosophy of the Enlightenment had set up a new man, subject only to ascertainable natural laws, and distinguished from brute beasts by the searchlight of the power of reason. Locke and Hume studied the human mind with scientific objectivity. God retreated. Free will advanced. Finally the child, a creature *sui generis*, with rights and privileges of its own, jumped through the pages of Jean Jacques Rousseau's *Emile* (1762) to the centre of a stage that it has dominated ever since. The relation of the medical advances to the popularization of Locke's and Rousseau's theories of education was reciprocal. Buchan, Nelson and other doctors specifically referred to Locke and Rousseau when they wrote; their whole cast of thought was moulded around the twin concepts of Nature and Reason. But if improved obstetrics, enlightened infant care, and the reduction of diseases such as smallpox had not slashed the infant mortality rate, parents would have been less interested in reading about how the philosophers thought they should handle their children.

Locke's *Some Thoughts Concerning Education*, published in 1693, contained a good deal of advice on dealing with small babies, as well as the better-known descants on the education of young men. The pursuit of reason which he advocated governed both the manual writers' approach to early education and their testing of existing practices in child-rearing. Buchan admired Locke deeply, remarking on 'the extraordinary precision of his manner of reasoning on any topic'. Locke was evidently read by mothers—the *Ladies' Library* popularized Locke's ideas, albeit anonymously, in a pamphlet which ran through eight editions between 1714 and 1772.

Locke, who had no children of his own, was occasionally accused of being unrealistic. Brouzet criticized him for 'opinion not built on observation, and having in it more of the metaphysician than the physician'. The opinion in question was a scheme of Locke's to preserve the child's freedom of will by preventing it from forming the habit of eating at the same time every day, and so being subject to its stomach's demands. James Nelson warned that 'Mr Locke, amidst great good sense, has some notions a little rigorous'—he disagreed with Locke's theory that children should be dressed in very light clothes and shoes, so that they would learn to bear wet feet and bodies with equanimity. Locke also felt that beds should be both hard and varied, so that a child could learn to sleep easily anywhere. He didn't go so far as to recommend icy baths, although he remarked that it was commonplace in Germany, Ireland and among 'ladies in the Highlands of Scotland' to do so. The reaction to his suggestion of cold baths is an interesting revelation of the tenderness then current among mothers: 'How fond Mothers are likely to receive this Doctrine is not hard to foresee. What can it be less, than to murder their tender Babes, to use them thus? What! Put their feet in cold water in frost and snow when all one can do is to keep them warm?' The real interest which Locke held for the eighteenth century was not in these rather erratic details, but in the theory of mind which lay behind them.

Locke declared that the differences between men were due to their education more than anything else, so that 'great care is to be had of the forming of Children's Minds, and giving them seasoning early, which shall influence their lives always hereafter'. Very small children were not susceptible to reason, and should be taught by 'fear and awe'. Later esteem

15

and disgrace could replace the commoner rewards and punishments of sweetmeats and beatings. Again and again Locke told parents that they must quell their instinctive love for their children in the interests of writing the right character on their minds: 'Parents being wisely ordained by Nature to love their children, are very apt, if Reason not watch their natural Affection very warily, are apt, I say, to let it run into Fondness.'

The remarkable popularity of Rousseau's *Emile*, a gripping account of how Rousseau would have educated an imaginary boy, was due to its call to the wild, its apotheosis of Nature. The Stuarts had been replaced by democracy in 1688, the cracks in the *ancien régime* in France were widening, and in America a brave new world was open for those with the enterprise to explore it. As enlightened men threw off the accretions of the old perverted society, they looked to primitive tribes, even to animals, for relevant analogies. The major reference work of the day was the Comte de Buffon's *Natural History*, which was published in Paris from 1749 onwards. Its forty-four quarto volumes, beautifully illustrated, were the first comprehensive collection of current knowledge about the natural sciences. Rousseau quoted from Buffon when he encouraged mothers to leave their babies free to kick on the floor, rather than swaddling them:

> The ancient Peruvians wrapped their children in loose swaddling bands, leaving the arms quite free. Later they placed them unswaddled in a hole in the ground, so that the lower part of the body was in the hole, and their arms were free, and they could move the head and bend the body at will without hurting themselves.

Buchan repeated the quotation in *Advice to Mothers*, adding an analogy with animals: 'The instinct of brutes is an unerring guide in whatever regards the preservation of animal life. Do they employ any artificial means to mould the limbs of their young?' Again, when urging mothers to breast-feed, he pointed out how animals, 'obedient in everything to the impulse of nature, nurse their offspring . . . Not only the inhabitants of the howling wilderness, the she-wolf and the

16

fell tigress, but even the monsters of the great deep, draw out the breast and give suck to their young'. A whole chapter of his book was devoted to contrasting the health and strength of 'those nations that approach nearest a state of nature' with the 'dwarfishness and deformity of civilized nations'.

Hugh Downman, whose didactic poem *Infancy* had run through several editions by 1809, was similarly impressed by the primitive:

> The savage still her clinging babe sustains,
> Some, this communicated warmth affirm
> Is needful, and that Man's else-drooping Race
> Requires the general contact.

This sounds surprisingly like a recognition of infant marasmus, the wasting-away of neglected babies which was not officially identified until the 1930s. Like Armstrong's perception of the sick child's need for its parent, it was an insight lost on the increasingly blinkered generations that followed.

Cadogan declared his aim of introducing 'a more reasonable, more natural method of nursing' on the first page of *Essay on Nursing*, and repeatedly referred to 'unerring Nature'. Health and posterity were the reward of the labouring poor, 'whose want of superfluity confines them within the limits of Nature'. Dressed in rags, and necessarily breast-fed, their children contrasted in health, strength and independence with 'the puny insect, the heir and hope of a rich family, who lies languishing under a load of finery that overpowers his limbs, abhorring and rejecting the dainties he is crammed with, until he dies a victim to the mistaken care and tenderness of his fond mother'. Locke's fond parents seem to have been converted into Cadogan's fond mother. Cadogan attacked swaddling—'as if Nature, exact Nature, had produced her chief work, a human creature, so carelessly unfinished, as to want those idle aids to make it perfect'. Feeding too should be a natural process. Breast-milk

> is poured forth from an exuberant overflowing Urn, by a bountiful hand, that never provides sparingly. The Call of Nature should be waited for to feed it with anything more

17

substantial, and the Appetite ever precede the Food ...
Thus far Nature, if she be not interrupted, will do the
whole business perfectly well; and there seems to be
nothing left for a Nurse to do, but to keep the child sweet
and clean, and to tumble and toss it about a good deal, play
with it, and keep it in good Humour.

Rousseau's *Emile* was probably the most widely read child-
rearing manual of its age, and was qualitatively different from
the medical handbooks. Although it included a good deal of
advice on the minutiae of baby-care, it was the fruit of theory,
not of dispassionate observation. Rousseau's mother died
shortly after his birth, and his father deserted him. He
returned the compliment by leaving his own five illegitimate
children to the tender mercies of a foundling hospital. His
dream children were born free, natural and innocent, but
'from birth you are always checking them, your first gifts are
fetters your first treatment torture'. Doctors could support
his pleas to abolish swaddling clothes (already accomplished
in England), to breast-feed, to allow the infant freedom to
kick about and play in easy, unrestricting clothes. They were
less enthusiastic about his distrust of physicians ('the only
useful part of medicine is the hygiene') or his careless
acceptance of infant death:

Fix your eyes on Nature, follow the path traced by her. She
keeps children at work, she hardens them by all sorts of
difficulties, she soon teaches them the meaning of pain and
grief. They cut their teeth and are feverish, sharp colics
bring on convulsions, they are choked by fits of coughing or
troubled by worms, evil humours corrupt the blood, germs
of various kinds ferment in it ... One half of the children
who are born die before their eighth year ... This is
nature's law; why try to contradict it? ... Experience shows
that children delicately nurtured are more likely to die.
Accustom them therefore to the hardships they will have to
face ... Dip them into the waters of the Styx.

The theory that children required hardening was borrowed
from Locke, or from the literature of ancient Greece and

Rome, studied with renewed enthusiasm in a self-consciously democratic age. It did not imply the brutality of corporal punishment. Both Locke and Rousseau preferred to establish good behaviour on the pains and pleasures principle: even small babies could be quickly brought to associate certain actions with inevitable consequences. Hardening meant light clothes, uncertain mealtimes, freedom to have accidents and cold baths. Occasionally it was carried too far—blanket-tossing to strengthen frail nerves, or firing pistols near the head to promote endurance. Rousseau believed that from two to twelve years children should be free to play as they wished in natural surroundings. They were to have no academic training; all their actions had to spring from necessity rather than obedience. The supreme good was freedom.

Rousseaumania swept England in the late eighteenth century. Educational novels in the style of *Emile* were two a penny. His appeal to sensibility and nature came at a time when the shades of cities were closing fast over the hitherto unappreciated countryside. Blake, Wordsworth and the painters who saluted the 'picturesque' reflected the fight against industrial engulfment. Unfortunately, parents and educators rapidly became disillusioned by their experiments with nobly savage children. Richard Lovell Edgeworth's boy became so unmanageable that he was sent away to boarding school. David Williams described one little child of nature who, aged thirteen, slept on the floor, spoke 'a jargon he had formed out of the several dialects of the family', could neither read nor write, and was 'a little emaciated figure, his countenance betraying marks of premature decay, or depraved passions; his teeth discoloured, his hearing almost gone'. But a legacy remained. Most of the manuals, medical or moral, echoed Rousseau on the importance of following Nature's way—they just tidied him up to fit society.

The Child of Nature and Reason

So how, in conclusion, would the first baby experts have liked small children to be brought up? Preferably by their mothers, or with her close supervision.

In Rome's majestic days, long fleeted by,
Did not her mighty dames sing lullaby?
No mean-bred hags then nursed the guiltless child,
No kitchen slang its innocence despoiled.
'Twas deemed a glory that the babe should rest
In slumbering beauty on the MOTHER'S breast.
But *England's* mighty dam is too GENTEEL
To nurse and guard and like a mother feel.

(James Montgomery, quoted by Buchan, *Domestic Medicine*)

Montgomery's history was inaccurate—Roman women were every bit as likely to have wet-nurses as English dams, but he reflected the campaign for breast-feeding which had spread so far through fashionable society that Underwood could write in 1784: 'in this country there is no ground for a general complaint on this head'. Breast-feeding no longer turned husbands off; Brouzet confided that he had not avoided lying with his wife at these times, yet their children had been well suckled. Women might even enjoy it, according to Buchan: 'The thrilling sensations that accompany the act of giving suck can be conceived only by those who have felt them, while the mental raptures of a fond mother at such moments are far beyond the powers of description or fancy.'

There was some dispute over the timing of feeds. Buchan thought that the child should be given freely 'what nature freely produces'. Demand feeding was clearly indicated in *Paedotrophia*:

No fix'd hour prescribe,
This Nature teaches best the nursing tribe,
Let her your mistress be, and when with cries
The hungry child demands his due supplies,
Forbear not you the wish'd for relief to bring,
But for his use unlock the sacred spring.

Naturally, children in foundling hospitals would be fed on a more routine basis, and Cadogan suggested four feeds a day, decreasing to two or three after three months. One drawback to the application of hospital practice to the home was that it could reduce care to the minimum necessary. However, for the moment the domestic ideal prevailed—reason was tempered by nature. Cadogan was no Truby King.

The cutting of teeth 'gives a sort of hint of the use to which they may be applied', wrote Buchan, and mixed feeding could wait until they arrived. Paps and panadas should be avoided. Carefully selected cow's milk was a better food for infants if breast-feeding was not possible. The safest method was direct feeding from the udder of a goat or ass. Alphonse LeRoy described his success at the foundling hospital at Aix in 1775: 'Each goat which comes to feed enters bleating and goes to hunt the infant which has been given to it, pushes back the covering with its horns and straddles the crib to give suck to the infant. Since that time they have raised very large numbers in that hospital' (quoted by Wickes, *Infant Feeding*). Suitable first foods were barley gruel, veal broth with rice boiled in it, or rusks soaked in scalded cow's milk.

Teething remained a problem, the subject of a whole chapter in most of the manuals. Only Cadogan dismissed it as 'a natural process', and significantly the diet he prescribed for the children at his hospital was unusually rich in fruit and vegetables. Buchan's cure for teething started with a gentle purge, then bleeding, then a few drops of hartshorn or laudanum. 'In obstinate cases' the gums were lanced. This could be done with a fingernail, the edge of a sixpenny piece worn thin, or any sharp body, but 'a lancet in a skilful hand is certainly the most proper'. The *Female Instructor* had a gruesome anecdote about a chubby nine month old who went into a decline for six months. At last his teeth were lanced and sixteen were 'sprung from his gums'. The child expressed immediate relief, 'took notice and ate vigorously', but died the next morning. The moral—lance gums promptly.

Medicinally, babies were badly off. Rousseau was probably right in dismissing doctors' attentions and in general the fewer the drugs prescribed the safer the child. Apart from drugs, the main cure-alls of the physicians were bleedings,

21

emetics and the all-purpose purge. Leeches were recommended to cure convulsions, measles and teething. Spring and autumn purges were as regular as house-cleanings. Laxatives were also thought to be useful for teething, worms and as a preliminary to smallpox inoculation.

Smallpox was a major scourge in the eighteenth century, and one of the few success stories of medical practice was use of first inoculation and later vaccination to bring it under control. Inoculation was introduced into the country by Lady Mary Wortley Montagu, who had been so impressed by its use in Constantinople that she had had her own children inoculated. She persuaded the Princess of Wales to have the royal children treated, but not before the Princess had taken the precaution of asking George I to pardon six Newgate criminals under sentence of death if they would undergo the operation first. The criminals survived, and so did the royal children. Although inoculation fluctuated in popularity—its drawback was that the lightly inoculated subject could infect anyone around him—it was recommended by Cadogan, Buchan and others as safer than risking uncontrolled infection. In 1798 Jenner introduced the much safer vaccination.

The abandonment of swaddling clothes led to the adoption of 'rational dress' for infants. A loose flannel waistcoat, a petticoat, and a light and flimsy gown only a trifle longer than the baby, was Cadogan's suggestion, 'laying aside all those swathes, bandages, stays and contrivances'. He resigned himself to children wearing 'more genteel and fashionable dress' at the age of three, although he regretted the inevitable stays that would have to be adopted to procure the 'sugarloaf shape'. Laced stays gave way to bandages at the end of the eighteenth century. Buchan wrote, 'we no longer see the once familiar spectacle of a mother laying her daughter down upon a carpet, then putting her foot on the girl's back and breaking half a dozen laces to give her a slender waist. Instead, 'diagonal bandages, or ribands, fastened across the breast and shoulders with straining violence ... cause an unnatural prominence before, frightful indentation behind, and a weary stiffness in the motions of the pinioned limbs'. Empire-style clothes were a little kinder to small girls, but boys had to suffer the stiff tightness of 'hussar dress', aping the military obsessions of the Napoleonic age. Shoes, according to Buchan, could be left off entirely at first, but when they were adopted they were to be shaped to the foot, and not changed from one foot to the other in order to make them wear evenly. Dispensing with swaddling clothes meant that more attention had to be paid to cleanliness. Cadogan thought babies couldn't be changed too often, by which he meant at least once a day. Buchan reflected that long clothes too often served to disguise a dirty cloth, and the *Complete Servant* recommended clean cloths morning and evening. Mrs Parkes, whose *Domestic Duties* (1825) was one of the earliest and best books by a woman on the subject of baby-care, allowed for six dozen in a layette. There was no mention of over-zealous potty training. Locke was one of the very few who mentioned the subject at all, and he was clearly talking about a child old enough to be told to 'go to stool' every morning. He announced the idea of a regular visit at the same time of day as a novelty, but there is seventeenth-century evidence from France that when Louis XIII was a child his training began at eighteen months, and was completed by the time he was three. Silence on the subject of excretion has been interpreted by some psycho-historians as an indication of unhealthy repressions, and the frequent use of purges as good indirect evidence of severe toilet training, since this produces constipation. I am not convinced by this. The standard starchy diet was equally likely to cause constipation, and the silence on the matter need mean no more than the silence on wiping noses, or clearing up dribbles or vomit. With the abandonment of swaddling clothes, it seems likely that nurses would try to save themselves labour by catching what they could. By the late nineteenth century this was to become a fine art.

Dipping in the waters of the Styx was not the inevitable fate of eighteenth-century babies, although several manuals saw cold baths as a desirable goal to be achieved. For the first few weeks the bath was to be tepid. By slow degrees the water could get colder, until the child was enjoying its freezing dip. The baby was to be watched for signs of languor, and the baths discontinued in that case. 'Lively singing' was to accompany the experience, so the idea of pleasure would become associated with bathing. Underwood stood out against cold dips altogether: 'To see a little infant . . . washed up to breast and loins in cold water, exposed for several minutes, perhaps in the middle of winter itself, in one continued scream, and the fond mother covering her ears under the bedclothes that she might not be distressed by its cries, has ever struck me as a piece of unnecessary severity.'

'The cry of an infant should never be disregarded,' warned Mrs Parkes. 'It is Nature's voice.' She analysed the different types of cry: short and wrangling was due to hunger, continued and long-drawn-out meant a pain of some sort. A contented baby would quietly and placidly close its eyes, and should be allowed to sleep as long as it pleased. Cradles became dramatically unfashionable with the decline of swaddling. Rousseau was convinced that 'it is never necessary and often harmful to rock children in the cradle'. It was consciousness of the occasional abuse of cradles by servants that led to their disgrace. 'Banish far/The lazy cradle,' ordered Downman. It was 'useless but to give/Relief to th'indolent attendant race'. Nurses were now called upon to play with their charges, to amuse them rather than to lull them. Babies should be encouraged to stay awake all day, advised Cadogan, so they would be the readier to sleep at night. Not every expert condemned the cradle. Although Underwood was against the violent rocking that led infants to be 'jumbled in the cradle like travellers in a mail-coach', he felt there was something 'so truly natural, as well as pleasant, in the wavy motion of a cradle . . . and so like what children had been used to before they were born', that they could still be of some use. The mood in general was that the baby should be taken out and about much more, without the aid of go-carts or leading strings. It could travel on the mother or nurse's arm, to 'green fields and sunny eminences', where it could roll on the grass and learn to walk at its own speed.

With one exception, all that these early baby-care manuals were concerned with was the physical well-being of the baby. They trespassed on moral upbringing only when it influenced health; thus children should be taught obedience so that they would swallow disgusting medicines without demur. Locke and Rousseau, on the other hand, were philosophers. They were interested in the 'clay-cottage' of the body only in so far as a healthy mind could not exist inside a sickly body. In general, the manual writers referred to Locke and Rousseau not because of what they had to say about free will or human understanding, but because they seemed to make sense on the general health front. There were people who were interested in the moral upbringing of children, and in their intellectual education, but at this stage in the development of baby-care manuals they did not link moral development with physical concerns. They argued their cases on their own merits, without borrowing the authority that the doctors could wield because of their professional training. This point becomes important when we try to sort out truth from opinion in a modern compendium on the scale of Dr Spock, for example, because it is difficult to avoid being influenced by his knowledge of the symptoms of measles when we read what he had to say on temper tantrums.

The exception was James Nelson's *Essay on Government*, which effortlessly crossed the boundary between physical and moral to include 'the whole of a parent's care for their offspring' (sic). He was always primarily a father, an apothecary rather than a physician. His *Essay* is the more interesting in that it appeared so early—ten years before Rousseau wrote *Emile*. He was certainly influenced by Locke, although, as noted, he found that the great philosopher was a little impractical in his daily precepts. He agreed that children showed reason earlier than generally expected, and that their education should begin 'as soon as they have a being'. He saw the parents as sharing the task of bringing up their children. The Law of Nature had assigned them a joint portion of power, 'father's authority and mother's sweetness being discreetly blended'. But power was to be wielded with care. 'A coarse, clamorous method of enforcing obedience is to be avoided,' he warned. 'Severe and frequent whipping is, I think, a very bad practice; it inflames the skin, puts the blood in a ferment, and there is besides a meanness, a degree of ignominy attending it.' But he admitted that there might be occasions when it was necessary.

Nelson was quite happy to set down his own ideas on child-rearing without feeling that he need quote experts or be the mouthpiece of some philosopher. Nor did he posit a model child. Children, he felt, were born with different dispositions—some sweet and mild, others with 'a redundancy of acrimony'. These different tempers 'are sometimes a kindness bestowed on us by nature, on purpose for us to act some certain part on the great stage of life'. That his point of view was fairly typical of eighteenth-century parents is suggested by Hester Thrale's diary, or *Family Book*. She was a close friend of Dr Johnson, well read, and a businesswoman in her own right. Yet she found the time to record immensely detailed observations on her thirteen children and clearly found them fascinating—in a much more objective, guilt-free way than most parents manage today. She liked some, loathed others, and accepted their differences philosophically, all within the umbrella of her general caring. Such psychological openmindedness was not to survive the theories of mind which grew to dominate child-care theories in the next century.

Better known today among the educational authorities of the late eighteenth century are the whole tribe of religiously motivated moralists, both Evangelical and traditional. Rousseau's ideas divided the intellectual world into two camps. John Wesley, for instance, described *Emile* as 'the most empty, silly, most injudicious thing that a self-conceited infidel wrote'. Hannah More agreed with him, and deplored the difficulty of conveying to young people the corruption and helplessness of human nature in the face of the wild claims of Rousseau and the Enlightenment thinkers. By their lights childhood was no more than a preparation for adult life, and education was meant to instruct morally and intellectually rather than be of any intrinsic interest.

Opposing them with some vigour were the Edgeworths, whose first shock to their opponents was the simple omission of any reference to religious education from their *Essays on Practical Education* (1789). Maria followed the same principle in her very popular *Moral Tales*, which fictionalized the message of *Practical Education*. 'She does not attack religion, nor inveigh against it,' complained a Baptist minister, 'but makes it unnecessary by exhibiting perfect virtue without it.'

The first volume of *Practical Education* dealt with Toys,

Tasks, Attention, Servants, Obedience, and Truth in relation to the pre-school child. One of the Edgeworths' most striking ideas was that of a 'rational toyshop', stocked with 'sturdy carts, small gardening tools, printing presses, looms and furniture which takes to pieces and reassembles . . . pencils, scissors, paste, tools and workbenches'. The nursery was to be filled with toys that led to experiment. Round ivory or wooden sticks of different sizes could be placed in the mouth by a baby to feel their differences. Squares, circles, and triangles of wood were made with holes in them to fit the sticks into. The Edgeworths warned against the tendency of nurses to stun children's ears with various noises, and dazzle their eyes with glaring colours or stimulating light. This fatigued the babies' senses: 'the pleasure of exercising their senses is in itself sufficient to children without any factitious stimulus, which only exhausts their excitability, and renders them incapable of being amused by any common objects'. The mother had to oversee such matters herself—no servant could be entrusted with such an important care. The ideas in *Practical Education* read like a modern Galt toyshop catalogue—chemistry sets, jigsaws, basket-making kits, scale models of houses with separate architectural features, 'balls, pulleys, wheels, and strings, and strong little carts apportioned to their age'.

Although the Edgeworths disapproved of the intellectual cramming which produced such prodigies as Queenie Thrale, playtime had to end when the serious business of education started. At the age of four the moment arrived—the child had to learn to read. Richard Edgeworth's disillusion with his own son's education can be glimpsed behind the businesslike approach to the alphabet. 'It has been the fashion of late to attempt teaching everything to children in play, and ingenious people have contrived to insinuate much useful knowledge without betraying a desire to instruct.' He felt that 'counters, coaxing and gingerbread' were no more effective teachers of reading than 'reiterated pain and terror'. The Edgeworths offered their own very sensible reading scheme, which was to remain popular as long as their book did. What was to be read was circumscribed by utilitarian principles—one of the few matters that the Edgeworths and Hannah More agreed upon was the banishment of fairytales. Dr Johnson pleaded against this: 'Babies don't want to read about babies; they like to be told of giants and castles, and of something which will stretch their little minds.' In vain—away went the old tales.

The Edgeworths' advice on matters of discipline, obedience and truth-telling showed remarkable sensitivity, and a recognition of the child as a person with rights of its own. Obedience should be associated with pleasure—instead of telling children to go to bed, take them there. Instead of demanding instant obedience when a child is immersed in some activity, be patient, use 'praise and looks of affection' and so encourage attempts to obey. The old long lectures on morality should be replaced, as Locke and Rousseau suggested, with simple, practical examples. If something is broken don't seek a culprit, but be pleased if someone owns up. Ignore falsehoods with 'cool contempt' and praise truthfulness. The current theory of punishment was not vengeance or expiation but a utilitarian view that the greatest possible happiness of society was the object achieved by the partial evil of punishment. For children below the age of reason, punishment had to work on the association-of-ideas principle, by 'immediately, repeatedly and uniformly associating punishment with the actions we want them to avoid'.

Truth, they believed, was not instinctive to the mind. To give children too perfect a theory of morality before they had sufficient strength to adhere to it in practice was to make them hypocrites, or to give them 'a fatal mistrust of themselves'. Beware of using 'the delicate, secret, influence of conscience'. No punishment should be too longlasting, but it should be fitted to the individual. Withdrawing the love and esteem that was the reward for good behaviour had to be judged carefully—long disapproval suited the reflective nature, 'short sharp pain for the torpid'.

Practical Education remains worth reading, because it describes how the fourteen children in the Edgeworth family were brought up, at a time when approaches to child-rearing were refreshingly open—perhaps more free in experiment than they ever would be again. Locke, Rousseau and the men who relayed their ideas to parents eager for instruction had in common a tremendous faith in the potential of the babies being born. 'We know not what Nature allows us to be,' wrote Rousseau. 'None of us has measured the possible difference between man and man.' The parents who lapped up their words, and carried out their instructions with 'rational tenderness', set out on their task with cheerful confidence in the possibility of success. All the *Angst* was to come later, when the nineteenth century tidied up the Nature myth into the Garden metaphor, and brought in a priggish God to proscribe free will.

2
Mothers in Command
1820–70

THE DOCILE HUSBAND.

New Authorities

Napoleon had the greatest respect for his mother: 'The future good or bad conduct of a child depends entirely on the mother,' he observed, citing himself as evidence. Asked by Madame de Staël how moral values were to be improved, he replied: 'Instruct the Mothers of France.' Nineteenth-century England and America both had the greatest respect for Napoleon, and applied his advice to their own domestic modes. In family life after the Napoleonic wars, the most remarkable aspect of conservative retrenchment was the promotion of the middle-class mother to a semi-divine position. In upper-class family life, both parents were based at home and could be each other's companions. Children remained on the periphery of the circle. What was new about the growing middle class was that, rather than husband and wife working at home in some domestic trade, wealth was brought into the home by the husband's daily absence from it. This left his wife at home, with enough money not to have to work. All her energies were thus turned inwards, to the improvement of her home, her social status—and her children. She was concerned not only with their physical health, but with moulding the characters of future men, 'whose energies may turn for good or evil the destinies of a nation' (Beecher): new Napoleons perhaps.

Later feminists would rebel against the domestic conservatives who trapped women in the home with talk of sacred duty, fireside education, the home as nest. Anything so calculated seems unlikely. Long before the suffragettes invented her, a 'new woman' had emerged. Educated with her brothers until they left for public school, then by a governess, she was a thoughtful creature who had to find something to do or die of leisured boredom. Good works were one resort, rigorous etiquette another, but most popular was diving deeply into the responsibilities of motherhood, righting the wrongs of society by rearing quasi-perfect children.

Fathers continued, in theory, to occupy a powerful position, and were clearly extremely interested in the development of their children. Louisa May Alcott's father, Bronson, gave up his job and took over her upbringing until his wife could stand his interference no longer. William Cobbett was never willingly separated from his children. Nevertheless, because most fathers had to go out to work, their power was far less than that of the mother in practice. Some were used as distant thunder, some as treats to be looked forward to. The Reverend John C. Abbott wrote of American fathers: 'Paternal neglect is at the present time one of the most abundant sources of domestic sorrow. The father ... eager in the pursuit of business, toils early and late, and finds no time to fulfil ... duties to his children' (*The Mother's Magazine*, 1842).

What gave mothers the confidence to adopt a new, positive, intrusive mode of parenthood while their husbands were so frequently absent? William Cadogan's belief that, once feeding was established, 'there seems nothing left for a Nurse to do but to keep the child clean and sweet, to tumble it and toss it about a good deal, play with it, and keep it in good humour', was totally inadequate by the 1830s. Science and religion had combined by then to make child-rearing a matter of continual nourishing and pruning, staking up and cutting back.

Firstly, science—anatomy and clinical observation produced a science of the body: physiology, which analysed how the limbs, the organs, the blood, and the muscles functioned and interrelated. The message of physiology was that the body's mechanism was ruled by laws. Once understood, these laws could be followed in order to achieve perfect development. Related to physiology was phrenology, which established similar laws for the development of the mind. The Scottish brothers, George and Andrew Combe, popularized both sciences in two widely read books, *The Constitution of Man* and *Principles of Physiology*. They explained to a fascinated world that bumps on the head were related to faculties of the brain. They isolated thirty-five 'powers and organs of the mind', and pinpointed their positions on the skull: individuality lay between the eyes, amativeness well

34

down at the back of the neck. Different characters could be explained by the different degrees to which these faculties were developed. Each had a potentially 'morbid' or 'benevolent' tendency. What gave mothers some of their new sense of power was their supposed ability to influence the relative development of these powers and organs by applying the right stimuli.

If we wish to call out and give healthy development to the kindly and affectionate feelings in an infant, we must treat it, and every other person in its presence, with habitual kindliness and affection, because these are the natural stimuli to such feelings, just as the light is to the eye, or sound to the ear. (Combe, *Treatise on Infancy*)

By following the laws of health revealed by physiology and the laws of mind set up by phrenology, mothers could hope to bring up uniquely healthy and well-balanced babies.

Secondly, religion—the crumbling towers of eighteenth-century rationalism were abandoned for the tidy Evangelical chapels and the soaring spires of the Oxford Movement. The rediscovery of religious faith was as powerful in the home as in community life. 'To judge from the memoirs and biographies, the Evangelical families of England were conspicuously happy families, and it was in the hearts of Victorian mothers that Evangelical piety won its most signal and gracious triumph' (Smyth). Notorious bigots, such as the fathers of Samuel Butler, Edmund Gosse or Elizabeth Barrett Browning, were notorious because they were bigoted. Far more typical of the period were the mothers who imposed the gentle shackles of a religious outlook on their children's minds while they were still in the cradle. In 1846 *Mothers of the Wise and Good* by Jabez Burns went through four editions. In it mothers could read how early example had produced the world's heroes, and learn how to influence their own children from its chapters on Maternal Piety, Early Religious Impressions, A Mother's Love, The Mother's Charge, and so on. Had Byron and Washington been exchanged in their cradles, Abbott claimed, 'Washington might have been the licentious profligate, and Byron the exemplar of virtue and the benefactor of nations'.

Scientific laws and religious beliefs are uneasy bedfellows. A logical mind might say, and logical minds did say, how exactly can God keep his place in a world where science explains everything? If reverence is no more than a spot on the brain, how can a man remain a Christian if, by a blow on the head, that faculty is destroyed? Fortunately for mothers' peace of mind, this problem had already been faced up to by the geologists, who had found no evidence for the Flood in the fossil record, and by naturalists, who found it difficult to explain the crab except in terms of a practical joke. Man, they said, was doing nothing more than observing the design of the universe in his scientific probings. William Paley's *Natural Theology* (1802) sketched this scenario with a famous story: the discovery of a watch dropped on a heath. The fact that it was clearly made for a purpose implied a maker. So, in looking at natural history, evidence of design, of laws of development, implied a designer: God. 'In breast-feeding,' observed Dr Bull, 'the evidence of design is manifest. It is plainly intended to cherish and increase the love of the parent herself, and to establish in the helpless infant . . . affection and confidence.' The concern that Bull and many other child-care writers exhibited in sorting out this scientific/religious confrontation is an interesting undercurrent to the superficial self-confidence shown by parents—especially mothers.

Other anxieties arose. It was perhaps worse to feel that a child's death or depravity was due to the parents' mismanagement rather than to circumstances comfortably beyond their control—Rousseau's profligate Nature. Power could be misused. Convenience battled with maternal commitment, as nurses were ever more easily available, and domestic state less subject to children's intrusions. But until Darwin and genetics knocked her omnipotence so soundly on the head, the intelligent mother could find her fireside throne adequate and fulfilling.

So many more books were written about babies once the new century got into its stride that it seems worth isolating the most important writers. Baby-care was no longer a spin-off from medical concern for infant mortality, it was a field in its own right. A new category of author joined the predictable doctors and armchair philosophers—mothers. The emergence of mothers as writers reflected their new importance, their right to talk about their methods; they give an immediacy, a sense of personal experience that many earlier manuals lacked.

Not only were there more books—a huge ephemeral literature of pamphlets and magazines appeared: *Mother's Magazine, Parents' Assistant, The Family Magazine,* and many more. Packed with advice, direct or in fictional form, they also provided a forum for questions and opinions from parents. They debated such topics as methods of discipline, when to start religious instruction, or suitable first books. They were theoretical rather than practical, their consuming interest the child's moral and spiritual welfare.

Although the number of writers was growing, there was not yet the voluminous fringe of plagiarists and outright lunatics who were cluttering up the baby-care scene by the start of the twentieth century. Fads certainly existed, but they were the semi-respectable ones of the ancient hardening school, or homoeopathy, or the dwindling hard-core Puritans. These New England and Wesleyan schools of advice have received more attention than I think they deserve because they were such prolific writers. The mainstream I have chosen is faithful but not fanatical, whether couched in the poesy of Lydia Sigourney, 'sweet singer of Hertford', or economically phrased by Samuel Smiles. As one would expect, some eighteenth-century writers continued to be read. Underwood, Buchan and Smith were all brought up to date in new editions. Rousseau ('though sometimes a dangerous guide . . . often an excellent observer'—Saussure) was allowed a qualified usefulness. *Practical Education* increased in popularity; Hannah More continued to have her followers.

Even before it was translated, Albertine Necker de Saussure's *Progressive Education* was a well-known book. Mrs Gaskell read it in the original French, and the first American edition was embellished with a diary of infant life by Almira Phelps. Albertine de Saussure was a cousin of the 'first woman of Europe', Madame Staël. Born in 1766, she was something of an elder stateswoman when she wrote her book on education—certainly well past revolutionary enthusiasm. 'A little too perfect, a little too poised, a little too precise, a little too well-adjusted not to be a little irritating,' was a French historian's reaction on meeting her. In spite of this, she was the ancestress of all child psychologists. She analysed the first three years of life in extraordinary detail in order to track down and describe 'the secret springs that move the character to action'. Her method was fashionably scientific: 'I shall describe as accurately as I can the infant's moral constitution at different ages; and draw from such observations the practical results which evidently arise from them.'

She brought up her own children 'without imagining that I was studying children in general', but, like too many modern parent psychologists, on considering her experiences decided that 'in the constancy of the phenomena presented to our view by infancy, the effect of general laws was perceptible'. Instinct and individuality receded—Hester Thrale's calm acceptance of her children's separate vagaries disappeared. Rules and model infants arrived. Despite this pontifical approach, *Progressive Education* was a very good book— 'quite the nicest book on the subject', wrote Mrs Gaskell, who used it constantly while bringing up her small daughter, Marianne. De Saussure was exceptionally sympathetic to the infant mind and its development, and much of what she said is still illuminating today. For all its scientific method, it was an intensely religious book. Originally it was intended to extend over a dozen volumes, tracing human moral development—and its continuous (progressive) education— from cradle to grave. However, she got so carried away by early childhood that the later volumes were abandoned. Her thesis—that a scientific approach to physical, moral and intellectual education would lead to Christian perfection— saddled her natural perception with a rather ill-fitting yoke. It was typical of the uneasy contemporary alliance between science and religion.

If de Saussure was forward-looking, setting a trend, William Cobbett was backward-looking, fighting against it. Arguably, I should have considered his *Advice to a Father* as an eighteenth-century work, although it was written in 1829. But like Cobbett, himself, it doesn't really fit in there either.

Cobbett was the *enfant terrible* of his age, a perpetual rebel, but he was also the embodiment of the early nineteenth-century myth of the home as refuge from the troubles of the world. He shot down the government in *Twopenny Trash*, blasted the complacency of the gentry in *Rural Rides* and eulogized domestic self-sufficiency in *Cottage Economy*.

As much a case history as a manual, *Advice to a Father* was based explicitly on Cobbett's own experience of raising children, and the resounding success he felt that he made of it. He moved to the country because he felt that it was the best place for children to grow up; he worked at home because a child should have a father at home; he never let the children out of his or his wife's sight until they were old enough to look after themselves. If friends didn't want his children to stay, then he didn't go either. Servants and doctors were equally suspect influences, and there was no need for schools while parents were there to interpret nature and the world. Few parents today have Cobbett's self-confidence after the bludgeoning they have had since then by the experts. Nor could his advice be taken in a world of squashed-together town-houses, and fathers whose work is necessarily divorced from domestic life. But *Advice to a Father* has one unique aspect—of all the nineteenth-century manuals it is perhaps the only one to become a classic, still reprinted from time to time by publishers of elegant ephemera.

Andrew Combe, on the other hand, was a man of his time. Like Freud fifty years later, he made his mark in pathology and the treatment of the insane before applying his theories of mind universally. He was the fifteenth child (of seventeen) born to a family of tenant farmers near Edinburgh. Apparently the size of the family stopped his mother from showing 'that sympathetic tenderness towards her children which she really felt . . . her sway was one of general kindness and justice rather than endearment'. As a baby, Andrew was put out to nurse with Mary Robertson, a well-known Edinburgh foster-parent. He remained in touch with her all his life, and suggested many of her methods in his treatise.

The immense amount of detail that survives about Combe's early life was directly related to his belief in phrenology, to which he was converted once he had qualified as a doctor. If everyone would record their early impressions, or the early impressions of their children, he believed, then an accurate science of the mind could be set up by comparing their achievements in life and the shape of their skull with these first influences. Condemned to die young from lung disease, he co-operated to provide his brother George with as much detail of his early life as they could both remember, and just after his death George published the first true psycho-history, the *Life of Andrew Combe*—complete with a phreno-logical chart of his brother's head, measurement of his bumps, and a character assessment based upon them.

As Queen's Physician in Scotland, Andrew Combe was no quack, and his theories of the laws governing physical and mental development lay behind all the baby-care books of the time. Demand was immense for the *Principles of Physiology*—20,000 copies were sold in its first two and a half years. Mrs Gaskell referred to it almost as much as to de Saussure. The *Treatise on the Physiological and Moral Management of Infancy*, which concentrated more on baby-care, was equally respected.

Samuel Smiles was the epitome of energetic, high-minded, Victorian middle-class philosopher. His *Self-help* (1859) was one of the most popular books of the nineteenth century, and we are still influenced by its glorification of individualism and independence. He is less well known as a doctor and baby-care expert. One of eleven children, he qualified as a doctor at Edinburgh at the same time as Andrew Combe. In *Physical Education* he aimed to give parents the scientific facts, the laws of infant development, which would enable them to bring up their children properly. In this he is reminiscent of twentieth-century writers like Arnold Gesell—the facts were certainly different, but the intention was the same. For example, instead of simply suggesting that the baby be fed on a mixture of cow's milk and water four times a day, he explained why. His chapter on feeding opens: 'The stomach is an oblong bag, lying obliquely across the lower part of the chest, capable of containing when filled about half a pint.' Few mothers would try to force in pints of milk after absorbing that simple fact. Further on, he criticized a current vegetarian fad which assigned all moral evil to man's eating meat as: 'Mere twaddle, founded on an ignorance of nature and the constitution of man.' A proper knowledge of the formation of the jaw and alimentary canal showed parents that as the child's grinding teeth develop, and 'he exerts himself in infant romps', he should be given animal food.

Samuel Smiles was a conventionally religious man, quoting Paley on his title page, so it is not surprising that he fought a little shy of the implications of science for the brain. 'Much regarding this organ has yet to be revealed to us by further study and investigation—if such knowledge be within our reach even by these means.' How far could man understand the tool of his understanding? He did agree with the Combes that physical education was the basis of mental cultivation, and that the approach to both was the same: learn the laws that regulate the system.

> Whoever undertakes to train the tender mind of the child should have some correct idea of its powers; its propensities and faculties; at what period they come into operation; and what progress in the acquisition of knowledge the mind is calculated to make in the early stages of life.

Physical Education was perhaps the most demanding of the early infant-care manuals. Smiles suggested other books to read, and made no concessions to the limits of female comprehension which were assumed by other doctors. The implication of such a book was clear: instinct and nature were no longer enough, mothers had to be trained for their role.

American editions of English works on infant-care were common; but in the nineteenth century fewer American experts were read in England. One writer who was popular, presumably because her unabashed gush appealed to the emotional perinatal mood, was Lydia Sigourney. She was an Episcopalian, a society lady, and a popular poetess; a contemporary wrote that she 'combined wealth, beauty, refinement, talent and religion in one beautiful assemblage'. She edited *Mother's Magazine*, one of the many contemporary, religious, domestic papers, and 'laid aside the poet's lyre' to write *Letters to Mothers* in 1838. It flashed through six editions in ten years, and one can see why—few better collections of unadulteratedly beautiful thoughts on babies have been produced. 'As a germ quickened by spring, the infant opens the folding doors of its little heart, and puts forward the thought, the preference, the affection, like filmy radicles, or timid tendrils, seeking where to twine.' Despite her gift for hyperbole, Sigourney's gist was sensible enough. She had read Rousseau, Combe and St Augustine, and digested them all agreeably, although her bent was predictably religious. She represented the sentimental approach to death typical of the time very vividly. 'We must make it the subject of daily contemplation, praying for divine grace, to consider it as . . . the end for which we were born.' Religious instruction was the first duty of a mother—'Mothers! If there is one grave in the churchyard shorter than your child, hasten to instruct him in religion.' There was little of the Puritan fear of hell; it was a matter of preparing the child to join the 'glorious company of heaven'.

Pye Henry Chavasse, a Birmingham obstetrician, was something of a fan of Mrs Sigourney's, quoting her with relish in his later editions. His own *Advice to Mothers* was perhaps the most popular handbook of the age. It had gone through eighteen editions by 1896 (much extended and altered) and was widely read in America. There was even a final 'amended edition' in 1948, so a nostalgic granny could have given one to a mother with the first edition of Spock in her hands. 'We wish that a copy were in the hands of every matron in the Empire,' declared the *Dublin Evening Packet*, and such reviews gave a clue to its success. 'Plain simple advice of great value to mothers and nurses' (*London Medical Review*); 'anything that substitutes common sense for calomel is a great boon' (*Literary Gazette*); 'One of the chief merits of this work is its plain, simple common sense. Fresh air, plain food, and exercise are constantly insisted on, and the numberless indulgences allowed by foolish parents to their children are steadily condemned' (*Aris's Birmingham Gazette*).

Chavasse was not the iron man that these reviews suggested. He was clearly exceptionally well read, and when he felt that a tag from Longfellow or Tennyson made his point as well as an extract from the *Lancet* or *The Times*, he didn't hesitate to pop it into a footnote. Successive editions of the book were thoroughly amended with up-to-date ideas, and to read them all is to gain an accurate chart of the shifts of current opinion. Moreover, they make exciting reading—one never knows when a dramatic anecdote will be introduced, or a poem (often the author's own) put in to highlight advice. His sentimentality is a little overpowering at times, but was clearly popular. A supplementary work, *Counsel to Mothers*, was a marvellous ragbag of tips on everything from the merits of seakale and the demerits of perambulators to the expulsion of fleas and the need for public playgrounds. It was also a vehicle for his *chef d'oeuvre*, a 370-line poem apostrophizing the joys of childhood:

> A wheedling, coaxing little Puck;
> Full of mischief and full of pluck;
> Brimful of play and full of love;
> And bright as sunbeam from above . . .
> Breaking his cups, breaking his toys;
> Kicking up din and riot and noise;
> Almost breaking the drum of one's ear,
> Making one feel extremely queer.

Not great verse when read aloud, but an important corrective to modern visions of Victorian physicians. Chavasse used question-and-answer form in all his books, just as the National Childbirth Trust's 'Know-How' series does today, which gave a cosy armchair atmosphere, the feel of a conversation. Perhaps the mothers were talked down to somewhat, technicalities avoided, reasons rarely given— Smiles for the simple. But his firmness of opinion was clearly lapped up by the uncertain, increasingly isolated mothers for whom he was writing.

Thomas Bull, a London 'physician-accoucheur', wrote a manual which was not much less popular than Chavasse's— *Maternal Management of Children*. Written in 1840, it had run to eight editions by 1877. More down to earth than Chavasse, it stated its purpose firmly in its opening pages: to save infant life. The death of more than a third of the country's children before they reached the age of five could not be regarded with patient submission: 'We are justified in inferring, from the perfection of structure observed in the human frame . . . that it is not . . . the design of our Creator.' It was due to a want of knowledge, 'a lamentable ignorance of the nature of the human frame', and not want of affection, 'for the tenderest of human feelings flow out instinctively towards a helpless offspring'. Bull is good evidence too for a shift in metaphor from parent as she-tigress instinctively protecting, to gardener knowledgeabl rearing a healthy vigorous stock. 'Tender human feelings are as useless as the blind caresses that cause animals to strangle their own young without the knowledge that we assume a gardener must have of plants.' His book was therefore full of the whys and wherefores as well as the hows of baby-care—much potted phrenology and physiology. He stuck to his medical brief more firmly than Chavasse, not allowing himself to be drawn into moral management. Instead, he gave very detailed information on the treatment of illnesses—dosages as well as the usual nursing advice. These could be essential when a doctor could not be contacted, but dangerous if wrongly administered. Later manuals were far more cautious.

Mrs Sarah Ellis was typical of the small army of redoubtable society matrons of the mid-nineteenth century who mirrored the new fashion for domestic respectability. Her titles put one in mind of a cavalry general marshalling flagging female troops for a mindless gallop into the jaws of male dominance and female duty: *Daughters of England, Wives of England, Mothers of England*; she even considered sequels called *Hints to Stepmothers* and *Consolations for Old Maids*. An unabashed woman of the world, she was not much concerned with religious training, rather 'the tendency of modern education, and the peculiar social and domestic requirements of the country and the times'. *Mothers of England* was more about older children than infants, but had something to say on early moral management, and is a very good example of the new importance attached to the mother's role. Mrs Ellis urged mothers to look after their own children, criticizing women who 'appear to consider themselves called upon to do anything rather than attend the training of their children; who find time for morning calls, when they have none for the nursery or the schoolroom; and even make dresses for their infants rather than answer the questions dictated by their opening minds'.

Mrs Eliza Warren was a step or two down the social ladder from Mrs Ellis. It was by no means certain that the mother she was writing for would have a carriage to pay morning calls in. Her first book was *How I Managed My Home on £200 a Year*, which was something an office clerk living in a terraced house in Kennington would be interested in hearing about. Using the 'Archers'' technique of information through fiction, *How I Managed My Children from Infancy to Marriage* described a young mother's mismanagement of herself and her child through pregnancy and puerperium. Sacrificing this first-born rather ruthlessly (he remained a sickly worry until late 'teens, when he died of that early mismanagement, just as he was about to become famous as an artist), she then embarked upon how sensibly her second pregnancy was managed, and how she ended with eight model children. It is never a dull book. Chapter by chapter this child or that comes down with croup, measles, teething troubles or religious *Angst*, to be efficiently dealt with by helpful nurse, granny-figure neighbour (significantly the heroine's own mother lived too far away to be of any help) and eventually the experienced mother herself. The climax of her book is the plea for girls to be educated and trained for a career just as boys were. 'The greatest curse to society and to the Maidens of England has been the diffusion of the silly, sinful Dogma that Woman loses caste by honestly earning her bread.' There was very little theory in Warren's writing, but what she told mothers to do was in the tradition of Saussure and Combe, with a touch of Sigourney in her reminder of the mother's Christian duty:

> Narrow indeed is the path which a mother must walk—not making her child an idol to be worshipped, or a toy of caprice. Sober, orderly, and in the love of her Maker must she journey, knowing that she holds in her hand and cherishes at her breast an immortal spirit . . . that she has created either a follower of Christ or a companion of fiends.

Religious and socially conscious women were not the only

45

ones to be interested in infant minds. Harriet Martineau represented the intellectual agnostic, the independent-minded woman who set the cause of child-care in an early feminist setting. Written in 1837, *Society in America* gives interesting insights into American mothers' attitudes, while *Feats on the Fjords* was a children's bestseller calculated to carry out her advice that 'the child's imagination must be engaged on behalf of everything that is noble, heroic and openly glorious before the eyes of men'. *Household Education* was a controversial book—its utilitarian ethics, its advocacy of individualism damned it in conventional Christian quarters—but it was no less read for that. It deserves consideration, partly to redress the balance against pious weighting, partly to anticipate the feminist mood to come.

This particular collection of writers are far from being the only authors worth considering—many other names will crop up as the mood of the time is established—but I think they represent the breadth of available opinions fairly. Their diversity is important. Mothers could be expected to pick and choose their authority. By the end of the nineteenth century, when infant care became a science, they would be allowed no such independence.

'*Our bodies are our gardens*'

Physical habits have always held moral significance—the Seven Deadly Sins are example enough. The revival of religious conscience gave new force to old fears about gluttony, sloth, and sexuality, which could now be expressed in the categories of phrenology. Over-eating became the overdevelopment of the faculty of 'alimentiveness', onanism was now the fault of too much 'amativeness'. It became the mother's duty to cultivate a healthy body for her child's healthy mind to inhabit by seizing the once-in-a-lifetime chance which the infant's early malleability offered.

Bodies gained a new respect because of this coincidence of scientific and religious ideas about their importance. 'If anything in the body is wrong, it affects our thoughts and feelings,' wrote Dr Alcott in *The Young Mother*. Once connections between soul, mind, brain and therefore body were accepted, the mother became the guardian of 'a miniature temple, where the ethereal spirit is a lodger', as Sigourney put it. This respect was reflected in the better surroundings recommended for children, and more suitable clothes, food and amusements. Nevertheless, as a look at the details of the prescriptions will show, the emphasis was inescapably on training the baby up into a well-formed specimen. References to young animals tumbling about are few, interest in aborigines wanes. These are the decades of the sensitive plant, of the parent as gardener.

Breast-feeding was a baby's birthright, declared Cobbett. It was better to bring up by hand than to resort to the 'hireling breast'. Even if the experience was painful, it was worth enduring, impressing as it did both father and other children with what a mother did for them. 'Of all the sights that this world affords, the most delightful is a mother with her clean and fat baby lugging at her breast, leaving off now and then and smiling, and she half-smothering it with kisses.'

The exhortatory tone of earlier writers was no longer necessary. 'At least an attempt is made by most mothers to suckle their offspring, and generally with complete success,' wrote Combe. More and more mothers were feeding their own babies, partly convinced that it was safer than any other form of feeding, partly revelling in what Sigourney called 'a halcyon period . . . of peculiar, inexpressible felicity'. Other advantages were stressed. The mother who breast-fed was physically fitter, more attractive, and less likely to get pregnant, suffer from milk fever, 'broken breasts' or cancer of the breast, according to Dr Bull.

Unfortunately, the very enthusiasm for breast-feeding contributed to its undoing. In well-meaning attempts to inform and advise mothers, the manuals produced enough difficulties to discourage them. Take Dr Bull's approach: 'From the first moment the infant is applied [note that distancing word] to the breast, it must be nursed upon a certain plan. The baby must take a little thin gruel, or a mixture of one-third water and two-thirds cow's milk, sweetened with loaf sugar until the breast-milk is fully established.' After a mere week of demand feeding, 'it is essentially necessary to nurse the infant at regular intervals of three or four hours, day and night'. In fact the timing of breast-fed babies' feeds ought not to be a problem. Hungry babies feed, bigger ones probably more often than small ones. The problem only arises when writers of baby-care manuals, having told the mother how often to bathe the baby and when to take it for walks, decide to tell her how often to feed it. Doctors observed the behaviour of the orphans in their hospitals and jotted it down as a rough guide to practice (that it suited the nurses to feed babies at regular intervals was discounted). So we arrive at Dr Bull's position that it was 'essentially necessary' for mothers to nurse an infant at regular intervals.

There were still doctors who were more in touch with reality. Chavasse advised mothers to breast-feed as soon after the baby was born as possible, and not to give it anything else until then. 'We frequently hear of a babe having no notion of sucking. This "no notion" may generally be traced to bad management, to stuffing him with food, and thus giving him a disinclination to take the nipple at all.' Chavasse suggested that a baby might suckle every hour and a half for the first month, two-hourly for the second month, and gradually arrive at a four-hourly average. John Darwall, author of *Plain Instructions for the Management of Infants*, agreed that two-hourly feeds might well be necessary for breast-fed babies for the first two months. He added that artificially fed babies needed feeding less frequently because they took longer to digest the food that they were given. This important distinction was not made by anyone else. Hence many mothers would tend to be discouraged from breast-feeding, feeling that they were having to feed too often, and that their supply of milk must be inadequate.

Nursing mothers were treated like candidates for the Olympic Games. None of the old-fashioned pint of porter per day; instead plenty of exercise and a cold, salt-water shower bath every morning. Combe advised against excessive novel-reading, Lydia Child told them to 'avoid all over-heating from running, dancing, excessive fatigue, etc.; likewise the indulgence of violent passions and emotions' (*The Mother's*

Book). The child might have convulsions if fed after such excesses. An even more insidious doubt entered mothers' heads when it was suggested that milk might appear plentiful, but have no nutritional value.

Inadequate nipples were a further cause for concern. John Walsh claimed that 'in the present state of society, from the pressure of stays carried through several generations, the nipples are so shortened and injured in their development that, if left to itself, many a child would actually starve' (*Manual of Domestic Economy*). He recommended, and illustrated, a breast pump for use in the first few days. Eliza Warren no doubt intended to be equally helpful by suggesting that mothers with inverted nipples copy her 'charming Norwegian lady friend, who got two large nutmegs, scooped them out like thimbles, then put them in brandy for a week, and afterwards dried them. The breasts were then rubbed every morning with glycerine, and the nipples washed over with brandy, and, when dry, the nutmegs were placed one on each nipple. This drew them out, and hardened them.'

For mothers who did not succeed in breast-feeding, wet-nurses were still around. They fitted less well into city than country life, and the current belief in the importance of closeness between mother and child in the first few months was against them. The popular French practice of suckling children directly on to goats and asses—still the best alternative to human milk—did not catch on in England, so artificial foods were increasingly relied on. By the 1850s the improvement in patent baby-foods was felt to be so great that the manuals began to recommend them increasingly positively. Chavasse's ninth edition listed seventeen substitutes for mother's milk, some of them still household names today—Liebig's Food, Revalenta Arabica, Horlicks, Mellin's, Robinson's Patent Groats. The scientific halo which doctors raised over these concoctions, combined with the well-publicized difficulties of breast-feeding, contributed to a swing after the middle of the century from the uncertainties of suckling to the security of the bottle. The change was accurately mapped by Mrs Beeton's pronouncement on the matter—it still paid lip service to the 'natural course of rearing children', but her true opinion was unmistakable:

All we desire to prove is that a child *can* be brought up as well on a spoonfed dietary as the best example to be found of those reared on the breast; having more strength, indeed, from the more nutritious food on which it lives. It will be thus less liable to infectious diseases, and more capable of resisting the virulence of any danger that may attack it; and without in any way depreciating the nutriment of its natural food, we wish to impress on the mother's mind that there are many cases of infantine debility which might eventuate in rickets, curvature of the spine, or mesenteric disease, where the addition, or total substitute, of an artificial and more stimulating aliment, would not only give tone and strength to the constitution, but render any mechanical means unnecessary. (*Household Management*)

Of course the opposite was true—breast milk was more likely to give protective antibodies than any artificial food; but opinion and the temptingly packaged convenience foods won the day.

Infant mortality figures made a sharp upturn towards the end of the century. As much to blame as the artificial baby-foods were the extraordinary feeding-bottles into which they were put. Once theorists decided that a baby needed time to use its saliva to digest food, bottles were preferred to the old pap-boats or spoons. Ironically, whatever advantage the baby gained in ease of digestion it more than lost in life expectancy—the design of the bottles and teats made them chronic harbourers of germs. The most common early nineteenth-century bottle was the simple 'submarine' type. This was a long lozenge of stoneware or glass, with a small spout at one end over which a leather teat was tied, and a hole at the top, stoppered by a cork with a valve or tube through it.

An exotic variation was the Lacteal, patented in the United States in 1841. It amounted to an artificial breast, 'to practise a useful deception on the child, viz, inducing the child to think that it derives nourishment directly from its mother'. The usefulness of this was left obscure; perhaps it was a last attempt at nourishing the little radicles of love and trust beloved of Lydia Sigourney. From the patent drawing, the bottle appears to have been glass, slightly concave to fit over the breast. On the normal nipple site was a soft teat of deerskin, stuffed with a sponge to control the flow of the milk. In order to perfect the deception, the inventor provided a flesh-coloured elasticated pad to fit over the bottle as an optional extra.

By 1868, Chavasse mentioned three patent feeding bottles: Maws's Fountain, Morgan Brothers' Anglo-French, and Mather's Infant Feeder. Like most of the mid-century bottles, these were made of glass rather than china, so mothers could at least see any dirt inside them. But they all featured the deadly long tube between teat and bottle which meant that they could not be properly cleaned. The design was significant—related to the shift in baby-handling practice represented by perambulators and nursery wings. It meant that the baby could be left in pram or cot to feed itself. The teat was just like a dummy, which a baby can be relied upon to keep in its mouth *ad nauseam*; the bottle could be tucked in at its side. No time needed to be wasted cuddling the baby at feed times.

The teat itself was a matter for much debate and experiment. Rubber teats were made possible by the vulcanization of rubber by Goodyear in 1839, and were patented in America in 1845. They were not at all popular at first; they tasted and smelt disgusting, stiffened after repeated use, and perished internally. Bull continued to recommend the old chamois leather teats, or calf's teats pickled in spirit. Both teat and the sponge placed inside to slow down the milk flow should be changed every day he warned, 'otherwise the food will be tainted, and the bowel deranged'. Even Mrs Beeton preferred a genuine calf's teat to the unnatural-looking black ones of 'gutta-percha' or 'caout-chouc', as early domestic rubber was known. Walsh felt that a rubber teat varnished white suited the hygienic requirements of the age best. What the babies thought is not recorded.

The experts did not even begin to agree on what older children should eat, although overall bland farinaceous foods, broths, the least windy vegetables, and well-cooked fruit were the rule. Some said no meat until second dentition (that is at six or seven years old), others let children tuck into mutton chops as soon as they had a tooth in their gums. Monotony was felt to be the key to a successful toddlers' diet, but a little more variety was allowed after the age of two.

Combe pointed out that French children were allowed much more ripe fruit than English, and that they had correspondingly fewer bowel problems. Most of the manuals recommended diets which only laxatives could have shifted, and included long sections on the use of purgatives. A theory has been put forward that these were made necessary by intensive early toilet training, but it is worth pointing out that the sort of food small children were allowed to eat made what Mrs Ellis clearly regarded as a national constipation problem inevitable.

> There certainly exists among the English people something unfavourable to the healthy action of the digestive powers, and hence follows a long catalogue of uncomfortable sensations, scarcely to be classified under the head of disease, which beset the mind as well as the body, and assail most effectively what are called the animal spirits. (*Mothers of England*)

Could a stodgy dietary for young children in mid-century Vienna have led to Freud's isolation of anal traumas? Only further research will tell.

Nursery cookery was also 'a means, indirectly, of forming human character', according to Mrs Horace Mann, author of *Moral Culture of Infancy* and *Christianity in the Kitchen.* Plain, lightly seasoned food was supposed to promote self-denial. Parents were warned not to pamper and indulge their children by slipping them dainties from their own table. The traditional entry of the children with the dessert was phased out as mealtimes became later. Although experts conscious of the design of the universe could point to the 'wise and beneficial arrangement' of Providence which let children enjoy the food that kept them alive, food could be 'over-stimulating'. Parents had to encourage nobler appetites as the children grew older—and never to use food as reward. Samuel Smiles advised parents to 'trace the analogy between the feeling of the child who is taught to set the highest values on lollipop and sugar candy, and that of full-grown children whose opinions can be readily changed, and whose minds are rendered open to all kinds of conviction under the influence of a good dinner': a defence against the expense-account lunch was clearly already necessary.

Sleep was not yet a moral issue—the iron routines of the early twentieth century were still to come—but a fundamental divorce of mother and child did take place. In the eighteenth century babies slept in beds with their mothers or nurses as a matter of course. Cold houses made that a sensible precaution; moreover a baby sleeps well nestled up to an adult. 'The bosom of the mother is the natural pillow of her offspring,' wrote Dr Conquest. Smiles, Bull and Combe agreed—the new baby had a low body temperature and could not generate much heat itself. After six or eight weeks, it might be moved to a cot or cradle. Chavasse originally left the baby on its 'natural pillow' until it was weaned at nine months; but he changed his mind. The seventh edition of *Advice to Mothers* altered that nine to 'a few', and a lengthy warning of the dangers of suffocating was added. 'Careless, heavy-sleeping girls' were partly to blame—as were mothers who allowed the baby to suckle while they slept.

The mood was changing. Mrs Barwell liked her babies in a separate room from the start. She observed their 'instinctive knowledge' that the breast was in the room, which kept them awake when near their mothers. Walsh was also concerned that the baby should fit in conveniently, as one might expect of a book concerned primarily with the smooth running of a home, and of the 'committee of ladies' who contributed to it. Like Mrs Beeton's damnation of breast-feeding, this passage is a perfect index to the switch in priorities.

No-one of experience will hold the opinion that the mother's arms are not the natural shelter for her child, and therefore at first sight it might be supposed that it would be better for the baby to go to sleep there; and if only early infancy was to be considered no-one could object to it. But if allowed at that age, there is a great difficulty in breaking through the habit, and therefore it is better to begin early, at a time when no habits are formed, and when the child really is quite as comfortable in his soft little bed as on his

mother or nurse's lap. It is astonishing how soon some
children find out the way to obtain what they want, and as
all infants instinctively crave for their mother's presence,
so they will certainly prefer her lap, and will cry for it at
first, in almost all cases. But if, very early after birth, that is,
by the second week, they are left to go to sleep in their cots,
and allowed to find out that they do not get their way by
crying, they at once become reconciled, and after a short
time will go to bed even more readily in the cot than on the
lap. (*Manual of Domestic Economy*)

'That they do not get their way by crying'—bedtime was now
an opportunity to show who was boss. Although the baby's
instinctive craving for its mother's presence was recognized,
it was more important to ingrain it with the convenient habit
of sleeping alone in a cot.

Eliza Warren offered a graphic scene of the triumph of
professionalism over mother love in *How I Managed my
Children*. The monthly nurse had just departed, leaving the
baby tucked up on an ingenious little bed made by turning
two armchairs to face each other beside the parents' bed—a
nice glimpse of the improvisation necessary in a small house.
The silly young mother decided that it would be much nicer
to have the baby nestled up close beside her. Would he settle
down? Not at all. In the sleepless nights that followed, I
was pleased to read that the young husband took his turn
at walking up and down with the baby, 'making that
hshshshshshing sound of comfort that parents know only too
well'. But this wouldn't do—his career began to suffer.
Luckily a kind and experienced neighbour heard the 'constant crying' and came round. Her diagnosis was 'too much
cuddling', her solution—to leave the baby 'absolutely still'
and alone, lest convulsions or brain disease result. A myth-
ology for neglect was being created.

Whether babies were to be left alone in cots or cradles was
still not settled. There was concern that rocking was habit-
forming, and Dr Conquest recalled that 'an apparatus of this
kind was contrived and at one time made use of to subdue
furious lunatics'. He felt that a child should not need to be
rocked to sleep—if it wouldn't fall asleep naturally, then it

must need something—more food, or warmth. Scientifically based care could encourage sleep, however:

> When he is asleep, the motions of the heart and breathing are less, and so his animal heat is reduced. Darken the room; like a plant, the child is affected by light, and we know how easily the sleep of plants can be reversed by producing artificial night and day. Quiet and subdued colours should surround the sleeping infant, and the foot of the cot should be pointed towards the window to prevent squinting. (*Letters to a Mother*)

Realization that the baby could be manipulated was much more general now. This sort of passage encouraged action from parents, pushing and pruning their offspring up 'in the way they should go'. On the other hand, a more passive, observer's stance was equally acceptable. The *Mother's Oracle* justified the cradle because 'it invites, by its motion, repose, resembling in that respect, the situation of the child before birth, when it is suspended in a fluid and floats, so the cradle feels only to the child as a continuation of the exercise that it has been accustomed to'.

The marked bossiness of the experts on the subject of keeping children up late in the evenings, indulging the parents' vanity by letting them be 'fondled and admired' at dinner parties, again pointed to a change in opinion. Cobbett certainly never minded having his children around him, but now Eliza Warren spoke with the majority when she 'never allowed them to interfere with [her] time' once her husband came home. Although it was not until later in the century that children were to be generally banished from adult company, the lessening of free and easiness could already be perceived.

In attitudes to crying, the experts revealed more ambivalence. Physiologists introduced the idea that it was less a plea for help than a form of exercise. As Samuel Smiles wrote:

> Instead of being feared, the practice of crying in children in want of muscular exercise is most beneficial in its effects. Sickly and weak children cry a good deal, and but for this, it is almost certain that they could not live long. The very first

act which an infant performs at birth is to cry, and many of them continue to do so at an average rate of four or five hours a day during the first years of their existence. It cannot for a moment be imagined that all their cries arise from a feeling of pain. It would be an anomaly in the benevolent working plan of creation and an unmerited infliction of pain on the little innocents, were this the case. Not at all. They cry in default of exercise, or rather, for exercise. (*Physical Education*)

The echoes of Paley are evident. Smiles was not only a believer in the innocence of new-born babies and a merciful Providence, he was also a doctor looking for an organic reason for the crying that seemed an inevitable part of babies' lives. Eighteenth-century parents had been able to put down the infant's bawls to original sin, or just to cuddle the baby until its crying stopped. But if the baby was to be fitted into a routine from the word go (remember Walsh's advice), then parents had to resign themselves to a good deal of crying. Smiles's idea was one which suited changes in infant management well, and gave them both Christian and scientific respectability.

Not everyone was convinced. Dr Conquest looked back to Mrs Parkes for support.

It has been justly said (by Mrs Parkes) that the cries of an infant are the voice of Nature supplicating relief. It can express its wants in no other language. A healthy child scarcely ever cries. Though some have supposed that crying is a wise provision of nature, by which circulation is accelerated, it is more consonant with reason to consider it as a sign of uneasiness.

He showed an interestingly early consideration of the psychological effects of too much crying—of course such an observation could not be made until it was becoming a matter of course to let babies cry for long periods: 'Their violent efforts to get relief equally spoil their temper and disorder their constitution. When a child's turbulent passions are so early awakened and aroused, there is reason to fear that they will materially influence its future disposition.'

Other experts followed their own noses. Combe, as one would expect, endorsed Smiles by describing crying as 'a provision of nature, called into play by every new sensation of force'. Chavasse gave a hair-raising analysis of every possible cry that a baby could make, from everyday hunger and teething to 'the cry of inflammation of the membrane of the brain, a piercing shriek, most pitiful to hear', and ignored the exercise argument completely. Bull made a subtle compromise. Tears were nearly always a sign of temper and should be ignored. Crying had to be attended to. There was no agreement. The sentimental mother could still comfort her child; the iron lady could relegate it to its cot for exercise.

For the impatient there were always opiates. 'I sell in retail alone five gallons of "quietness", and a half gallon of "Godfrey's",' a respectable druggist in a middle-class district of Manchester told Bull. 'The former preparation being so strong as to contain 100 drops of laudanum in one ounce; a single teaspoonful is the prescribed dose, so that, allowing one ounce weekly to each family, this one druggist supplies 700 families every week.' Combe quoted the inquest statistics of 1837–8—there had been seventy-two cases of children poisoned by drugs given by mothers or nurses. Wet-nurses smeared their nipples with laudanum to ensure success in settling off their charges, mothers were warned, and nursemaids were likely to have bottles of cordial tucked under their beds. Responsible mothers made quite sure that nurses were supervised—others dosed their babies themselves.

The position of the early nineteenth-century manual writers on bathtime is best shown by quoting Cobbett. This is a passage full of illuminating details—a reference to Rousseau, the mistaken tenderness of mothers who quail at the prospect of cold baths, the fact that both Anne and William took their turn at bathing their babies, and finally the vision of the parent reassured by the book that he has been doing the right thing—ominous shadow of the future:

A great deal in providing for the health and strength of children depends on their being duly and daily washed, when well, in cold water from head to foot. Their cries testify to what degree they dislike this. They squall and twist and kick about at a fine rate, and many mothers, too many, neglect this, partly from reluctance to encounter the squalling, and partly, much too often, from what I will not call idleness, but which I cannot apply a milder term than neglect. Well and duly performed it is an hour's good tight work; for besides the bodily labour, which is not very slight when the child gets to be five or six months old, there is the singing to overpower the voice of the child. The moment the stripping of the child used to begin, the singing used to begin, and the latter never ceased until the former ceased. After having heard this go on with all my children, Rousseau taught me the philosophy of it. I happened by accident to look into his *Emile* and there I found him saying, that the nurse subdues the child and makes it quiet by drowning its voice in hers, and therefore making it perceive that it could not be heard, and that continuing to cry was of no avail. 'Here, Nancy,' said I, going to her book in hand, 'you have been a great philosopher all your life without either of us knowing it!'

Significant numbers of writers quailed at Cobbett's buoyant enjoyment of cold water. Madame de Saussure hesitantly asked: 'Should we, in spite of their continued crying, persevere in subjecting children to such treatments as cold baths, or should the constant distress of the child be a warning to desist?' Although most writers clung on to the cold bath as an ultimate goal, it was to be reached by easy stages, and delicate or nervous children might be spared altogether.

However, popular science gave water semi-magical properties. One expert's analysis of the skin had calculated that there were some twenty-eight miles of tiny 'perspiratory tube' to be kept clean by regular washing, and bathing was thought very stimulating to the circulation of the blood, and a 'tonic to the organs'. A new school of medical treatment, hydropathy or water-cure, claimed success in treating almost every childhood ailment by a combination of bathing, friction rubs, cold and hot compresses, and sudden unexpected douches. Prescribing sea-bathing became a fine art. Filey was for tougher constitutions than Margate. Brighton or Little-hampton could be relied upon for the most delicate. Failing sea-bathing, salt was added to the daily bath to imitate the 'invigorating' marine effect.

Added to scientific enthusiasm was the 'excellent moral influence' that entire cleanliness was calculated to exert upon the mind, as Bull put it. Perhaps there was a baptismal element in it, a washing away of sins. Given the unpleasant-ness of the hour-long process of washing and dressing, it was seriously considered as an opportunity to show patience in adversity.

> Even at this tender age, the little creature may be taught to be patient, and even gay, under suffering. Let it be remembered that every act of the nurse towards the infant is productive of good or evil upon its character as well as its health. Even the act of washing and clothing may be made to discipline and improve the temper, or to try and impair it, and therefore may be very influential on its happiness in future life. (*Letters to a Mother on the Watchful Care of her Child*, n.d., *c.* 1840)

In practical terms, the possibility of hot baths had to wait for the plumbing to provide them. Kitchen ranges took some time to warm up in the mornings, and first claims would be for father's shaving water and mother's early-morning tea. No doubt enough water could be heated up on a little nursery fire to take the chill off the baby's bath water, but for older children it must have been almost necessary to assert the physically and morally bracing effects of cold water. As piped hot water developed in the second half of the century, opinion could and did change.

Nappies and toilet training were aspects of infant manage-ment equally tied to reality. After swaddling clothes and before washing machines, keeping babies clean and dry was a major chore. Nappies were made of diaper doubled over, stitched on three sides, turned inside out and oversewn into a neat square. Loops and ties were sewn on to the corners in preference to pins, then far from safe. Some nursemaids stitched the baby into its nappy, but this was felt to be a disincentive to frequent changes. In default of plastic pants, a heavy flannel pilcher was tied and buttoned over the nappy. Dr Conquest suggested oiled silk as a substitute for flannel, because he felt that the weight of the pilcher tended to 'heat and enfeeble the loins, as well as inducing diseases of the lower spinal marrow and rendering the child prone to paralysis'. Walsh criticized this innovation: 'Some fine lady-nurses confine the disagreeables with oiled silk, but this keeps the baby too wet, and makes it difficult to know when to change it.'

Nappy rash was to be treated by frequent rain-water washes, and a dusting of powdered zinc. Or it could be avoided altogether by the very early training which began to be recommended around the 1840s. Although 'in very early infancy, evacuations are frequent and involuntary', Combe found that 'after a short time, an attentive nurse can generally discover some indications of what is about to begin, and take measures accordingly'. Conquest agreed that 'an infant may be brought at a very early age to be so cleanly as to go without any guard, if regularly put on a chair, or if a little pan be placed under it as it lays on the lap. In many well-managed nurseries, this practice begins so early that the necessity for napkins is altogether superseded by the time the children attain the age of four months'.

Chavasse provides a useful reflection of the new practice. He didn't mention the subject at all in his early editions, but became very decided later on. The baby was to be held out at least a dozen times a day at three months old; if this were done, there need be no more nappies at four months, 'a great desideratum', and he would be inducted (another good distancing word) into clean habits, 'a great blessing to himself, a comfort to all around, and a great saver of dresses and furniture'. He quoted Mrs Balfour's *Hints on Household Management*: ' "Teach your child to be clean. A dirty child is the mother's disgrace." Truer words were never written—A DIRTY CHILD IS THE MOTHER'S DISGRACE!' Although I have found no suggestion at this time that children or babies ought to be punished for failing to perform, it is clear that if disgrace was being introduced into the matter with such intensity, there was a great deal of unspoken feeling.

Significantly, bedwetting began to be mentioned as a problem. 'Punishment should *not* be inflicted,' protested Lydia Child, but her remedies were severe. The child was to sleep on straw, with flannel next to its skin. Its 'whole person' was to be frequently rubbed with a stiff brush. A plaster of Burgundy pitch could be placed low on the back, or the abdomen rubbed with oil of rosemary. Cantharides (see p. 69) might have to be resorted to for obstinate cases. Finally, she suggested a twice-daily bath of the loins and kidneys with spirits of turpentine and hartshorn mixed with soap. Conquest, with the psychological acuteness he had shown over crying, reflected that bedwetting was 'more often due to deficient care and want of moral training than to any real state of disease'. But all the cure he offered was a cold douche to the loins from a height of five or six feet. Bull, milder and more resigned, agreed that a shower might help, or a cold hip-bath before going to bed, but added a practical tip (tolerance made easier by technology)—slip the 'useful new invention, Macintosh sheeting' between mattress and sheet.

Nursery Life

Shifting points of view on child-rearing in the nineteenth century have been concealed by the blanket assumption that most middle- and upper-class children spent their time shut up in their nurseries with nannies, and only saw their parents for an hour in the evening. Although it is possible that at the height of the nanny's rule, the late nineteenth and early twentieth centuries, a great many upper-class families organized their families in this way, I think it is misleading to accept it as usual in family life earlier on. Magazine illustrations, cartoons and fashion plates all show mothers and children in drawing-rooms, out for walks, and in the nursery, together. Children were to be seen, although hopefully not heard. Fathers joined in when they came home from work, but this children's hour was far from the only time that mothers were in evidence. They usually reckoned to teach their children to read and write themselves, which with large families was a considerable task.

Architectural evidence also belies the nursery wing as the norm. In the average three- or four-storey terraced house there was no room for remote nursery and servant quarters. Families with four, five or more children must have lived very much on top of each other in such houses. According to Eliza Warren, children 'rambled all over the house from attic to kitchen'. Not that she thought this was a good idea. To stop the 'poundings overhead' and the 'sliding down banisters at the risk of broken heads', she suggested arranging the back parlour as a nursery. Here the children could have direct access to the garden, which was to be divided into plots for each of them. Another idea was that the dining-room should double as a nursery, and Combe suggested that if it was raining the drawing-room could provide the change of scene necessary for small children. The newly discovered laws of health forbade basement nurseries, and it was thought better to sacrifice a rarely used guest-room rather than banish children into small, stuffy attics.

And, from the statistics which Patricia Branca gives in *Silent Sisterhood*, it does not seem likely that any but the wealthiest families had full-time nursery staff. A monthly nurse was a general rule, but there do not seem to have been many professional nursemaids in the middle of the nineteenth century: 35,937 in 1851, 67,785 in 1861, 75,491 in 1871. Their numbers were increasing, but so was the population as a whole. In 1871 there were 150,000 families classified as upper-middle class. Not all families had small children, and no doubt there were many girls working as nursemaids who avoided the census. Nevertheless, the picture is not one of general remoteness of mother from child.

The advice in the manuals supports this impression. Mothers were the accepted moral guides and physical guardians of their children—nurses were auxiliaries, not stand-ins. One of the reasons for the stress laid upon children's good behaviour was that they would be with their parents in the drawing-room, or even paying calls on other families.

Q. When ought a child to commence to dine with his parents?

A. As soon as he be old enough to sit up at the table,
    provided the mother and father either dine or lunch in
    the middle of the day. 'I always prefer having children
    about me at mealtimes. I think it makes them little
    gentlewomen and gentlemen in a manner that nothing
    else will.' (Dinah Mulock, quoted in Chavasse, *Counsel
    to Mothers*, 1869)

The importance now firmly attached to the early years
strengthened eighteenth-century suspicions that the influence of servants could be disastrous on a child's character.
Middle-class mothers wealthy enough to afford several
servants were constantly warned against leaving them with
the children. Eliza Warren's arrangement was probably a
fairly common one. She had two girls, one a kitchen maid and
one a nursery maid, who supported her running of both
spheres. As soon as the children were old enough, she
dispensed with all but a 'general', and taught the daughters to
run the house themselves.

Even books such as Mrs Barwell's *Nursery Government* and
Louisa Hoare's *Hints on Nursery Discipline*, which were
specifically 'addressed to nurses, were conscious of the
dangers of maternal neglect. Significantly, Mrs Hoare re-
dedicated the second edition of her book to mothers, and put
her advice to nurses in an appendix. Even where a separate
nursery staff was assumed, mothers were not encouraged to
leave nurses in sole charge. No doubt some mothers were too
busy socializing or politicizing to see much of their children,
and no doubt many nurses abused their position of trust—but
the ideal was one of closeness between mother and small
child. Mrs Gaskell and her daughter Marianne, rather than
sad Samuel Butler, should be taken as the norm for the
period.

Even if mother was there too, small children undoubtedly
spent a good deal of their time in the nursery. The room had
to be chosen with care. 'A dull and confined prospect will be a
source of dullness and ennui to the naturally active mind of
the child,' wrote Combe. Light was important. 'The windows
of the nursery are generally too small,' complained Chavasse.
'Gardeners are well aware of the great importance of light in

the construction of their greenhouses; and yet children, who require it as much, and are of much greater importance, are cooped up in dark rooms.' Decorations were painstakingly considered. Green wallpaper was forbidden, coloured as it was with arsenic of copper. 'Four children in one family have just lost their lives from sucking green paper-hangings,' Chavasse declared. (Did it taste as well as look good?) Bull emphasized the useful moral function of nursery pictures. 'A fine engraving and a good painting elevate the mind. We all know that first impresssions are the most vivid and the most lasting. A taste in early life for everything refined and beautiful purifies his mind, cultivates his intellect, keeps him from low company, and makes him grow up a gentleman.'

What did children do in the nursery? Mrs Warren had one low cupboard full of books, and another for toys. 'I never thought money badly spent on inexpensive toys. I remember my own delight in them, and also in storybooks—not sensible ones, I must confess, but *Bluebeard, Jack and the Beanstalk, The House that Jack Built*, and others of that kind.' She thought that their rough woodcut illustrations encouraged the 'imitative faculty' more than the highly finished colour plates then becoming popular.

Each child in her nursery had a peg of its own with its name on it, and a place for its garden tools. Written up on the walls was the motto, 'A Place for Everything, and Everything in its Place'. 'I do not mean to say', she hurried on defensively,

that anything *like* continuous order was kept, or that constant reproof went on in consequence of shortcomings, but good habits were given, if they were not always followed. I frequently put away the things myself, saying kindly—'Mamma likes to see the room tidy; let us all help to make it so.' Then the little feet pattered about, and the little hands were ready to be useful; then a kiss was given to each, and such a joyful clapping and shouting at the end of our labour.

As far as toys went, the experts preferred the old favourites: hoops and skipping ropes, Noah's arks for Sundays, simple carts to be loaded and unloaded with bricks. Already the child learnt through play; he was encouraged to test out the laws of mechanics with his little hammers and bricks, she could practise the 'mysteries of handling, fondling and soothing a baby' on her doll, 'life in miniature'. A rocking horse in front of the open window was excellent exercise for delicate children who could manage no more demanding mount. This puts a rather macabre light on the many riderless steeds that outlived their small owners, but no doubt they had more energetic riders too.

It is clear from the caveats of the writers that vast numbers of toys were being made for children. Many were disapproved of as potentially dangerous, possibly finished with poisonous paints. Others were over-elaborate, leaving the child with little to do but admire them. Enthusiasm for educational toys increased, despite the occasional lonely voice dismissing them, and parents rushed to buy their children kaleidoscopic toys, jigsawn maps, and movable letters. 'It is certain that a great deal of valuable information, even on abstruse subjects, can be imparted easily and pleasantly by means of playthings,' wrote Hamilton Fyfe in *Good Words*. They were also an opportunity—yet another opportunity—to mould the character. 'It is easy to see how truth, courage, self-denial, generosity and other moral qualities, may be instilled while the children are at play,' he continued—but then turned the tables nicely on the pedagogues by declaring the society of children, 'a fine moral shower-bath, into which one might go jaded, chilly and torpid, but from which one is sure to come out refreshed and glowing, with a brisker circulation and a lighter heart'. His article illustrated the deep affection and tolerance felt for children at the time. They were the hopes of the future, the fine instruments which, properly tuned, could lead to a better world.

Fresh air and exercise were nursery essentials. Windows were flung open as soon as a child left the room—fears of chills still prevented open windows while it was inside. Tiny babies were rubbed all over to improve their circulation, and carried about on cushions in front of open windows to get their daily dose of fresh air; or a small oblong basket, with sides high enough to allow a cover loosely over the limbs, could be carried around. 'By this contrivance, a gentle and agreeable swinging and undulating motion will be communicated,' wrote Combe. At three or four weeks, the baby was carried about on a nurse's arm. When old enough to enjoy it, a baby could crawl and tumble about on a rug, or outside on the grass. Clothes had to be short enough not to impede it and loose enough for easy movement.

Leading strings and other mechanical aids to walking were disapproved of—the child was to be left to go at its own speed. Eliza Warren sketched a model description of the process. At first the mother just held up the baby to make him walk. Then she used a silk scarf to support him, but could see that it hurt his chest. A friend told her to let him crawl—'I said I wanted him to walk, not crawl'—but she gave in, and admitted that 'it gave him much pleasure'. When the child seemed more ready to walk, she gave him a little practice session, six or seven minutes every hour—useful evidence of how much that mother expected to be with her child.

Babies were necessarily carried and cuddled a good deal at this time, because there were not cleverly designed alternatives for them. Whether it was cause or effect of the distancing process, inventiveness now began to be applied to keeping infants content without human contact. Dr Conquest recommended Rogers's Patent Infant Gymnasium, or Baby Jumper, recently introduced from America. A strong elastic spring was attached to the ceiling, supporting a little canvas seat. This was disguised as a dress or coat, to preserve decency, and a baby of three or four months could be strapped into it to bounce up and down. It was exactly the same as the modern 'baby bouncer'.

The most influential of all baby-care appliances was the perambulator, and its history is worth a little digression. No doubt babies had been put in carts of sorts ever since the invention of the wheel—a clay model of a baby-cart has been dug up in Athens, and there is pictorial evidence of their use in fourteenth-century India and Ceylon. Perhaps they were first introduced into England by some homecoming nabob. The earliest examples in that country were those made in the carpenters' shops of the very rich—the baby-carriages built for Lady Georgina Cavendish at Chatsworth were coaches in miniature.

The decade of their general introduction was the 1850s, and their popularity increased rapidly. There had been many experiments in the 1840s, some three-wheeled, some pulled rather than pushed, but the first patent for the perambulator as we know it was Charles Burton's, in 1853. He opened a showroom in Oxford Street, where four other manufacturers had joined him by 1856. By the end of the next decade, there were at least thirty British pram-makers, soon publishing a trade gazette of their own, rather than just a supplement to the *Journal of Domestic Appliances.*

Undoubtedly, there were hazards to be faced—lack of springs, arsenic-coated harnesses, and the dangers of increased neglect by nursemaids. But the early prams were things of considerable grace and beauty. Liveried wooden casings were hemmed with miniature balustrades, lined with buttoned leather, and trimmed in gleaming brass. Bassinet versions, especially popular in the United States and the colonies, were reed-woven in shell-coiled arabesques, with parasols or canopies fluttering overhead. The experts were divided on their merits. To Walsh they were 'one of the most extraordinary inventions of the age', an unqualified blessing. But Chavasse maintained that a child should be carried until it could walk:

> It is painful to notice a babe of a few months in one of these new-fangled carriages. His little head is bobbing about, first on one side and then on another—at one moment it is dropping on his chest, the next it is forcibly jolted behind: he looks and doubtless feels, wretched and uncomfortable. Again, these wretched perambulators are dangerous in crowded thoroughfares. They are a public nuisance, in as much as they are wheeled against and between people's legs, and are a fruitful source of the breaking of shins, of the spraining of ankles, of the crushing of corns, and of the ruffling of tempers of all the foot passengers who unfortunately come within their reach; while in all probability gaping nurses are staring the other way, and every way indeed but the right.

Eliza Warren produced a 'long-legged pig' snuffling under

the covers of one pram while the nurse chatted to her mother in a rough part of town. Until roads and springs improved, babies must have had very bumpy rides. However, prams had come to stay. Their use, if not their abuse, was accepted in most of the later books. Finally the royal seal of approval was given by Queen Victoria's purchase of three Burton carriages, and an engraving in the *Illustrated London News* which showed the Princess of Wales processing beside one in St James's Park.

'Life is soon extinguished in Infancy'

Confirmation of the central importance of the mother at this time was the extent of her medical responsibility. The contents of contemporary domestic medicine chests show that she was free to administer frighteningly dangerous drugs. Doctors were not sufficiently respected at the start of the nineteenth century to be an automatic resort in times of emergency—moreover, they were expensive to consult. Conquest blamed the medical profession for this popular lack of confidence.

> Until of late, in no country has the attention of medical men been so little directed to the state of infancy as this; and much mortality is due to lack of popular instruction. Many eminent men, even of the present day, feel an aversion to being consulted in cases of infantile disease.

The chapters on sickness and disease in the manuals therefore often contained detailed prescriptions for cures, assuming that the average mother would be her own physician. When one considers what babies were likely to suffer from, this situation becomes even more alarming. Although smallpox was now curbed by vaccination, there were plenty of lethal threats left. The digestive system could suffer from jaundice, worms of all shapes and sizes, diarrhoea or dysentery. Lungs were attacked by croup, whooping cough, pneumonia and consumption. Other common killers were measles, rickets, hydrocephalus, scarlet fever, erysipelas, gangrene and convulsions. By modern standards, medical defences against these were risible. They centred round the well-tried cure-alls of leeches, purgatives and blisters, enhanced by opium and calomel. John Darwall gave details of their use in his *Plain Instructions for the Management of Infants.*

Leeches were seen as a kindly measure, gentler than bloodletting by steel. In order not to frighten the child, the leech was concealed in the mouth of a small bottle, applied to the skin, and allowed to gorge itself until it dropped off. A touch of salt encouraged its collapse if its appetite was too hearty. Leeches were applied to every part of the body. Cradle cap in its worst form, *porrigo furfuracea*, required their application to the head. Catarrh, 'the malignant snuffles' which could kill in four days, called for a leech on the nose. The even more dreaded croup called for eight leeches on the windpipe. 'Watery gripes' were treated by leeches set to the abdomen and rectum, and urinary infections in little girls were helped by a couple on the vulva. Purgatives were not only used in cases of constipation, but as a preliminary to almost every cure. On the blanket principle that if something was wrong inside the child, the more that could come out the better, they were recommended even in cases of diarrhoea. Gentle aperients were preferred to the most common nursery stand-by, calomel, which several books warned mothers not to use. Magnesia and rhubarb, senna teas, soapstick suppositories, enemas and castor-oil biscuits were all familiar prescriptions.

Blisters, or plasters, were distinctly odd affairs. They were a preparation made from cantharides beetles, nicknamed Spanish flies. These beautiful insects, bright gold and iridescent blue in colour, were gathered from the shores of the Mediterranean at twilight as they drowsed on bushes. They were scooped into muslin bags, dipped in vinegar and dried. Then, compressed in bottles, they could be bought from chemists' shops, their quality being judged by the intensity of the blueness. Applied in poultices, they raised a large blister on the skin. Why was this done? It has been variously explained as being a counter-irritant, summoning blood away from the seat of infection, or as acting by contracting the arteries. However it acted, the effect seems to have been to lower body temperature.

Darwall did not believe himself to be a physician who dosed unduly, and he criticized doctors who did. All his remedies had the same 'anti-phlogistic' aim—that is, to reduce the heat of the blood and so lower the temperature. He described with some pride how he saved the life of a child with pneumonia by a warm bath, two or three leeches and some syrup of poppies. Her two older sisters had died of the excessive zeal of their physicians: 'bleeding, blistering, the whole anti-phlogistic regimen had been most carefully and repeatedly practised, and the two children died at the end of a fortnight in a state of complete exhaustion.'

Darwall's book was written for doctors and nurses, but he hoped that mothers would read it too. Andrew Combe disagreed. Mothers resorted to medicines far too easily, he felt. To force them to seek professional advice he refused to give any specific cures. In general they interfered far too much:

> they seem to regard [the body] as a machine acting upon no fixed principles, and requiring now and then to be driven by some foreign impulse in the shape of medicine. Under this impression, they are on the watch to see what *they can do* to keep it moving; and are altogether distrustful of the Creator's arrangement.

With conventional medicine (perhaps rightly) held in disrepute, mothers subscribed to other authorities. Alternatives were provided by quacks such as Alfred Fennings, the ancient herbal remedies of Lydia Child (particularly useful in the remote American settlements) or the semi-respectable and very popular new science of homoeopathy. Fennings wrote his *Every Mother's Book, or the Child's Best Doctor* in order to sell his own patent medicines, which he recommended for every childhood complaint. Their efficiency may have been improved by his directive to mothers not to let leeches, calomel or blisters anywhere near their children. He believed that the mother was the child's best doctor, and that tender loving care was half the battle—the other half, of course, was a Fennings' Cooling Powder, a Fennings' Lung-healer, or a Fennings' Whooping-cough Powder.

Lydia Child concentrated on herbal specifics: for croup, a poultice of tobacco leaves, replaced after a time by a cloth covered with goose or hen oil, plentifully sprinkled with Scottish snuff; for colic, warm mint-tea, or an infusion of fennel or caraway. The pulp of rotten apples eased inflammation of the eyes, and persistent whooping cough could be cleared by munching garlic. Perhaps she was ambitious in offering a cure for dropsy in the head (hydrocephalus)—certainly she was a little hesitant: 'I have heard of one child, given over by his physician, whose life was thought to have been saved by having his head shaved and covered with a poultice of onions stewed with vinegar, and his feet bathed in warm water with mustard in it.'

Arguably far less harm was done by these measures than by the official prescriptions of calomel and 'quietness' (opium syrup). Many doctors ascribed the considerable vogue for homoeopathy to the 'natural medical law' that, left alone, the body's mechanism would put itself right if possible. Homoeopathy was conceived of by Hahnemann in 1796. His theory was that like should be treated with like. Foreshadowing the use of serum to treat and prevent such diseases as lockjaw, typhus and bubonic plague, it was also modern in its belief that drugs ought to be tested on healthy people before sick ones. The dosages recommended were minute, certainly unlikely to do any positive harm. Walter Johnson's child-care manual 'on homoeopathic and hydropathic principles' was written in 1857, at the height of the movement's success. Mrs Beeton approved it enough to include a chapter on it in *Household Management*, and recommended its use for children's diseases. The domestic medicine chest that homoeopathic enthusiasts used certainly compared favourably with the lethal cabinets of the orthodox. Packed with tiny phials, they allowed plenty of margin for error.

Although ignorance could cause death by not recognizing illnesses for what they were, it was also true that the well-meant chapters on diseases and their cures encouraged mothers to take dangerous action too often. Calomel, for example, although an efficient cure for many stomach troubles, and as such widely used in nurseries, was in fact a compound of mercury—mercurous chloride—and a cumulative poison, like arsenic. It is interesting, although only speculation, to consider that the symptoms of mercury poisoning are tenderness of the teeth, spongy bleeding gums, and excess salivation. Perhaps many of the 'teething deaths' should have been laid at the door of those useful 'grey powders'. Cantharides was fatal when taken internally, and the risks of laudanum are well known. Mothers were not competent to deal with such things. As medical understanding increased, more and more manuals left out all details of dosages. Given the situation—crowded city life, epidemic diseases, rising infant mortality, general ignorance of the hygienic and dietetic precautions necessary to stop complications developing—this was probably right. The mother was no longer the 'child's best doctor'.

'*As the twig is bent*'

Religion and science combined to postpone infant intellectual accomplishment. Smiles wrote: 'The tender minds of children are too often early tasked and wrought beyond their abilities, their memories laden with words like the veriest packhorse, drugged with knowledge, through the medium of sounds which convey little or no meaning.' The new thinkers felt the dry intellectual precocity of the eighteenth-century prodigies was as inappropriate to infancy as the total freedom advocated by Rousseau. The early years were to be devoted to 'cherishing amiable moral feelings', and to leading the senses to feed the 'inner storehouses of the mind' by giving the child toys to play with which would stimulate its understanding of the concrete world.

Conservative opinion remained sceptical. Bookstores were full of textbooks on botany, geometry and astronomy for two and three year olds. Because of the 'high mental excitement which pervades the age', parents 'anxiously resort to every method which will enable their offspring to become prodigies in mental endowments, while in every other respect they remain weak and delicate infants' (quoted in Stewart). When Harriet Martineau visited the United States, she shocked one rural widow because of the lack of booklearning of a six-year-old boy in her party, even though she explained that 'Charley's head was full of knowledge of other kinds'. By the mid-century there was nothing extraordinary in a child not learning to read until it was six. Phrenology had added its weight to the argument for holding back on words and ideas until the child's mind could really grasp what it was being taught. If the faculties were merely in bud, then their education should proceed by gentle and easy stages. The baby's observation, curiosity, imagination and memory could be gradually exercised. Combe pointed to the baby's instinctive efforts to do this: 'It delights to exercise its eyes on brilliant objects and colours, to train its ear to the discrimination of sounds by every variety of noise, and to educate the sense of touch by feeling and handling everything within reach.'

Phrenology backed up a movement in education which had started in the previous century. Rousseau, Pestalozzi and the Edgeworths had all believed in education by things rather than words. Froebel's kindergarten system was exhibited at the Society of Arts educational exhibition in 1854, and although it was not widely adopted until the later decades of the century, his ideas influenced the manuals of child-care much earlier on. Samuel Wilderspin, whose movement for infant schools at the start of the century paralleled Thomas Coram's innovation of foundling hospitals in its benefit to 'the nation's babies ... thus redeemed from ignorance and vice', very soon found that he had to adapt his methods to suit his audience. His account of how he and his wife started their first school reveals his inner resource. Eighty small children aged between two and seven were deposited by their (working) mothers in the new schoolroom. There was a moment's silence after the last mother left. Then as one child the entire gang hurled themselves at the door in a united wail of protest. Wilderspin could not even make himself heard. He slipped out to consider what to do, and on consultation with his wife decided that surprise was the only hope. So he put one of her largest bonnets on his own head—backwards—and suddenly appeared behind the desolate mob with a gay shout. Silence. Then laughter.

Wilderspin realized that he would have to rethink conventional rote-teaching methods. He used objects, pictures, and talk—about colour, form, properties—and kept the lessons short. Singing and dancing and the fashionable callisthenic exercises made the school enough of a success to inspire others all over the country. Wilderspin travelled energetically, appointing teachers, and advising philanthropic ladies on how to manage their schools. The extent and importance of the infant-school movement can be calculated when one recalls how often heroines in novels are preoccupied by their management, either before or after their love-affairs.

Although the infant schools were intended for the children of the poor, they were apparently regarded as something of a threat by middle-class mothers. Isaac Taylor claimed that many were sending their children to them, in case they became less intellectually accomplished than 'stocking-weaver Willie or Kitty'. Harriet Martineau allowed that they had done a good deal of good for the 'little creatures who would be locked up all day while their parents were at work, liable to falls, or fire, or who would be tumbling about the streets dirty, quarrelsome, and exposed to bad company'. But she criticized mothers who sent their children to such schools rather than teaching them themselves at home. Her reasoning was not class-consciousness but the belief that the family had more to offer than the peer-group:

> Nature makes households, family groups where no two children are of the same age, and where, with the utmost activity, there is a certain degree of quietness, retirement, and repose; whereas, in the Infant School there is a crowd of little creatures, dozens of whom are of the same age; and quietness can only be obtained by drilling, while play occasions an uproar which no nerves can easily stand. The brains and nerves of infants are tender and irritable, and in the quietest home a sensible mother takes care that the little creature is protected from hurry, and loud noises and fear, and fatigue of its faculties. (*Household Education*)

Fireside Education was the ideal, sketched by Samuel Goodrich in 1838. 'The mother sways the dominion of the heart, the father that of the intellect,' he declared. Perhaps this traditional division encouraged the dropping of intellectual cramming, and the intensifying of gentle teaching, by affection rather than coercion. A more significant reason for the mother taking over as intellectual mentor could have been that, since education was now seen as a continuous process from infancy, she was obviously more suited to initiate and continue handling it. Mrs Phelps's 'Observations on an Infant' was an American parallel to Mrs Gaskell's *My Diary*—detailed observations of her own child, inspired by Madame de Saussure's suggestion that mothers keep diaries. It showed the mother as both observer and attendant. Besides recording, she intervened to multiply the experiences and thus exercise the faculties of the child. For example, she gave her boy a box of wafers and let him shake and pull at the box until he was able to open it. When 'hundreds of bright round pieces fell about him in glorious confusion' she felt that he 'had conquered a difficulty and had made a discovery'. This sort of loving attention and stimulus from mothers would disappear underground later on in the century, when nannies relieved parents punch-drunk from Darwin and professional kindergarteners.

Until then, the keynote was simplicity. Nature study had not yet been organized into expeditions to name and forget things. Mrs Ellis asked that children should 'roam the hills, listening to waterfalls and holding converse with the spirit of nature', rather than being taken 'in the heat of summer to fashionable bathing-places, to wear their best clothes, walk out in tight shoes, and hear their mammas and aunts discourse on the elegance of the Duchess of Devonshire's equipage'. Isaac Taylor advised parents to avoid the 'doggrel history, the gingling grammar and geographies' and educational toys. 'Let play be play and nothing else. On a rainy day I had rather see a boy amusing himself with cats' cradle than with a geometrical, or geographical or historical puzzle.'

Although mothers were usually the managers of infant education at this point, Cobbett's *Advice to a Father* painted the domestic ideal of the age. It was in a rural setting, however, and with a father present all day—both increasingly uncommon as cities grew. It also reinforced Harriet Martineau's belief that children of different ages learn better from each other than from their peers. And it was true—it was how Cobbett spent his life, making scholars of his children without the help of teachers:

I accomplished my purpose indirectly. The first thing of all was health, which was secured by the deeply interesting and never-ending sports of the field and pleasures of the garden. Luckily these things were treated of in books and pictures of endless variety; so that on wet days, and in the evenings, these came into play. A large strong table in the middle of the room, their mother sitting at her work, used to be surrounded by them, the baby, if big enough, set up in a high chair. Here were inkstands, pens, pencils, India-rubber and paper, all in abundance, and every-one scrambled about as he or she pleased. There were prints of animals of all sorts, books treating of them; others treating of gardening, of flowers, of husbandry, of hunting, shooting, fishing, coursing, planting, and in short, of everything with regard to which *we had something to do*. One would be trying to imitate my writing, another drawing pictures of some of our dogs or horses, a third poking over Bewick's *Quadrupeds*, and picking out what he had to say about them; but our book of never-failing resource was the French *Maison Rustique* ... Here were all the four-legged animals from the horse down to the mouse, portraits and all; all the birds, reptiles and insects; all the modes of taking the wild ones, ditto rearing, managing and using the tame ones, and of destroying those that are mischievous etc. etc., and there was I, in my leisure moments, to join this inquisitive group, to read the French and tell them what it meant in English ...

What need had we of schools? What need of teachers? What need of scolding and force to teach the children to read and write and love books?

Bathtime as a lesson in cheerful fortitude, bedtime as an opportunity for tyranny, a risk of sensual appetite over lunch:

it is clear that there was no longer a distinction between mind and body in bringing up children. Rousseau had felt it a waste of time to do much about the moral education of small children. Once the necessary safety net, obedience, had been draped around them, they were left to discover as much as they could about the nature of the world for themselves—if they survived. The Puritan approach had been equally lacking in subtlety. They had beaten out evil and ladled in the Scriptures indiscriminately. Early nineteenth-century parents, fortified by the truths of phrenology, also had a more benevolent religious approach to their children. The doctrine of infant depravity was no longer generally acceptable— by the 1820s it had been dropped even from Evangelical theory.

I ask . . . if children were demons fit for hell, would God have given them that attractive sweetness, that mild beauty which renders them the most interesting objects on earth, and which compels us to shrink with horror from the thought of their everlasting ruin? ('Dissertation on the Sinfulness of Infants', *Christian Disciple*, 2 Aug 1814)

Childhood became a saccharin-sweet state of purity and innocence, 'which speaks to us of heaven, which tells us of those pure angelic beings which surround the throne of God, untouched by sin, untainted by the breath of corruption', (*Ladies' Magazine*, June 1833). Literature, for adults and children alike, became stuffed with small heroes and heroines, usually (mercifully) moribund, who redeemed those about them with their essential goodness. Little Nell, Little Eva, Eppie in George Eliot's *Silas Marner*—'In old days there were angels who came and took men by the hand and led them away from the city of destruction. We see no white-winged angels now. But yet men are led away from threatening destruction: a hand is put into theirs, which leads them forth gently towards a calm and bright land, so that they look no more backward; and the hand may be a little child's'—these were the more respectable of the genre. A random dip into the family periodicals reveals many more.

Fire and brimstone addicts continued to exist, as they do to this day in odd corners; but such bigotry was not well represented in the popular manuals. In fact, the tedious recurrence of the names of Elizabeth Grant, Augustus Hare and Samuel Butler in social histories perpetuating the myth of the heavy Victorian father suggests a paucity rather than an abundance of evidence on the subject. Elizabeth Grant's father was a backwoods Highland peer with his feet and riding crop firmly in the eighteenth-century hardening school. Augustus Hare was raised by a semi-lunatic aunt who hung his pet cat and committed suicide. Samuel Butler is generally reckoned by his biographers to have cruelly exaggerated the characters of his father and mother in *The Way of All Flesh*. How about recalling instead the humanity of Mr Micawber, of Mr Pooter in *The Diary of a Nobody*, or Trollope's *Warden*? Extreme oppression of children for their own good was not a typical approach of the well-meaning middle-class parent, as Mrs Ellis indicated when she wrote in 1843:

> It was the custom, with many well-intentioned parents, some fifty years ago, to bring up children under the mistaken notion of rooting up evil, before good could be introduced; of breaking the natural will, crossing the natural inclination, and subduing pride by constant mortification. Yet, notwithstanding the various modes of discipline adopted in carrying out this notion, people were just as self-willed, as proud, as determined to please themselves, as they are now. It has by degrees become evident to persons of common sense, that such violent measures are not adapted to produce the desired effect. Indeed, some of us have gone so far as to believe that pride is no more likely to be eradicated by constant mortification, than the appetite is likely to be destroyed by a scanty supply of food.

Persons of common sense came down somewhere between the child martyrs and the imps of Satan. Their favourite metaphor was that of the seedbed. De Saussure and Mrs Ellis used it, as did Combe. The parent as gardener had to be constantly on the alert to stake up deserving mental qualities and weed out those that were undesirable.

Phrenology made this easier by dividing the infant mind into three categories, as separate from each other, they believed, as the five distinct senses of the body. The powers of Emotion were the subject of moral training. The powers of Thought governed intellectual development, and the powers of Observation were the medium through which understanding of God was achieved. By example rather than precept— showing, not telling—Combe believed that 'the appropriate stimuli' could be applied to each faculty. Each had its optimum time of approach. Benevolence, for example, was believed not to develop until the infant was two years old. Careful conditioning at that age could increase its strength. Mrs Sigourney described a mother who had been so successful in teaching her child kindliness at that age that when she described a bird catching flies, her child 'lisped, with a kind of horror on his baby face, "Oh! kill flies! Will God forgive it?" '

The first and most powerful of the infant faculties was that of imitation. Kind faces were to surround the baby, harsh voices were never to be used in its presence. Children began to retreat from the harsh realities of the adult world. Who looked after the baby was no longer decided by whether they could efficiently cope with it physically—it was a matter of soul nourishment. At the aristocratic level this led to new anxiety over the character of the infant's nurse, but to the middle classes it was a triumphant vindication of the mother as moral, spiritual and intellectual mentor: 'moulding the whole mass of mind in its first formation', as Mrs Sigourney put it. 'If she can fix her lever judiciously, though she may not, like Archimedes, aspire to move the earth, she may hope to raise one of the inhabitants to heaven.' All the manuals united in encouraging mothers to be with their infants as much as possible. 'The conduct and spirit of the mother give a tone to that domestic atmosphere by which the soul in its early experiences is sustained,' wrote Mrs Ellis.

Faith in the child's capacity for imitation explained the flood of moralizing literature, with its crude blacks and whites to ensure that even the least sensitive of children grasped the point. Mrs Sherwood's *Fairchild Family* is often quoted as typical, with its visit to the gibbet to discourage sibling rivalry, and threats of damnation for stealing an apple. But it was written in 1818, by an Indian Army officer's wife, who could hardly be said to have been in touch with forward-looking ideas in child-rearing. Moreover, although the book continued to sell well throughout the nineteenth century, the more extreme passages had been dropped by 1847. Most of the moral tales were a good deal milder—and a good deal duller. Fairytales remained unfashionable in the first half of the century. Catherine Sinclair attempted to correct the imbalance with *Holiday House* (1839), written about 'that species of noisy, frolicsome, mischievous children which is now almost extinct' in literature. It must have appealed as much to children as the Fairchild family did to their parents, but it too had a moral purpose—and a deathbed scene. Jacob Abbott (1803–79), an American preacher, schoolteacher, and writer on child-care, wrote the series of Rollo books from 1834 onwards, and together with the Jonas and the Lucy books they illustrate far better than more purple fiction the sort of everyday life that parents hoped for for their children at this time, 'exemplifying the principles of honest integrity and practical good sense'.

'Will shows itself very early. Fear has to be guarded against, and Love to be cherished, from the first days that mind appears.' Coping with these basics summarized by Harriet Martineau was the essence of moral management. First will—the sticky matter of obedience. *Emile* could be forgotten, as far as Madame de Saussure was concerned. 'Perhaps Rousseau has made you uneasy as to the lawfulness of your authority. But if your child be exposed to a real danger, or even a trifling or imaginary inconvenience, you snatch him up in your arms and carry him away; your scruples, your resolution, your theories are all forgotten.' Reasoning was inappropriate at this age—it was unfair to treat the child as an equal when in any emergency the parent would simply resort to physical force. 'In your conduct then, there exists a degree of treachery; and the resistance of the child shows that he feels it.' Here was a dilemma which will be familiar to any parent who has started with Spock in hand and ended with a real child on the knee. De Saussure betrayed her astringent tendencies when she made the remark typical of such theorists that 'domestic discipline, formerly too rigorous, is now, perhaps, carried to the other extreme'. Andrew Combe, on the other hand, felt that although allowing the child's will unlimited sway was too common an error in bringing up children, there was more danger in 'substituting the mother's feeling, inclination and judgement for the child's, and regulating even the minutest and most unimportant details by a rigid adherence to rules.' He went on to show his commitment to the 'child's eye-view' position:

> Adaptation to the wants, feelings and nature of the infant—so different in many ways from those of the adult—ought to be made the leading principle of our management ... accordingly the child ought as far as possible to be allowed the choice of its own occupations and amusements and to become the chief agent in the development and formation of its own character. In later life, the independent child will show far more promptitude and energy than the 'puppet' dominated by parents and trained in moral slavery.

A quite different emphasis appeared in the ninth edition of Combe's *Treatise on Infancy*, edited and revised after his death by Queen Victoria's own physician, Sir James Clark. A remarkable number of insertions refer to the 'tyrannical propensities' of infants, sure sign of the iron man at work. It provides a fascinating example of how similar facts can be made to work to very different general effect, depending on the personal point of view of the writer.

Harriet Martineau dealt with the matter of obedience in a neutral way which reflected her agnosticism.

> When the child wills what is right and innocent, let the faculty work freely. When it wills what is wrong and hurtful, appeal to the other faculties and let this one sleep; excite the child's *attention*, engage its *memory*, or its *hope*, or its *affection*. If the infant is bent on having something that it ought not, put the forbidden object out of sight and amuse the child with something else.

The technique of distraction is still familiar today, although we wouldn't put it into terms of distinct faculties in quite the same way.

The theorists were firmly against corporal punishment for small children. James Nelson's lonely voice on its meanness and ignominy now had an almost united body of thinkers to support it. There were still parents who beat their children savagely (there still are today), but an anecdote in Martineau's *Household Education* illustrates a change in public opinion as well as in expert theory. It concerned an American clergyman set on breaking the will of his *eleven-month-old* daughter by forcing her to eat a crust of bread:

Hours of crying, shrieking and moaning were followed by its being shut up in a closet. It was brought out by candlelight, stretched helpless across the nurse's arms, its voice lost, its eyes sunk and staring, its muscles shrunk, its appearance that of a dead child. It was now near midnight. The bit of bread was thrust into the powerless hand; no resistance was offered by the unconscious sufferer; and the victory over the evil powers of the flesh and the devil were declared to be gained.

As it stands, the story does nothing but reinforce popular ideas of Victorian fathers. But the sequel is more significant. An indignant servant leaked the tale to the town, and the clergyman was publicly pilloried. Hershey was out of style: wills were no longer broken.

A subtler, possibly more dangerous, means of discipline was introduced instead—conscience. Perhaps the change reflected the retreat of the father from the forefront of domestic management. Traditionally women were less violent than men; they were the gentle rulers, soothing men's coarser natures. Through the cradle they could rule the world. 'The nations, instead of being controlled by fear, are ere long to be controlled by the law of love and kindness. In this revolution . . . woman is to perform the most important, if not the principal part. She is to wield the sceptre, first over her husband, and next over the children whom God may give her' (Alcott, *The Young Mother*). Conscience was 'the greatest and noblest of the moral powers of man' and could be stimulated very early in childhood—recall Mrs Sigourney's satisfaction over the two year old's sympathy for the flies. His concern for God's forgiveness was as striking as his youthful benevolence.

The astringent Eliza Warren took some pride in the success of her disciplinary techniques. 'Children can, as they are trained to good or left to run wild, make or mar the happiness of every home.' Naturally signs of rebellion had appeared among her eight very different children, 'but I never allowed the child to become master'. God figured highly in her method. She told them that His eye was literally on them all the time. When one of the children sneaked to her that little Richard had carved his name on the bench, she swept in on the culprit and announced that in a personal interview with her, God had told her of his sin.

Less untruthful, but more morally crippling, was the approach recommended by a prize essay written to the American *Mother's Assistant* in 1844. In it the mother deepened the offender's sense of repentance by backing up a necessary beating with an appeal to conscience. 'Mrs Robinson' did not like using the rod, considering it 'perverting to the moral feelings of the child', so she engineered matters to make the child request to be beaten to appease his conscience. She called her small son Willie to her, explained what he had done, and that she had to beat him for it, and settled a time on the next day. His sister was sent to fetch a rod, and it was hung in a prominent place. So Willie had until the next day to look at the rod and reflect upon his sins. Next day:

his mother took him into her chamber, and holding him affectionately in her lap, discussed at length the nature of his offence. She read and explained to him the account of Eli's death saying, 'Would you rather have God punish your mother, or have her punish you?' Willie chose to be punished, and before inflicting the chastisement, she knelt and prayed with him. (Kuhn, *Mother's Role in Childhood Education*)

This was heady stuff. Without the rod, it was also standard disciplinary technique—never before or since was so much demanded of the infant moral sense. It could only be successful, however, if the child's affection for its parents was profound enough to make it want to obey for their sake. The 'this hurts me more than it hurts you' method of punishment only has any point if the child minds its mother feeling hurt. It would be cynical to reduce the theorists' concern for developing the faculty of love in their children to a desire for obedience, but de Saussure appeared to do so when she wrote:

> If the favourable season of sympathy has been allowed to pass away without our having gathered the fruits which it ought to have produced, such as a desire to please and oblige, a wish to relieve the afflicted, the power of giving up a pleasure in order to bestow it on another, we shall soon arrive at a troublesome season, when our children will . . . understand our exhortations, but will receive no moral impression from them.

This sympathy had to be established within the first year. The writers concerned with encouraging love between mother and child recognized that it might not be an immediate reaction from either—it was a good to be worked towards. Naturally, the mother's presence was a necessity. 'Trust not your treasure too much to the charge of hirelings,' pleaded Lydia Sigourney. 'Have it under your superintendence night and day. Its little heart will soon reach out the slender radicles of love and trust.'

The phrenologists had found a faculty of philoprogenitiveness—love of having offspring—among the bumps on mothers' heads (interesting that they looked for one). So a very small bump could explain an undemonstrative, harsh mother, and an over-developed one an over-fond, excessively indulgent mother. The discovery of this built-in affection of a mother for her child was a useful scientific ally for the current Christian projection of a world ruled by love and affection. Infancy, according to Lydia Child, was a period of 'unfoldment' when the exercise of gentleness and love acted on the child's soul 'like sunshine on a rosebud'. Mrs Sigourney opened *Letters to Mothers* with the words: 'You are sitting with your child in your arms. So am I. And I have never been so happy before ... How this affection seems to spread a soft fresh green over the soul ... What a loss, had we passed through the world without tasting this purest, most exquisite fount of love.'

Even Samuel Smiles, so calmly and dispassionately rational in most of *Physical Education*, waxed suddenly poetic in considering the baby's need for affection. 'Love is the element God has designed them to move in, for parents, for friends, for playfellows, and that this so often appears wanting in children, arises from erroneous or perverse systems of moral training, which neglect and pass unheedingly the little flowers of human nature, trampling and injuring them.'

Deep affection for children made fear, and its converse fortitude, important to parents. No doubt a child would be likely to suffer severe pain from illness at some time in its life; the shadow of revolution was far from dispelled by the death of Napoleon, and grumbling industrial strife did not die down until the 1850s. Preserving the growing empire required an army of brave men led by worthy officers. Perhaps this background goes some way to explaining the almost morbid interest in infant fears which now appeared in the manuals. It was a faculty like any other, to be developed to the correct extent.

The shadow of the hardening school still stretched over Harriet Martineau when she wrote that, although a bold child was a delight, he had to have some fear in him. In order to become great (remember *Feats on the Fjords*), 'he must learn and endure much that can be learned and endured only through fear and the conquest of it ... The parent must silently seek out, and train it up into that awe and modesty which are necessary to the high courage of a whole life.' With a timid child, the work would be a slow one, but the parent should be comforted that 'the noblest courage of man and woman has often grown out of the excessive fears of a child'. It was absolutely essential in teaching an infant to overcome its fears—and here the link between fear and affection was very clear—to give the child complete confidence in its mother as a constant refuge and unfailing support. A trifling action by a parent—she gave as an example a mother who slapped her five month old out of vexation at its poor table manners in front of visitors—could do 'fatal mischief' by 'impairing the child's security'.

Fear was also seen as necessary to the imagination—something was lacking in a totally fearless child. Harriet Martineau made a familiar modern point when she noted that an apparently listless and apathetic child could in fact be profoundly fearful of some trivial object or occurrence. Suppressed worries ought to be watched for by the careful parent. 'No creature is so intensely reserved as the proud and timid child, and the cases are few in which the parents know anything of the agonies of its little heart, the spasms of its nerves, the soulsickness of its days, the horrors of its nights.' Chavasse warned against foolish nurses who frightened their charges with stories of hobgoblins, or put on masks to keep them scared in bed while they enjoyed themselves elsewhere. A child, he added, ought never to be put in a dark place, or frightened by tales of rats, ogres, and such. Sudden fright could cause dangerous illness. If the child suffered from 'night-terrors', he was to be left with the light on, and some kind person—preferably his mother—should be at hand to comfort him. 'Do not scold him for being frightened—he cannot help it; but soothe him, calm him, take him in your arms, and let him feel that he has someone to rest upon, to defend him, and protect him.'

It is interesting how much psychology, of a sort, had a place in child-rearing literature before the much trumpeted discovery of the unconscious and its shadowy allies at the end of the century. Books like de Saussure's *Progressive Education* provided a reasonable and sophisticated theory of the different stages in children's mental development. With de Saussure, Combe, Chavasse or Martineau at their sides, it is difficult to see how parents could have been the caricatures that so many social historians make them. The message that emerges most clearly is that of affection—powerfully tinged with Christian respectability, but affection none the less.

3
Science and Sensibility
1870–1920

By courtesy of the Committee.

Limbo, 1870–90

This is not a neat part of the story, but a necessary one. The decades from 1870 to 1890 were characterized neither by the confident Christian morality that preceded them, nor by the curious co-existence of science and sentiment that followed. They were years when parents and popularizers alike digested Darwin, and wondered if families really needed to be so large and expensive. Whether through a crisis of faith or through love of fashionable life, mothers became demoralized. In a flush of feminist enthusiasm, they considered their own roles in life rather than the immortal souls of their children. As E. L. Linton's famous essay in the *Saturday Review* made clear, they put women, not children, first. 'Society has put maternity out of fashion, and the nursery is nine times out of ten a place of punishment, not pleasure, to the modern mother.'

Popular interest in babies waned perceptibly, perhaps because there were far too many of them about. The opening lines of F. M. Mayor's *The Third Mrs Symons* set a typical scene:

> Henrietta was the third daughter and fifth child of Mr and Mrs Symons, so that enthusiasm for babies had declined by the time she arrived . . . If she had been one of two, or one of three, in a present-day family, she would have been more precious. But as one of four daughters—another girl was born when she was eight—she was not much wanted. Mr Symons was a solicitor in a country town, and the problem of providing for his seven darkened the years of childhood for the whole Symons family. The children felt that their parents found them something of a burden, and in those days there was no cult of childhood to soften the harsh reality.

Writing at the height of the cult of childhood in 1913, F. M. Mayor was looking back to the 1870s, the uncertain world in

89

which she was brought up. Drawing-rooms were then uncomfortably full of unqualified daughters who had missed the nuptial boat, and idle younger sons. Men could be sent out to the colonies, but the great question of the age was what to do with 'redundant' or 'superfluous' women.

One answer was, of course, to have fewer babies. *Large or Small Families: on Which Side lies the Balance of Comfort?* was the challenging title of Austin Holyoake's book of 1870. 'Have We Too Many Children?' asked a controversial article in the *Englishwoman's Domestic Magazine* in 1877. The explosion which rocked the idol of large family life right off its pedestal was the trial of Charles Bradlaugh and Annie Besant in 1877 for their republication of a useful little pamphlet on the techniques of family planning, *The Fruits of Philosophy*. They were convicted of obscene publication, but fought the verdict successfully. The case was a *cause célèbre*, and the press thundered its opinions for and against. Nice girls and wives were told to block their eyes and ears to the debate, but nothing could stop the quiet revolution which was already taking place. Families began to grow smaller; by the 1920s the birth rate was roughly half that of the 1870s.

The whys and wherefores of the falling birth rate do not directly concern us here. J. A. Banks has made out a convincing case for the part played by economic necessity in *Prosperity and Parenthood*. The increasing comfort in which the middle and upper classes felt called upon to keep their children as well as themselves was threatened, he believed, by trade recession, political upheavals in Europe, and an atmosphere of uncertainty at home. The struggle to maintain social position was most easily resolved by cutting down the size of one's family. In a second book, *Feminism and Family Planning*, he links the woman's movement of the day to the issue, albeit indirectly, and here concepts and valuations of motherhood arise which are extremely relevant to how mothers, and their mentors, saw their role. 'Do we not see', wrote Mona Caird, 'that the mother of half a dozen children, who struggles to cultivate her faculties, to be an intelligent human being, nearly always breaks down under the burden, or shows very marked intellectual limitations?'

A hundred years before Germaine Greer's *The Female*

Eunuch, women's rights caught the fashionable imagination. The under-occupied girls of the over-populated drawing-rooms were not slow to feel that they were as worthy of consideration as the working-men enfranchised by the 1867 Reform Bill, and sent to school by the 1870 Education Act. Professional training for women became an issue to be fought for. Proper girls' schools were founded by such bodies as the Girls' Public Day School Trust, and women were at least allowed to attend university lectures, even if they were not yet supposed to be capable of taking degrees. Sophia Jex-Blake and Elizabeth Blackwell—both writers of manuals on child-care—were among the first women doctors allowed to qualify and practise.

Prosperous cities and new public amenities brought the 'girls of the period' away from 'samplers and schoolrooms' to 'skating rinks, lawn-tennis grounds, bicycle grounds, and supper after the play at restaurants' (Cunnington, *Feminine Attitudes*). They became personalities in their own right, rather than merely daughters of a house. Marriage on these terms was very different from being inspected for accomplishments on one's domestic hearth, and being quietly transposed to another fireside. Unwilling to give up exciting careers and social delights, such young women postponed motherhood—occasionally for ever.

Pleas were also made that mothers should recognize their importance in themselves. 'Do not drown in your child, do not sacrifice your own work, exchanging a present good for a prospective and merely possible one,' wrote Thomas Wentworth Higginson, champion of feminism, in *Common Sense about Women* (1882). 'We must do the work and train the children betimes.' The fact that, for half the years of her life, woman was incapable of child-bearing, proved to him that 'even for the most prolific and devoted mother, there are duties other than maternal'.

Just as 'new women' were deciding that they had plenty to do sorting out their own rather than their children's problems, traditionalists were trying to recover from the body-blow to the old ideas of Christian nurture administered by Charles Darwin. The publication of *The Origin of Species* in 1859 sparked off a long-drawn-out debate on the implications of the theory of evolution for man. Geologists, botanists and natural theologians had been tussling with evolution for years, but now the debate seized the popular imagination. If men were merely upstart apes, it was difficult to maintain the old Wordsworthian image of the baby fresh from heaven, 'trailing clouds of glory', and still half-conscious of 'God, who is our home'. The first popular digests of Darwin and heredity maintained that the child's nature was a foregone conclusion—'Life is eight parts cards and two parts play,' as Samuel Butler laconically put it. Its early years were merely a recapitulation of the primitive barbarity of the race's history. The child, wrote Henry Ashby—an iron man if ever there was one—'is destitute of any sort of conscience, its pleasures are those of the appetite, it has a short sharp temper, and will bite and "butt" when its angry passions are aroused ... Ages of civilization have not succeeded in eradicating some of the most characteristic and unpleasant impulses of the brute.'

Clearly Rousseau's enthusiasm for savages was not shared by eminent Victorians. Babies were not seen as noble, or even fun. 'Infants up to the age of one year should be neither amusing nor amused,' wrote one brisk society matron. Gone were Lydia Sigourney's 'filmy radicles and timid tendrils of affection, seeking where to twine'. All that was left in these tedious aboriginal years was the donkey-work of civilizing the unholy young apes. It became more and more frequent to hand the thankless task over to a nurse—these were the true, unchallenged years of the nanny. It may seem far-fetched to cite popular reaction to Darwin as one cause of the muted interest in babies, but there was a remarkable absence of baby-care writers with any enthusiasm for their task during these years. On the other hand two decades later mothers would be deluged with books on baby-care, all characterized by a preface outlining optimistic new theories of evolution and heredity mechanisms which gave parents plenty of elbow-room for interference. Like cookery books published after rationing ended, which revelled in cream with everything, the turn-of-the-century manuals oozed a relief at being allowed to influence babyhood again, which implied considerable inhibition earlier on.

Protests were put on record. 'What can be more unnatural', asked kindly Mrs Bowdich, in *Confidential Chats with Mothers*,

> than the present fashion daily gaining ground of handing one's baby almost as soon as it is born into another's arms, often a total stranger's care? When only a month old, the little, soft, helpless mite, needing so greatly all the divine, instinctive love of a mother's heart, and all the tender shelter of a mother's arms, is, according the approved system of the present day, ruthlessly turned over to the doubtful offices of a strange woman.

Mrs Bowdich, a precursor of John Bowlby, was unusual in giving credence to the maternal instinct. One of the most striking features of these limbo decades was the undermining of the mother's confidence in her own instinctive feelings for her baby. A few generations back instinct combined with reason had been enough to see mothers through. Now writers united to deny it. To produce the right kind of children required 'brain work and soul work, not the uncertain rudiments of a brute instinct', wrote Mrs Gilman in *The Home*. 'Mere instinctive love is not enough,' announced Samuel Smiles's last self-help manual, *Character*. Women ought to learn business methods and mathematics to enable them to run their homes properly and to train and educate their children. Baroness Marenholtz-Bulow, author of a very widely read kindergarten manual, *The Child and Child-nature*, insisted that 'the mother must no longer be content to meet her child's impulses with the maternal impulse—for impulse is blind, and the following of it cannot result in happiness for reasonable beings'.

If any one book were to be chosen to convey the mood of these years, it would be Marion Harland's *Common Sense in the Nursery*. It conveys the liberated mother of the 1880s briskly and wittily—and can still be read with profit. She had no time for mothers who wanted to spend all their time with their babies, and the woman who pleaded that 'no-one can understand [my baby] and his needs as I do!' was held up to ridicule. 'In the extravagance of her idolatry she pities the poor parent who can be happy when her child is out of sight. Her whole soul is wrapped up in the cherub (Octopus would be a fitter name for her) . . . The best mothers are not those in whom the maternal instinct is cultivated to an abnormal excrescence.'

In practice, the most striking evidence of the demoralization of maternal instinct was the increasingly pronounced swing against breast-feeding. In face of assurances from authorities as potent as Isabella Beeton that artificial foods were as good as if not better than breast-milk, mothers had already begun to waver. Nurses, eager for complete authority over their charges, were only too pleased to extend their province to feeding time. Breast-feeding was represented as out of date.

> A hundred years ago [wrote Harland], it was rare not to feed one's baby oneself. Failure to do so was mentioned as a misfortune, in the same category as a disease. Now custom, inherited weakness [a nice up-to-date touch], perhaps the results of excessive labour or imprudence on the part of those very foremothers, and perhaps climatic influence [a little wild]—has changed this in great measure. The query, 'How do you feed him?' is conventional. The answer no longer involves the child's chance of strength and life.

Perhaps the most outspoken of the anti-breast-feeding school was a redoubtable lady called Mrs Panton. She wrote as many manuals on how to run one's life as Mrs Ellis had a few decades earlier. Her model young couple, Edwin and Angelina, were led *From Kitchen to Garret* when they set up home, and told *The Way They Should Go* once their children arrived. Breast-feeding, still being lukewarmly recommended by doctors as 'natural', may have been so in a state of nature, she conceded:

> but we don't live in that time now, and we must adapt [a consciously evolutionary term] our doings to the age in which we were born . . . Let no mother condemn herself to be a common or ordinary 'cow' unless she has a real desire to nurse . . . Women have not the stamina they once

possessed; and I myself know of no greater misery than nursing a child, the physical collapse caused by which is often at the bottom of the drinking habits of which we hear so much.

Breast-feeding failed to recover from the many-sided attacks upon it until the crusade led by Truby King in the 1920s. All through the coming years of intense interest in children's minds and nursery management, this crucial link between mother and baby was undervalued. Nor were society matrons most to blame for its unfashionableness. 'Lactation', wrote the most eminent expert on feeding of the day, Dr Eric Pritchard, 'is far more likely to go wrong in a woman than in the teetotal, vegetarian, nerveless cow' (*Infant Education*). He advised women to make themselves as much like cows as possible, if they wanted to breast-feed successfully. They were to drop all social commitments, rest a lot and follow a bland and nourishing diet. Several optimistic baby-food manufacturers suggested in their advertisements that the best thing a breast-feeding mother could do was to eat their products herself. 'So nice!' ran one inspired piece of copy, 'While nursing, I have gruel for lunch and supper made from Robinson's Patent Groats, and don't require any other stimulant!' Dr Allbutt, despite being the author of the racy but banned *Wife's Handbook*, told women in *Every Mother's Handbook* that 'sexual emotion of frequent occurrence deteriorates the quality of the milk'. None of this advice was calculated to appeal to the new mood of independence among women. By 1914, Mary Gardner likened mothers to the Egyptian hens who had forgotten how to sit on their own eggs because they were kept warm for them by their keepers. 'In the same way, as a race we are becoming decadent with regard to breast-feeding, and the mothers who can't and the mothers who won't are causing successive generations to be less and less fit physically to nourish their infants naturally' (*Nursery Management*). Despite Darwin's emphatic belief that evolution was a process which had taken thousands and millions of years to happen, it is clear that in the popular mind, the action of every generation risked influencing the whole race. Unsure of their maternal role, women filled the space once occupied by fireside education and nourishing little souls with busy social lives and increasingly elaborate domestic life-styles. Children could hardly have been let loose in the cluttered drawing-rooms of the 1880s. Women's magazines reflected the change in mood. There were far fewer directly concerned with motherhood. The preoccupations of the new journals were fashion, etiquette, and the 'new woman'. In 1880, *Girl's Own Annual* ran a major serial on domestic matters, 'Margaret Trent, and How She Kept House', which might have been expected to tell the new bride something about babies. But its heroine had no thought for such things. When her sister came to visit, bringing her baby, Margaret found her small niece an annoying interruption to the important business of discussing the management of servants. 'It seemed to Margaret that baby Annie monopolised a good deal more than her fair share of her mother's attention.' Joanna eventually sent baby upstairs to mollify her angry elder sister, who merely reflected: 'Joanna was certainly *much* nicer when tyrannical baby Annie was upstairs in the nursery.'

Charlotte Yonge, author of classic novels of idealized large family life earlier in the century (*Pillars of the House*, *The Daisy Chain*), also wrote a little tract for the times (which she didn't much like)—*Womankind*. She pointed out the harm done to family life by the newly fashionable late dinner:

> When 'late' dinners were at what we now consider the barbarously early hour of five or six, they did not break up the home half so much, as they left an hour or two for the children to come down and amuse themselves quietly under their parents' eyes, be played with by their father, show him their performances, or perhaps be read to by him.

The old children's hour was becoming a thing of the past, or being rushed uneasily into dressing for dinnertime. 'The march of sanitary aesthetics has swept away the stock picture of the young mother plying her needle by the evening lamp, her foot on the rocker, a lullaby on her lips,' declared Harland, not without satisfaction.

'Give the children a morsel of your time, now and then,' suggested *Sylvia*, half apologetically. To make them less inclined to beg for more time in the drawing-room, make their nurseries more attractive—'poor little things, they are *so* tired of their own particular sanctum, its sameness, its dullness, its ugliness'. Too many families, she thought, especially those with 'no regular staff' packed children great and small off on a Sunday afternoon, regardless of the weather, 'some to church, some to walk, some in the perambulator', so that the parents could enjoy a rest. 'They become cross, fretful, and quarrelsome, because of the strain on their bodies. Their attendant is cross and peevish also (no wonder), and the whole troop of little ones come home not exhilarated and buoyant as they should after a pleasant journey, but quite the contrary . . . To treat children as if they were so many puppies can hardly be right.'

I may be accused of exaggerating its importance, but the pram in which the 'cross and peevish' attendant wheeled off the unwanted babies seems to have been an influential enabling agent in the growing divorce between parent and child. Exercise without prams, and with two or more children, must have necessarily been short in span. Mothers frequently went too, to lend a hand. Once prams allowed babies to be kept quiet for long periods of time, with little fatigue to child or nurse, the manuals suggested longer and longer walks. This took the heat off the domestic scene in a very pleasing fashion, and elegance could reign at home, uninterrupted by ructions from the upper storeys. It apparently became socially unacceptable for a smart mother to be seen wheeling her own pram. Mrs Linton contrasted English mothers with French ones, who promenaded beside their 'bonnes' as a matter of course. 'Here, the woman who once had one nursemaid now has two . . . the shabbiest little wife with her two financial ends gaping, must have her still shabbier little drudge to wheel her perambulator' (*Modern Mothers*). It would have been well worth hiring such a little drudge, to remove the babies from the scene while nurse or mother at home could get on with the endless chores.

Mrs Montgomery revived memories of the old maternal carefulness when she told mothers to be 'ever on the watch to detect every bent that is given to the thoughts or temper of your little one', but regretted that 'our present mode of society throws great obstacles in the way of this duty. Nurses and governesses intervene to cut off sympathy between mother and child. Her numerous other avocations, her share in her husband's pursuits and pleasures divert her thoughts and exclude her from the constant attention and personal superintendence over all that passes in her nursery' (*Early Influences*). Materially, it is worth pointing out, babies were better off than ever before. Standards of living were rising, and the state in which one's children were seen to be kept reflected one's social importance. Nursery staff multiplied— 'the woman who once had one nursemaid now has two'—and grand Victorian houses were constructed with whole wings to accommodate them. Purpose-built nursery furniture, elaborately decorated prams and mailcarts, exquisitely hand-made clothes, and patent baby-necessaries galore covered up the central hollowness, the mother's abdication.

There never was a time when children were made of so much individual importance in the family, yet were so little in direct relation to the mother—never a time when maternity did so little and social organization so much. Juvenile parties, the kind of moral obligation felt by all parents to provide heated and unhealthy amusements for their boys and girls ... extravagance in dress ... education ... all make children real burdens. (E. L. Linton, *Modern Mothers*, 1881)

The Century of the Child

Medical, scientific and political developments combined at the turn of the century to turn a floodlight of interest and anticipation on the small creatures hitherto left to tumble up together in their nurseries. The twentieth century, trumpeted the redoubtable Ellen Key, was to be the *Century of the Child*, the dawn of the *Renaissance of Motherhood*. Mere survival became much less of a hit or miss affair, so families could be planned small with some confidence. Scientists of the mind linked up evolutionary and genetic theories to develop a far more demanding analysis of the infant pysche than the phrenologists had ever contemplated. Psychology would replace spirituality. And with Europe fast moving towards military confrontation, the quality of the nation's heirs acquired a political significance—the Eugenics Movement initiated an ominous concern for the quality of the race.

More people than ever before put pen to paper on the subject of raising babies. The old dichotomy between discipline and indulgence was evident—Mrs Bowdich and Mrs Harland were merely replaced by the enthusiasm of Millicent Shinn and the dismissively orderly mind of Luther Emmett Holt. But both wrote within the new setting of the Child Study Movement and all-pervasive scientific officiousness. Before we can understand why mothers were told to bring up their babies as they were, these wider background developments need elaboration.

The last twenty years of the nineteenth century were marked by resounding medical triumphs. Koch and Pasteur made discoveries in bacteriology and immunology which reduced the risks of epidemic diseases. The diphtheria bacillus was identified in 1883, and by 1891 Behring of Berlin had discovered a successful anti-toxin. Meningitis could be cured by an anti-serum discovered in 1907, although it was some time before the highly risky lumbar puncture it involved became generally acceptable. Pioneer studies of infant metabolism were made in Strasborg around 1900, and by 1920 studies were established in chemistry and experimental nutrition which would affect infant feeding dramatically.

New 'milk technology' was probably the single most effective advance in saving infant life. Railways and refrigeration, combined with a better understanding of hygiene and pasteurization, meant that reliable milk began to be widely available—the alternative suggested to Edwin and Angelina by Mrs Panton had been to acquire their own cow (an Alderney, of course).

The improved dairies were inspired by an American paediatrician, Luther Emmett Holt, as famous in his day as

Dr Spock is in ours. He took over the New York Babies'
Hospital and made paediatrics his life's work. His textbook
for doctors, *Diseases of Infancy and Childhood*, was a standard
work, but the training manual which he originally wrote for
nurses in his hospital became 'the infant Bible of the nation'.
Care and Feeding of Children was revised twelve times during
Holt's lifetime, and expanded from sixty fairly terse pages to
200—an indication of the rapidly growing interest in baby-
care. As might be expected of a book that started life as a
nurse's training manual, it was a rather cool, formal, little
work, although its question-and-answer style made it quick
and easy to use. It appealed to the new fashion for scientific
precision, rather than the parallel sentimental fondness
which other manuals represented.

Holt helped to found the Walker-Gordon Laboratories,
which undertook to deliver pasteurized milk in sealed bottles
to the infant's doorstep. Walker-Gordon Laboratories were
established in England, at Wembley, by the time Mary
Gardner wrote *Nursery Management* in 1914. Commissions
were set up to certify milk, so even without a specialist dairy
mothers could be assured of the quality of the milk that
they bought. Free milk was provided by milk stations for
'deserving cases'.

As doctors proved that they knew better than mothers on
almost every front, an interesting rearguard action was fought
against state medical interference—unfortunately on the
shaky ground of vaccination. Vaccination for smallpox had
been made compulsory, and had done so much to reduce the
incidence of the disease that no impartial observer would
quarrel with it. But parents are not impartial, and in a debate
strikingly parallel to the present-day arguments for and
against whooping-cough and measles jabs, they fought for
their right to choose whether their children should be
vaccinated or not. They were concerned that, because
infected calf's lymph was used, vaccination transmitted
tetanus, syphilis, tuberculosis and other diseases. They
formed anti-vaccination societies (crushingly renamed Associations for the Propagation of Smallpox by Sophia Jex-
Blake) and sent postcards to the addresses of births announced in the newspapers. A Royal Commission was eventually

set up to examine the anti-vaccination case, and in 1896 it was recommended that the severe penalties previously imposed should cease. Special cases were allowed to escape vaccination. 'If your friends include a J.P.,' Mary Gardner confided, 'there will be no difficulty getting the signature exempting you on the form you are given with the birth certificate.' The less privileged could swear before the Commissioner of Oaths that the vaccination would be prejudicial to the child—a much easier proceeding than the long hours fathers had previously had to spend attending police courts.

More manual writers were for vaccination than against it. 'In civilized communities,' wrote Jex-Blake, 'the well-being of the many must over-ride the suicidal hobbies of the few. Just as people should be stopped from setting their own houses on fire, because of the danger to other people in the street, so parents should be forced to vaccinate their children for the general good.' Here, and in the move towards state-trained motherhood which will be examined a little later, baby-care moved from the negative undermining of mothers' initiative to the positive acceptance of medical interference whether the child was ill or not. It was, of course, all for the child's own good.

Once the initial shock of Darwin's theory of evolution was over, and it was realized that there was still no cut-and-dried answer to the questions why and how the human race developed, scientific investigations concentrated on 'the beginnings of all things'. History, anthropology, ethnology and archaeology all had their devotees, but to James Sully, 'the beginnings of a human mind, the first dim stages in the development of man's god-like reason, ought to be the most interesting of all' (*Studies of Childhood*). He acknowledged that infancy had its poetic side, sympathizing with Plato and Wordsworth and their valuation of each new soul, but what he and his fellow-scientists were interested in was 'the opening germ of intelligence from the colder point of view of science'.

Evolution, he felt, 'bids us view the unfolding of a human intelligence today as conditioned and prepared by long ages of human experience'. The successive stages of mental life answered roughly to vegetable, animal, human and civilized. The infant stage owed most to the first two, although its similarity to primitive man was often very striking. Such docketing of the baby into its evolutionary place seemed to have two effects. Firstly, it distanced the would-be student of humanity from the individual child. Secondly, it made much greater tolerance towards children possible—not altogether a healthy tolerance. In jotting down her first-born's temper tantrums as being strikingly analogous to the behaviour of the Dakota Indian under stress, the mother almost forgot to care whether it screamed or not.

Shifts to the optimistic in popular interpretations of heredity meant that child study became not merely an academic pursuit but a vital prerequisite of parenthood. W. B. Drummond criticized the first narrow views of what heredity meant—a sort of Fate, Nature being implacably stronger than Nurture. On the contrary, he believed that one merely inherited possibilities—'tendencies'was another favourite word—from nature, and these were realized or discouraged by upbringing. 'While we dare not trust to the good qualities of the parents reappearing without patient and careful training, we need not despair of eliminating defects which may have no root in the child's nature.' Instinctive acts were gradually replaced by habits acquired anew by the individuals of each generation, who were thereby enabled to adapt themselves to their environment. The child was 'like clay in the hand of the potter, to be moulded day by day, by the habits, the tastes, the passions, the ideals of those among whom he lives, to be impressed in a thousand ways for good or evil by all he sees and hears'. So the very first months, as well as the early years, were vitally important. They were the time for 'the reacquirement of the past acquirements of the race', and there ought to be 'far more earnestness in our endeavour to understand the child, the hope of the family and the nation'.

In *Practical Motherhood* Helen Campbell gave one of the best of the popular résumés of evolution and heredity as it affected baby-care—and this was in a very down-to-earth book, meant for everyday use, not for idle dreams. It was essential, she thought, that evolution be properly understood if mothers were to grasp the way their children's minds worked. She sketched the marvellous process 'from amoeba, noctiluca and globigerina to man', and extended physical to mental and moral evolution. The final object of the whole process was the human soul evolved through love: 'Human nature is ever climbing up the world's great altar stairs that slope through the darkness to God'. She quoted from Drummond:

> The most beautiful witness to the evolution of man is the mind of the child. The stealing in of that inexplicable light called consciousness, the first flicker of memory, the gradual governance of will, the silent ascendancy of reason—these are the studies of evolution . . . which make every mother an unconscious evolutionist and every little one a living witness to the Ascent.

The means by which parents were to succeed in evolving these little souls was the imposition of habits—routine reactions to life which would ensure eternal success. Her final metaphor was the now familiar one of manipulation: 'The clay is moist and soft, now make haste and form the pitcher, for the wheels turn fast.'

The implications of these theories were extremely important. Mothers could pick up the educational traces which they had dropped in despair. The reason for the long helplessness of the human baby was judged to be the enormous amount of input necessary to make it into a civilized human being, to help it develop beyond the animal or primitive savage stage. The first necessity was for a thorough understanding of how children should be expected to develop so that parents could do their work properly.

This was where the Child Study Movement came in. The 'scientific educator', James Sully's ideal, had to study the infant to adapt to the 'spontaneous processes' of the child mind. Not only its intellectual but its moral and emotional nature could be learnt by observation. Before mothers became too excited, Sully put them back into the ranks of second-class citizens. Who, he asked, was the right person to study the infant with scientific detachment and benevolent enthusiasm? A doctor would be too involved with the physical aspects of child-rearing. The mother was likely to be 'too involved, sentimental, and eulogistic'. Undoubtedly, the ideal candidate was the *father*—if the nurse would allow 'the intrusion of male footsteps into woman's domain' (she was going to have to allow a positive stampede of footsteps into her once neglected nursery when the Child Study Movement got properly under way). Sully relented a little. The father's restricted leisure compelled him to call in the mother as collaborator. 'Indeed, one may safely say that the mother's enthusiasm and patient, brooding watchfulness are needed quite as much as the father's keen analytic vision. The mother should note under the guidance of the father, he taking due care to test and verify.'

Darwin himself had kept a detailed record of the earliest months of one of his own children, which he had published in 1877 in the new quarterly review of psychology and philosophy, *Mind*. He was inspired to publish the 37-year-old diary by the publication of the French psychologist Hippolyte Taine's record of his daughter's first three years in the previous issue of *Mind*. Taine was particularly interested in the development of language, and ended his observations by saying: 'Speaking generally, the child presents in a passing state the mental characteristics that are found in a fixed state in a primitive civilization, very much as the human embryo presents in a passing state the physical characteristics that are found in a fixed state in the classes of inferior animals.' Notice that Taine promoted the infant to primitive man, never really considering him as vegetable. In England he was left as animal for much longer.

Darwin's main concern in his diary was with the development of expression, and with the comparison of relative development in different infants—the road was opening up for competitive 'milestones of development'. He observed signs of fear with interest, and commented on the dread shown by his 2½-year-old son on seeing large wild animals in the Zoological Gardens, even though they were safely behind bars. 'May we not suspect', he surmised, 'that the vague but very real fears of childhood, which are independent of experience, are the inherited effects of real dangers and abject superstitions during savage times?' Although several readers of the article criticized Darwin's suggestion on the grounds that any child in its senses would be frightened of large wild animals, it was clear that the march into the unconscious had begun.

'After Darwin published his study of the child,' wrote Honnor Morten in *Child Nurture* (1911), 'scientific fathers in Germany took to dropping their infants out of the windows to see if, like kittens, they would alight on all fours; or hanging them onto trees by their hands to prove their descent from monkeys.' These methods, she added, were hardly what parents wanted. The big names of child study—Sigismund, Drummond, Tiedemann, Fenelon, Preyer, Sully, Chamberlain, Perez, in Europe, Stanley Hall and Dewey in the United States, needed popularization before they could appeal to the lay parent. To do this—and to increase the scope of the research being undertaken—Child Study Associations and journals were founded. The British Child Study Association was founded in 1894, with its journal, the *Paidologist*. The Childhood Society and the Parents' National Educational Union soon followed. In America Faculties of Child Study were set up in several universities, and most substantial towns had a Child Study Association. What was wanted, the experts said, was as much observation of real children by real parents as possible, so that an accurate Science of Childhood could be set up.

Proud parents were not slow to oblige. Louise Hogan's *Study of a Child* immortalized every lisp of her son, as she 'sat reverently at the foot of infancy, watching and learning'. She dated every development of speech, and described the minutiae of his existence indefatigably. Other mothers, she felt, would do well to learn from her methods: no formal learning until the seventh year, but before that scrupulous attention to his questions; surroundings carefully planned to suit his growing needs, and a nightly plan to ensure that the next day, in apparently spontaneous play, carefully graded steps in achievement could take place. The child's sensitivity was 'wonderful'—he could tell people's character at a glance. If he disliked the look of a would-be servant, the girl was not engaged.

We have more continuous amateur records of the first few years of infant lives for this period than any other before or since. Other notable published accounts were Elizabeth Harrison's *Study of Child Nature*, and Millicent Shinn's 'Notes on the Development of a Child', which showed a mother who was following scientific precept in every way— she described Holt's manual as 'always by my side'.

The vast amount of information thus collected about babies and young children furnished manual writers with the nearest thing to statistics that they had so far had. Chapters on the norms of height, weight and general development began to be included in child-care books as a matter of course. Tables were printed out in deceptive simplicity, demanding that by so many weeks so many ounces should have been gained. 'Milestones' appeared. At six months your baby should be crawling, at ten months standing, at a year he should have two or three words.

To make it easier for parents to make notes, special books were provided—they are still sold today, but as souvenirs rather than for scientific purposes. Florence Hatton Ellis's *Record of a Child's Life* was a particularly lavish example of the genre. Her categories are roughly the same as today's, with a few period surprises: baby's weight, baby's height, when he first wore short clothes; his first hair-cut—space to attach a ringlet; his first Railway Journey, his first donkey ride. A whole page was provided to record every one of his 'falls, knocks and bruises'. Space followed for vaccinations and photographs, his autograph, and finally, his first school report. That wrapped up baby.

Naturally, mothers began to coax lethargic learners into action. They had to have something to write about, after all; nor did anybody want to feel that their child was developing more slowly than their neighbour's in the child study group, although some experts offered the comfort that slow learners often did better in the end. A relentless spotlight of expectancy was focused over the cradle of every thinking parent's baby. An editorial in the *Archives of Pediatrics* for 1898 registered some misgivings at the phenomenon of so much attention being devoted to children: the Child Study Movement, special teacher-training colleges, the 'hundredfold increase' in books and journals written for and about them. 'The general tendency is in the direction of bringing children into too great prominence, in making them the most important and first-to-be-considered members of the family, and in laying burdens on them too great for their strength.' The worst mistake was 'the habit of too great *camaraderie* with their children, and the growing tendency to remove the barriers between childhood and age'. This led to over-stimulation of children, and overstrain—this 'cannot fail to cause harmful effects during childhood, and frequently produces a neurasthenic and nervous temperament in later life'.

It was hardly surprising that the neurotic baby syndrome first appeared at the turn of the century. Earlier books did recognize the odd case—characterized for *Sylvia* by restlessness at night, headaches, low spirits for no good reason, and an inability to get on with its peers. Her analysis and cure were matter-of-fact:

> Many parents possess just such a bairn as this among their flock, and cannot understand it and its ways even a little. This child with the irritable, aching brain, is, unfortunately for itself, generally speaking *mischievous*. It has wild spells of tremendously *high* spirits now and then, and when it is thus, it stops at nothing.
>
> The parents' route to follow in this case is a careful, unheated dietary, a frequent washing of the child's head in weak vinegar, or weak gin and water. A shower bath, if obtainable, will do much service. Let the child take frequent, but short, walks, not tiring ones.

This was the pragmatic language of the nineteenth century. Contrast it with Drummond, Holt, Pritchard or Cunnington, who all spoke in terms of psychology. The infant nervous system was 'a delicate piece of machinery', quite unlike an adult's, and 'as yet not accustomed by habit to the ordinary wear and tear of life' (Cunnington, *Nursery Notes*). In what must have been a contemporarily happy simile, making use of Edison's new invention just as Pavlov had, Pritchard likened the adult nervous system to 'a great telephone organisation', in which external stimuli were analogous to the human voice, the nerves which transmitted these messages to the brain were the telephone wires, and the nerve cells in the spinal cord and brain were the local exchanges. 'The convolution of the brain' was the central bureau of information which co-ordinated everything. A baby's nervous system was then compared to 'a new telephone system, which has only been recently installed. All the telephones are in position, the wires laid and connected, and all the exchanges completed, but the operators are without experience, and the intelligence bureau without information or direction.' If the wrong early messages and information were given, a neurotic baby would result, as irreversibly ruined as a telephone exchange would be 'if all the wires were tangled in an inextricable jumble, if all the numbers on the instruments were changed, and if all the operators themselves were mentally deranged' (*Infant Education*).

Holt agreed that the brain was a very delicate structure in infants and young children, and that they required quiet and peaceful surroundings. Infants who were naturally nervous should be left much alone, should see but few people, and should be played with very little. In fact, he added, babies under six months should never be played with at all, and the less play at any age the better for the infant. Perhaps this was a doctor's reaction to all the over-stimulation of children that the editor of *Archives of Pediatrics* had noted.

It was certainly remarked on by many observers that there were more neurotic children about than there used to be. The causes remained obscure. Pritchard put it down to 'these strenuous days of over-civilization, and often of luxurious and intemperate living', which meant that children were born with a 'reserve of vitality'; they had 'a heritage of nervous instability'. Dr Laing Gordon, on the other hand, saw the increase in nervous disorders among children as a fault of environment rather than constitution. Cunnington felt that an important factor was the new phenomenon of the single-child family—'now becoming a marked feature in the middle and upper classes in this country'. It was as notable and as fashionable a topic of discussion as the single-parent family is today. Highly strung, easily frightened and fanciful, the only child had none of the rough and tumble of nursery life to 'obliterate yesterday's sensations'. Although it imitated the adult in drawing-room manners, it had no adult self-control, and was 'easily spoilt by such mental food'. It would exhibit 'that queer modern precocity, so strangely named old-fashionedness' which was drawn to the life in Frances Hodgson Burnett's *Sara Crewe*. Probably, Cunnington continued gloomily, the only child would grow into a frail adult with an ill-balanced intellect and weak morality, likely to make an injudicious marriage to escape loneliness.

No one could provide an adequate reason for there being so many neurotic children. Michael Powell's 1960 horror film, *Peeping Tom*, does, however, recreate unforgettably the misery of a small child that feels itself watched and experimented on by a psychologist father. Powell was born in 1905, and his scriptwriter was himself the son of a psychiatrist. Although few children were driven to the lengths of the hero's murderous neurosis, it must have been something of a strain to have one's every move put under a microscope, and examined for significance. Or maybe, on the other hand, children had always been neurotic, and it was just a name and a sympathy for the condition that had been absent. Perhaps the shock of learning the complexities of the infant mind made the experts assume the likelihood of children feeling strain and needing to rest.

One of the early child psychologists was of course Sigmund Freud. He wrote his 'Essay on Infant Sexuality' in 1906, but it was given the popular thumbs down. The world was not then ready for the complication of the unconscious and subconscious minds of their children—parents had barely got used to the idea that their babies had nervous systems which were to be treated with kid gloves. They were appalled at the idea that infants were born with sexual urges, and that their first sexual objects were their parents. All but an ultra-modern few tucked Freud severely into the backs of their minds, and concentrated on mechanistic psychology, applying the right stimuli to a known nervous system.

We will consider Freud more fully later on—how he was evaded in the 1920s and finally faced up to with a vengeance from the 1940s onwards. But perhaps one point should be made here. Freud saw childhood as the most difficult phase of development because the mind's apparatus for adjustment—the famous Ego—was at its weakest just when it was faced with enormous problems of accommodation to reality. Traumas of birth, toilet training, weaning and sibling rivalry were piled on to it, while it was forbidden to gratify itself by masturbation or sexual satisfaction with the parent of the opposite sex. He drew his conclusions largely from his experience of the pathologically insane, but also from his observation of family lives around him. One cannot help reflecting that he was observing relatively new phenomena in bringing up children. Babies had only recently been kicked out of their mothers' beds, training in 'good habits' was a new art, and breast-feeding was at one of its lowest ebbs. Freud could have been interpreted as warning parents against some damaging trends in baby-care—that he has remained relevant until recently reflects the fact that those trends continued regardless, rather than that Freud's insights were eternal verities.

Despite the Child Study Movement's optimism that heredity could be countered by careful upbringing, genetic tinkering was very much in fashion. 'The importance of a good stock must not be underestimated,' Drummond admitted. Parents were now to be made conscious of the implications of Mendel's work. Sir Francis Galton's *Inquiries into the Human Faculty* (1883) told them that the great hope for the improvement of the human race was careful 'eugenic' selection. He suggested forbidding 'inferior specimens of humanity from transmitting their vices or diseases, their intellectual or physical weaknesses'.

Galton was president of the Eugenics Education Society—their philosopher was predictably Friedrich Nietzsche, whose *Thus Spoke Zarathustra* (1884) glorified the Superman.

Man is something to be surpassed. What have ye done to surpass man?

All beings hitherto have created something beyond themselves: and ye want to be the ebb of that great tide, and would rather go back to the beast than surpass man.

What is the ape to man? A laughing stock, a figure of shame. And just the same shall man be to the Superman.

Ye have made your way from the worm to man, and yet much within is still worm. Once ye were apes, and even yet man is more of an ape than any of the apes.

Even the wisest amongst you is only a disharmony and hybrid of plant and phantom.

Lo! I teach you the Superman! The Superman is the meaning of the earth!

Enthusiasm for Nietzsche's 'blond beast' was very general—he was repeatedly quoted by child-care manuals of this era. It reflected the popular misconception of the speed with which evolution took place, and the prevalent hope that by conscious action man could affect the direction that it took.

The marked trend to state interference in child-rearing was one direct result of the eugenics movement's claim that much could be done to improve the race. The new policy was partly philanthropic and partly militaristic in inspiration. A rampant Labour movement and a conscience-stricken middle class forced governments to take the plight of the industrial cities seriously. Housing, health and education conditions were so appalling that infant mortality was actually rising in the 1890s. The state had little alternative but to interfere with functions formerly regarded as belonging to the family in relation to food, health and welfare generally.

Moreover, as Germany's power increased, the quality of the nation's children—the soldiers of the future—became a matter for serious concern. According to William Boyd, the function of schools had been extended well beyond mere learning:

The beginnings of this extension of function may be traced to the progressive organization of the military resources of the modern state. Those nations which maintained great armies have found that many of their recruits come into service with impaired health. The effort to check this wastage has led to an active care for the health of modern school children.

111

It was logical to extend 'the work of improving the national physique' to the formative first years. 'The children are the property of the nation, to be brought up for the nation as is best for the nation, and not according to the whim of the individual parent', wrote Charlotte Mason, despite an otherwise independent spirit. Norah March's *Towards Racial Health* pleaded for an understanding of the factors that affected race improvement and race decay—'then we may be able so to weave into our care and guidance of child-life a thread of gold, a thread which shall make its way from the fabric ɔf our own lives into the fabric of theirs, a thread known as the Ideal'.

Attempts were made to go back even further. Many of the manuals began with an antenatal chapter on how mothers could do their duty to their unborn children. Books today still have them, but they no longer advise on selection of the fittest mate, or accuse one of racial suicide if one practises birth control. In fact the only people criticized for racial suicide were the rich. The poor were very welcome to limit their families as much as they could. Galton had suggested that intellectuality could be encouraged by making the possession of a large family a prerequisite for, rather than an obstacle to, holding an Oxford or Cambridge fellowship. From 1878 fellows were allowed to marry, and Gwen Raverat's *Period Piece* records that academic wives were eager to pursue the newest theories of child-care. In a free society, there was little the state could do to force genetically desirable alliances and forbid disastrous ones, but the extent to which such talk was in the air was reflected by Huxley's later satire on the subject, *Brave New World*. What could be done was to tell the masses how they should look after their babies. At this point the baby-care manual left the upper- and middle-class nursery shelf and was distributed in the city slums.

Perhaps the first book written with such a missionary aim was Sophia Jex-Blake's *Care of Infants*. She had opened a dispensary for women and children in Edinburgh in 1878, and published her manual six years later, commenting in its preface on the scarcity of books on the subject. The best of the existing ones was, she felt, Andrew Combe's *Management of Infancy* (written forty-four years before), but even that she found too long, too expensive, and 'by no means as well-known as it deserves'. Her own book was a tiny red pocket volume, easy to handle and refer to, and sold at a price that most mothers could afford. Sympathetic but brisk, it aimed to reduce infant mortality by informing mothers of the basic facts of baby-care. 'Poor mothers, overwhelmed as they often are with the burden of their daily lives, may have treated their babies affectionately indeed, but with a crass ignorance which has been as fatal as intentional infanticide.'

Soon voluntary groups of well-intentioned matrons began to set up such institutions as the Ladies' Sanitary Association, and the Infant Health Societies of Marylebone and St Pancras. They issued pamphlets on infant care, and gave homely talks on 'How to Raise Our Little Ones'. The vulgar mind was not troubled by the theories of the Child Study Movement, but was given good, clean, hard-hitting orders on how best to rear infants. *Mrs Blossom on Babies* disguised the advice as fictional incidents in the life of a working-class granny, and its author, Helen Hodgson, a Durham health visitor, hoped that it would be read aloud at 'meetings for mothers and working girls'. It didn't mince words. A little baby overlaid by its mother, who had spent all her money on a showy mailcart for it, instead of a cot, was 'just as much murdered as if its head had been cut off'. There would be a police inquest at which 'its little body will be cut about'. Dummies were 'an invention of the devil to tempt mothers to harm their children. If the Lord had intended little babies to be always sucking something, He'd have sent them with dummies round their necks already.' Condescending stuff at best—perhaps it was not surprising that audiences for such readings were difficult to attract. Portsmouth prison did provide a captive one of women 'selected for good behaviour' in 1904 (Davin).

As the state flexed its muscles in its new role, local authorities supplemented the do-gooders with official health visitors. The duties of four Birmingham lady visitors appointed in 1899 suggest why such invasions were by no means popular. They were:

to carry with them disinfectant powder and use it where

113

required; to direct the attention of those they visit to the evils of bad smells, want of fresh air, and dirty conditions of all kinds; to give hints to mothers on the feeding and clothing of their children, and to use their influence to induce them to send their children to school.

More popular were institutions like the St Pancras School for Mothers, set up in 1907. Attendance at its Babies' Welcome was voluntary, and babies could be weighed and examined by a doctor free of charge; it was a forerunner, in fact, of today's baby clinics. Breast feeding was recommended to the masses much more energetically than to the well-to-do—advisedly, since, as we will see, successful artificial feeding was beginning to require a degree in chemistry. The St Pancras centre gave free dinners to breast-feeding mothers, conscious of the tendency of women to stint themselves, and, as one address by the School's medical officer made clear, was concerned with the progress of feminism:

> They [mothers] never treat themselves, either in the home or in public affairs, as of any importance, and consequently no-one thinks them important. One of the first steps needed to effect the political and social emancipation of women is a crusade on the part of man calling on her to eat. And there can never really be a strong race of Britons until she does. (Davin)

Lessons were given on food values, domestic health, house-wifery, and the preparation for and care of babies. A Provident Maternity Club helped families to save for the new expense of maternity. There were Fathers' Evening Conferences on 'the duties of the father to the mother, the babe, the children and the home (coffee handed round, smoking allowed)'. The emphasis was thus on practical help in a friendly, club-like atmosphere, and the school was popular as a result.

The significance of what was happening did not go unremarked. 'Let the State step in between the mother and her child, and domestic confidence is dissolved, family privacy is invaded and maternal responsibility assailed,' wrote Cooke-Taylor. 'For the tender care of the mother is substituted the tender mercies of the State; for the security of natural affection, the securities of an unnatural law. Better by far that many another infant should perish in its innocence and unconsciousness than to be victims of such a state of things.' Birth control and rising standards of living, collective bargaining and shorter working days, parks, libraries and other forms of state philanthropy, made life a more comfortable affair; but they did not strengthen the family. It looked outwards increasingly as it became smaller, better housed, and better equipped culturally and educationally. On the horizon was Lynd and Merrell's *Middletown* nightmare of the 'home as physical service station', a place where individuals were refuelled with food and sleep for an essentially lonely battle with the world outside. As far as child-rearing patterns were concerned, what emerged over this period was a habit of deference to authority—which was natural in a time when war threatened, but which was never to be discarded.

The Renaissance of Motherhood

Under fire both from their liberated and professional sisters, and from the scientific know-how of eugenics-mad bureaucracy, mothers were in need of a champion. Ellen Key, Swedish author of the best-selling *Century of the Child*, rose to the occasion in 1914 with her *Renaissance of Motherhood*. 'Has our race ever been afflicted by a more dangerous disease than the one which at present rages among women: the sick yearning to be "freed" from the most essential attribute of their sex?' she demanded. The truly free woman would have attained 'so fully developed a humanity' that she could not even dream of a desire to be 'liberated from the foremost essential quality of her womanhood—motherliness'. Criticizing Charlotte Gilman's scheme for mothers who were gifted educationalists to bring up about twenty other children together with their own, and so free other mothers to work, Key insisted that 'each young soul needs to be enveloped in its own mother's tenderness, just as surely as the human embryo

115

needed the mother's womb to grow in, and the baby the mother's breast to be nourished by'.

Ellen Key stood firmly in the line that leads from Lydia Sigourney to Penelope Leach, and wrote at a time when every opinion on child-raising was allowed to be heard. She sounds curiously modern, particularly when pleading for a state pension for mothers, and acknowledging their need for a fulfilling intellectual life. But she also stood insistently against the encroachment of the state on the mother's province—opposing state crèches or kindergartens. The mother must herself be her child's educator, and to do so should acquire an understanding of 'the principles of heredity, of race hygiene, child hygiene and child-psychology'. To combine motherhood and intellectual work merely made both mediocre and led to 'a lessening of values and enormous overstrain'. If Nietzsche's vision of the completed man—the Superman—was to be achieved, then 'the socially pernicious, racially wasteful and soul-withering consequences of the working of mothers outside the home must cease'.

Key had, and still has, her supporters. But in one important respect she failed. Like too many of her contemporaries, she insisted that instinct was not enough, it was not 'the surest guide to motherliness'. She recommended a year's social service for girls, a parallel to men's military service, so that they would be equipped by such training in parenthood to face motherhood. The confident early-nineteenth-century years, when mothers had enjoyed the responsibility of motherhood, were past. Although intense interest in babies had succeeded the apathy of the last two decades, the hallmark of motherhood was now anxiety—an anxiety produced in large part by the systematic demoralization of mothers concerning the quality, or even the existence, of their maternal instinct in face of the united front presented by the state, by doctors and by manual writers, on their inadequacies. The young mother had been 'shorn of her maternal instinct' according to the sympathetic Dr Laing Gordon. 'On the bookshelves' crowded shelves, treatises confuse and alarm; the heavy responsibilities stare out from every page. It may require firm resolve to prevent her resigning her offspring to an inferior intellect, and denying herself the most fascinating interest in life' (*The Modern Mother*).

For the first time, as far as I know, a description of 'third-day-blues', or postnatal depression, appeared, in Mrs Panton's *The Way They Should Go*. Again, the similarity of the turn-of-the-century mother's position with that of a mother in the 1980s is striking:

> She is more perplexed than pleased, more frightened than delighted, by the young person who develops such extraordinary powers of harassment that one wonders not only how one lived through the tremendous anxieties of birth; but how one is to live under the weight of alarm and responsibility which is suddenly placed on our shoulders ... The dreams that a young mother is supposed to dream over the cradle of her new-born baby are about as real as her supposedly passionate desire for children. She dreams principally about herself—she longs to be out of bondage. A little indignant at the manner in which the child engrosses everyone's time and attention, the while she is abjectly terrified of it, and as abjectly afraid that everyone who touches it will do it a mischief ... wondering how many more minutes it is going to live. She even wishes she never got married ... These thoughts may not be noble, but they are universal, and therefore the girl who feels them agitating her breast need not write herself down a monster—the phase will soon pass.

The 'weight of alarm and responsibility' which the worldly Mrs Panton hotly resented on her shoulders was added to by Herbert Spencer, the most important educational philosopher of the day. He declared that for too long 'the fate of a new generation has been left to the chances of unreasoning custom, impulse and fancy—joined with the suggestions of ignorant nurses and the prejudiced counsel of grandmothers'. It was that mothers were properly trained: 'an acquaintance with the first principles of physiology and the elementary truths of psychology is indispensable for the right bringing-up of children'.

As families became smaller, there were fewer little brothers and sisters for the older girls to practise on, and fewer small nieces and nephews for younger girls to adopt. Children were busy people—sent off to school punctually at seven, they were no longer available as child-minders, and so became less and less familiar with babies themselves. Sophia Jex-Blake pointed out that 'crass ignorance' of baby-care was not limited to poorer mothers. 'Many girls who are most highly educated are left to encounter the problems of motherhood with absolutely no training or preparation; and only learn by extreme anxiety, and perhaps most painful loss, the importance of what nobody has taught them.' Undeniably, in the crowded industrial world of the day, mothers needed information, just as they do today. It was a question of balance. Reinforcement of maternal confidence as well as scientific education was needed; sensibility as well as sense. The comforting writers who understood this were in a minority.

How did the enthusiasm for professional motherhood affect the position of the nurse? Nurses were by now a social institution, a way of life for the middle and upper classes, and could not easily be dispensed with. The sheer practical slog of turning-out a smart Edwardian baby fully occupied a nursemaid, even if its mother did choose to exert herself over its moral and intellectual well-being. More often than not, social commitments were still found to be inescapable—the fatal dinner party for which the Darlings left their children alone with the dog Nana was a symbol of a world from which children were excluded. In this uneasy period of adjustment, a wife's first duties were still towards her husband rather than her children.

Nevertheless, the implications of the medical and psychological discoveries of the day were that the average nurse was far from an adequate caretaker for a baby. 'It is very unlikely that lectures on nursery dietetics, ventilation, infusoria, and fixed hours will leaven the soggy dough of her mind. It is a puttyish mass that may be impressed, but seldom interfused, by any alternative agency,' thought Marion Harland. Mothers could only attempt to 'create a conscience' in her, and to make sure that she never physically chastised the infant.

There was a response to the new ideas—two new species of

caretaker appeared in the 1880s and 1890s: the trained monthly nurse, and the lady-nurse. Monthly nurses had ranged from the comfortingly motherly to the appalling Mrs Gamp caricatured by Charles Dickens. Trained nurses offered hospital discipline dear to doctors' hearts—but their clockwork efficiency was also subject to caricature:

> Mother and child are set down in her professional notebook as 'nos. 104 and 105'. The machinery of the twenty-four hours comprehends cleanliness, quiet, order, weights and measures of nourishment, examinations of pulse, temperature and other conditions. She administers food, and, when prescribed, medicine, with the same emotions and air, and come what may of rapture and anguish, life and death, never forgets her role. The mother knows herself to be in the custodian's sight a piece of jarred mechanism which must be readjusted into working order, and endures the consciousness better than the thought that her baby is but a smaller instrument just out of the factory, to be tested, proved, and carried by the expert for a given number of weeks before it is warranted to run evenly. (Harland, *Common Sense in the Nursery*)

In a development of the inadequate mother thesis, which showed the alarming degree to which mothers were prepared to quash their natural feelings for what science told them was the child's own good, several writers (including Harland) suggested that nurses were better able to induce the necessary early habits (regular feeds, sleep and 'cleanliness') because they were less emotionally involved with the child. A mother 'was bound to feel in and for the baby too deeply to carry calm pulses and judgement through the daily routine of "taking care" of that which is a dearer part of herself . . . Babies who are entirely tended by their mothers are almost without exception troublesome by reason of their ceaseless exactions.'

The lady-nurse was a happy thought which mediated between the acknowledged need of a baby for its mother and the disinclination of the mother to respond. Trained nurses of good, genteel background would be more like the mothers they were being substituted for, and would have the necessary scientific knowledge at their fingertips. Mrs Ballin, the influential editor of *Baby* magazine, pleaded for more trained nurses in her manual, *From Cradle to School*. She urged educated and redundant ladies to take up what was so far 'a relatively empty woman's profession'. By 1914 her advice had clearly been acted upon. Mary Gardner wrote in *Nursery Management*:

Nowadays the trained and well-educated nurse is more and more in request. Children have always copied their elders, and the advantages of having a refined, lady-like nurse in charge of them are obvious. She knows how to look after the health and food of the little ones, is able to teach them their first lessons, plays with them, knows how to give the children those good habits on which so much of their future happiness depends.

Colleges were set up to give training as a lady-nurse the status of further education. The Norland Institute at Notting Hill was one of the first, in 1892. Princess Christian Training College opened in Manchester in 1901, and the Wellgarth College in London in 1911. Others followed, all asserting the enormous advantage of a properly qualified and genteel nurse.

Lady-nurses had their domestic drawbacks. A union-style code of conduct allowed them to be assigned no scrubbing, grates or coal-carrying. They were to be allowed to go to church once on Sundays without the children, to have four weeks holiday a year, and half a day off each month. Their meals were to be served separately from the other servants, and they were to be addressed as 'Miss'. Their special status could lead to social dilemmas. What, asked one anxious lady, should happen when the children were sent to a party with their lady-nurse to dress and undress them? What should she do while they were playing? She could neither join the young revellers nor 'lose caste' by congregating with the house servants or the untrained nannies. Mary Gardner thought such etiquette 'absurdly upheld'. The lady-nurse should simply make herself pleasant to the nannies, allowing them to profit from her knowledge. No wonder the British found India easy to govern.

Despite such buttresses as the trained monthly nurse and the lady-nurse, the traditional nanny system was beginning to break up. The draw of more glamorous jobs reduced the quality of applicants for domestic service of all types. There were not enough good trained nurses to go round. Moreover, thanks to the observations made by the students of 'child-nature' and the rhetoric of Ellen Key and her supporters, the suspicion that mothers might, for all their inadequacies, be the best people to oversee their babies' needs—even to care for them altogether—began to filter through. Honnor Morten warned: 'When a child has been defrauded of the affection due to him, when he has starved for it and never been satisfied, a psychological need grows with the years, and he is *bound* to meet this craving somehow, wholesomely, or the reverse.'

Mrs Pepler's *His Majesty* faced up to the implications of the maternal murmurings fairly and squarely. She was a lap theorist, if ever there was one—but her first baby had not then been born, which may have made it easier to be sentimental. Have a nurse by all means, she conceded, but do not let her mind baby'. She could do the washing, take him out in the perambulator sometimes, or clean the house. Her ideal, however, was not to have a nurse at all:

You love the child more than anyone else in the world can love him, you will do your best for him in a way a nurse could not, you will learn to know him better, and he you; you will educate yourself away from your little failings, and so save him from tasting of them, and you will know that no liberties are being taken with his mind or constitution. Babyhood does not last for ever; if you have lived simply and worked hard, if you have done your very best during that period, I am sure you will have your reward. It will certainly be worth going without a nurse's help. A lady-nurse, with an evident love of children, might be allowed more liberties, but until we are all 'levelled-up', and have all enjoyed the same humanising education, and until there are many more refined homes in the land, it is best to confine your cockney to the kitchen, your would-be nurse-maid to the laundry.

Smaller families, more domestic appliances, and labour-saving homes would make Pepler's vision achievable for mothers in the next few decades. Unfortunately few of them could feel her simple conviction of rightness. Although they would return to their babies, they remained unconfident, in thrall to the advice of the experts.

If mothers and nurses required training for their jobs, what of fathers? Sully had presented them with an important task—that of being the 'scientific educator', and it would seem that the heavy Victorian father of myth stepped gratefully down from Olympus into his nursery/laboratory. Jean-Paul Richter's *Levana*, although written in 1814, only became popular in England in the 1880s. In a semi-Rousseauesque vein he pleaded for more sharing of roles: 'Mothers be fathers! we might cry, and fathers be mothers! for the two sexes complete each sex.' Ada Ballin decided to rename her 'Mothers' Parliament' in *Baby* magazine 'Parents' Parliament' because of the increasing number of letters written to her by fathers.

Nevertheless, from the evidence of the manuals the role of fathers seems to have remained disappointingly distant. Of necessity, the father was more often than not away from the home when the child was awake, and changing methods of discipline deprived him, for good or ill, of his retributive role. Mrs Arthur Acland felt she had to plead against 'a tendency towards putting the father outside the life of the child, a more or less clumsy interloper whose opinion and advice is to be taken critically, and with more or less conscious derision' (*Child Training*). Cunnington, not a sentimental man, decided that there was something particularly feminine about the patience required to deal with children. The child's nervous system, he asserted, could not stand sustained pressure; it needed constant change—of lessons, posture, or activities. Adults, on the other hand, liked to concentrate on one task for some time.

That is why a child and an adult find each other's society

irksome if it is maintained for any length of time. The child's nervous system is in constant fluctuation. Women can adapt themselves better than men to this curious rate of oscillation, and Nature has arranged that the mother, and not the father, should manage the nursery. (*Nursery Notes*)

Although fathers were not often to be found in the nursery, it is interesting that the authors of the intensely sentimental literature of childhood typical of the time were more often men than women. 'His Majesty, the Baby' wielded a romantic fascination reminiscent of the reaction to Rousseau's *Emile*. Hervey Elwes's anthology, *The Modern Child*, celebrated this with a selection of quotations from child-conscious contemporaries. In its preface he reflected:

In nothing is change in the last fifty years more marked than in the mental attitude of the English-speaking races towards children ... Nowadays nothing is too good for children, no sacrifice too great; money and time are poured like water before their tripping feet. Literature is flooded by a multitude of books about children, full of intuition, insight, and tenderest understanding.

These were the years of the *Child's Garden of Verses, Dream Days, Romance in the Nursery* and above all, *Peter Pan*. The first producer of *Peter Pan* is said to have fastened his lifebelt on the doomed *Lusitania* with Peter's own words: 'To die will be an awfully big adventure.' The audience on the first night was almost entirely adult—and clapped furiously to save fairy Tinker Bell's life at the line: 'Do you believe in fairies?' The cult—the institution as it has been called—of J. M. Barrie was only explicable in terms of the general nostalgia for childhood and infancy which prevailed just before war broke out. Barrie's complex was 'more than maternal; it seems to have been positively foetal'. According to Peter Coveney Peter Pan was not just a boy who did not want to grow up—he wished that he had never been born. The first version of the story, *The Little White Bird*, makes this clear. Peter flies out of the window and goes back to the island in Kensington Gardens, where all the little birds lived before they were sent to be babies. The age of two for Barrie was 'the beginning of the end'. And—at one here with Freud, albeit unconsciously—'Nothing that happens after twelve matters very much.'

Scientists and sentimentalists combined, then, to assert the importance of the baby—whether as a hope for the future or as a memento of the past. The distinction between their approaches is worth remarking. Although 'child study' was itself criticized by those who could not be bothered with it as being over-sentimental, obsessed by the 'child's eye view', in fact its observations and records did not lead to indulgence in the long run. They created norms, tables of statistics and 'milestones of development' which led parents to seek to fit their children into the pattern of the average. The nostalgia of the romantics opposed itself to such officiousness. It recognized the passing of an era—in many ways a rather pleasant and relaxed era—which I called the limbo decades, when children had not been greatly valued. Instead they had led self-sufficient nursery lives, cosseted for an hour by their parents and then forgotten about. There were clearly adults who missed the secret garden, the fantasy life once lived by children under the oblivious noses of their parents.

Nowadays there are unhappy children who are studied all day long; whose plays are arranged for them, always with a view to their 'development'; who may not even make mud-pies in seclusion, but must perforce and in gangs shape something out of gray india-rubber, and sit at a table to do it. What can they know, poor things, of the joys and terrors to be found in a dwarf-infested shrubbery, just at sunset, on a chill October day? (Harker, *A Romance of the Nursery*)

Practical Motherhood

The priorities of the new-wave manuals were feeding and cleanliness. Medical details were largely omitted as the necessity for doctors was conceded—a sketch of symptoms directed the mother to a likely cause of illness, but she was not encouraged to cure it herself. Her province was prevention—reflected in the fashion for 'rational clothing' (shades of Rousseau), fresh air, and hygiene—and habit-training. Bringing up baby was no longer a succession of moral lessons: infant fortitude and benevolence were lost concepts. Good behaviour became a matter induced by early practice rather than early understanding. Very little was expected of these elaborately dolled-up babies. Only towards the 1920s did a mood of impatience creep in, a semi-military no-nonsense approach, which foreshadowed the mentally and physically hygienic age to come.

Feeding was the most skilled art—discipline, rather—of infant management once breast-feeding went out of fashion. In 1881 *Sylvia* advised the young mother to be 'as systematic as you can—but do not go to extremes and be too rigid. Baby may have made a mistake in his calculations as to the length and breadth of his hunger.' But by 1907 Eric Pritchard, the most influential authority on infant feeding in Britain, said that 'it is essential not only that the food should be given at regular intervals, but that these intervals should be sufficiently spaced out to give the stomach time to become empty and to recover from fatigue' (*Infant Education*).

Pritchard encouraged mothers to establish a three-hourly feeding schedule with no night feeds 'from the first day of life, when such functional habits are most easily established'. He felt that the 'old-fashioned' two-hourly feeding gave the stomach far too little rest, and cow's milk took longer for babies to digest. The needs of breast-fed babies were largely ignored. When regular three-hourly feeds became regular four-hourly feeds more mothers than ever despaired of getting a breast-fed baby to last out that long, and took to the bottle.

Another reason for cutting down the number of feeds was the change in medical opinion over the best weight for babies. Fat babies became distinctly unfashionable, rather than 'bonny'. Marion Harland warned that 'chunky children laden with adipose tissue are apt to be more quiet than those who are reasonably plump, because their whole system is lethargic. They need less food and more air and exercise.' Holt, the most popular American oracle, described over-feeding as 'a habit gradually acquired which may increase until the child is being given twice as much food as is proper' (*Care and Feeding of Children*). Varying birth-weights were ignored—babies were to be fed by the book.

That in itself became something of an achievement. Chemical analysis of milk brought scientific exactitude to the old rule-of-thumb method of diluting cow's milk by half and sweetening it slightly. In order to give the baby a substance as like mother's milk as possible, 'modified milk' was created. This meant diluting the cow's milk to reduce the casein in it, adding a little cream to increase the fat, and using lactose (sugar of milk) to sweeten it. A little lime-water eased digestion and added mineral salts. According to Holt, the strength and the quantity of such artificial feeds was to be altered first daily, then weekly, then monthly according to how strong or delicate the child was. All proportions had to be exact, and it was hardly surprising that mothers who could afford to surrendered their role of milk-provider to the Walker-Gordon Milk Laboratories—they were sent baby's 'formula' daily, in sealed bottles, adjusted to the infant's doctor's prescription. With Holt's system, sick and well children alike required a doctor constantly in attendance.

The 'cult of similarity' in feeding was made more complex by Biedert's studies of the composition of milk in 1905. Mothers were told to mix top milk with ordinary milk, add whey here and cream there, peptonize the milk for one baby, add bicarbonate of soda for another, and to adjust casein, lactalbumen and sucrose as if they were professional chemists. One early twentieth-century manual offered two and a half pages of algebraic formulae for calculating a healthy baby's feed. There were dozens of methods; schools of feeding rose and fell in popularity with the latest manuals. 'Like metaphysics, it was the search in the absolutely black room for an absolutely black hat that wasn't there' (Goldblom). What was odd was that mothers were not driven back to their breasts in despair. Instead, they grappled with formula feeding scientifically and enthusiastically. If they did relapse, it was to use one of the many patent foods that spoke so well of themselves. Very nourishing they were too, admitted one manual—but not for babies.

One advance brought in by hygiene-conscious science was the disappearance of the long-tube-type feeding bottle. Holt recommended cylindrical bottles with wide necks and no angles or corners. What did become popular, to judge by the number of patents for them, were self-feeding bottles of different types. One had short legs at the base to stand up on the baby's chest at a suitable incline. Another hung round the neck on a ribbon. A third patent, in 1897, recorded that 'in the raising of infants sustained by the bottle it becomes a source of great inconvenience and labour to provide food at varying intervals, especially at night, when rest and recuperation are necessary'. It described a bottle with a groove around the middle, so that it could be suspended by a pulley from the ceiling over the baby's cot—nipple-end up, to prevent drips. All the baby had to do was yank it down and drink to its heart's content. Holt would hardly have approved of such freedom, but he certainly accepted the lack of contact with the baby which all such self-feeding devices implied:

> For the first two or three months, it is better, except at night, when it may be undesirable to take the infant from the crib, that it be held on the nurse's arm during feeding; later it may lie on its side in the crib, provided the bottle is held by the nurse until it empties.

Holt's babies were not to be fed for more than twenty minutes, nor for much less. If sleepy, they could be kept awake by 'gentle shaking' until the food was taken. There was to be no playing with them after a feed—they should be put back into their cribs and 'disturbed as little as possible'. Holt's ideal was based on his hospital experience—rows of neat infants wrapped tidily in identical cots, waking as one man on the feeding hour with a united wail. Hospital routine made such drilling necessary. The sad fact was that it became a model for family life. Just as the psychological treatment of young children would be ultimately derived from the abnormalities observed by Freud, just as Maria Montessori would apply the techniques that succeeded well with the subnormal to ordinary toddlers, so normal feeding practice was to be borrowed from orphanage discipline.

Breast-feeding of a sort did make a small comeback, but in a suitably organized form—the breast-milk bank. When all the formulae failed, doctors were forced to resort to nature. Mothers who did breast-feed their babies in hospitals were asked to strip their breasts when their child had had its fill, and sell their milk to the hospital. Breast-milk banks were set up in Boston in 1910, and at Queen Charlotte's, London, a few years later. They were not a great success. On the whole the wet nurses were 'homeless women of low intelligence and morale'. Boarding them in or near hospitals was an administrative nightmare, and they were not above boosting their earnings by watering their milk, or adding cow's milk to it. After the district nurse (another innovation) had collected the milk, she had to take it to laboratories for quality control. The whole clumsy manoeuvre was typical of the fatally critical and manipulative approach to breast-feeding.

The epitome of the anti-breast-feeding trend was the patenting of an 'anti-embarrassment device for nursing mothers' in 1910. This was a massive harness which cupped the breasts and provided rubber-tube extensions for the nipple, ending with a rubber teat by which the baby could be fed in public places 'avoiding the necessity of exposing the person'. If you weren't using artificial milk, you could at least appear to be doing so.

Once weaned from the bottle, babies' prospects improved. Ada Ballin criticized the old 'sameness in children's meals' as something that 'parents would never tolerate in their own'. She showed a homoeopathic respect for the body's needs, and didn't believe that children should be forced to eat what they didn't like. 'Organic idiosyncrasy' might make particular foods 'obnoxious to the system'. In a passage worthy of the old humoural medicine, she suggested that children of different temperaments should have different food. The constitutionally feverish and excitable child should be given an unstimulating diet—milk, eggs, and vegetables. The 'dull and lymphatic' child, disinclined to activity, should have as rousing a diet as possible—coffee at breakfast, tea at teatime, and, in extreme cases, wine at dinner.

The ancient commitment to gruel was brightened up by Mrs Ballin's recommendation of fruit and sugar as foods.

Fruit might avert the problems of this 'medicine-taking nation', she felt. And sugar, scientifically proved to produce heat energy, was better suited to children than the fat they generally abhorred. Dr Brockbank, in *Children, Their Care and Management*, agreed that a varied diet was necessary. Cooking was to be appetizing, vegetables 'fresh and tender', and milk puddings frequent—'there is no nicer light pudding than junket'. Tea should be bread and jam, and plain, well-made cakes. Some mothers, he reflected, only allowed either jam or cake.

Opinion remained divided on the 'eat-it-all-up' front. *Sylvia* believed that 'at the nursery table there must be inculcated a perfect horror respecting *waste*'. Good appetites could only be encouraged by no eating between meals, and she criticized badly brought-up children 'who are eating continually from morning to night, and the maternal pockets have always in readiness a biscuit or sugar plum'. One should allow ample time, she commanded oracularly, for the stomach 'to *rest* but not *play*' between meals. Mary Gardner and Cunnington reflected the increasing weariness with the 'child's eye-view' school that Ballin represented. Once the child was old enough to be reasoned with, Gardner felt 'it should be made to understand that if the food placed before it is not eaten, no other will be provided'. Cunnington scoffed at the idea of a child who couldn't drink milk. 'There are plenty who *will* not drink it, and many mothers who cannot submit to the fatigue of training their children.' Eric Pritchard turned basic psychology to good use in his devious compromise—he deserves the final word:

> Permanent tastes are acquired very easily at this time of life. As a rule, children dislike foods which are said to be good for them, or are forced on them, and they take strong fancies to foods which they are not allowed to eat; advantage should be taken of these tendencies. (*Infant Education*)

In attitudes to bathing, far more consideration was shown for the baby's feelings. There was no more lusty singing to drown the cries. There was no more cold water, for that matter, although an occasional enthusiast still offered cold-water douches to older children especially if they were inclined to wet their beds. The bath thermometer was to read a comfortable 94°–98°F (Americans preferred a slightly cooler 84°–90°, oddly enough), and every precaution was taken to prevent the infant from 'chilling'. Did piped hot water make this advice possible? Perhaps some mothers had always cheated—Marion Harland confessed to her own hypocrisy as a young mother, now that she could recommend hot water:

> When my first baby was born, the rage for the plunge bath was at its height. Having known for myself the discomfort of such an immersion, and the torture of the cold shower bath, inflicted with conscientious regularity by one of the most tender-hearted of mothers, I resolved that my boy should never have to suffer either. I bathed him myself, and under a playful pretext of nervousness in performing under the eyes of others a task to which I was not accustomed, I used to lock myself up with him in the nursery while washing and dressing him. My conscience flinches to this day in the recall of the deception practised on an exemplary matron who one day asked me how my baby liked his cold dip in the morning. I answered that he had 'never objected to it'. I had not the moral courage to avow that I washed him in tepid water.

From this anecdote, and from her tips on bathing, it is clear how much Marion Harland revelled in her own baby.

> Let him splash and flourish his naked limbs in the water to his and your delectation . . . Should he resist the motion to remove him—and the chances are he will do so—do not yield, but try some form of consolation—a toy, a game of bo-peep behind the flannel folds, a flow of chirrupy talk.

Such compromise, and such concessions to the baby's own feelings, were refreshing. So too was the unabashed tenderness of: 'When perfectly dry, his flesh sweet and pure with the

130

exquisite lustre imparted by the bath and friction, he is the most kissable object in nature.'

Mary Gardner suggested, if the baby was frightened of water, wrapping him up in a large, fluffy bath-towel, and lowering the whole bundle gradually into the bath, revealing the water at last by throwing back the corners of the towel over the edges. She even conceded bath toys—a little grudgingly perhaps: 'Loofah dolls and corkstuffed ducks are not an unmixed blessing, because the child will often refuse to part with these dripping creatures when emerging from the tub without a great deal of loudly expressed grief.' Clearly confrontation was to be avoided at bathtime. It was to be a pleasant experience, relaxing rather than bracing, and more often at bedtime than on waking. Brand names invaded the bathroom as they had the kitchen. Colgate, Pears, Vinolia and Allen & Hanbury's made washing more luxurious and more expensive. Mothers were put upon their mettle to give their babies the best, and wads of advertisements before and after the texts of the manuals made sure that they knew what to ask for.

Baby, although more comfortable at bathtime, continued inexorably in exile from his mother's bed. 'The place where baby most likes to sleep is where he must not be,' crowed the *Glaxo Baby Book* with looking-glass-world satisfaction. He was best off sleeping alone, in 'a quiet, dark, place', according to Marion Harland. To rock or not to rock was no longer a controversy—no one admitted to it any more. Nevertheless, Drummond, then one of the most important thinkers behind child-care practice, surmised in his theoretical musings that 'the earliest cradles of the race were rocked in rhyme to sleep'. The possible reason for 'a practice so troublesome' was that 'rocking and lulling were among the earliest waves that broke upon the child from the sea of feelings in which he found himself'. They were associated with the 'dawn of consciousness' and helped to awaken and strengthen the emotional links which joined mother and child together. This Leboyeresque sensitivity to the newborn baby failed to shake the orderly plans of the manual writers for baby's distant deployment.

Plenty of sleep was made a necessity. 'Many children grow up irascible in temper and disordered in their nervous system because they are habitually deprived of their lawful quantum of rest,' claimed Harland. Consider the baby's point of view, she suggested. He was the busiest member of the domestic workforce.

> Comparing his strength with yours, you would have paced ten or twelve miles of floor, composed and delivered an oration (with due regard for foreign idiom) on current events, and examined critically two or three hundred pictures, besides being opposed in a dozen designs and methods, in the four hours that separate breakfast from the midday nap.

Harland felt that the amount of sleep needed by a child depended on its heredity and should be varied accordingly. But this perception—only recently reasserted by the Spock generation—disappeared under the military uniformity demanded by Cunnington. He provided one of the first of the infamous tables showing the hours of sleep 'required' by children at different ages. It allowed no variation for more or less active children, and blamed caretakers for babies who failed to conform: 'Much of the difficulty in persuading some children to sleep is the outcome of bad habits; a feeble discipline in the nursery commonly results in irregularities in a child's sleeping' (*Nursery Notes*).

The baby's wardrobe, for many years an unexceptional miniature version of the adult's, was severely overhauled to suit the mood of the age. Although baby clothes in fashion plates looked as pretty as ever, underneath they were to be designed upon rational and scientific—occasionally theosophic—principles. Wool was to be worn rather than cotton or flannel for undergarments. It was warmer, softer, and absorbed perspiration better, 'which is why the Almighty clothed sheep in wool in preference to the inferior article'. Annie Hewer thought fine cashmere, gauze flannel, good nun's veiling, or washing silk were all 'far more cosy and soft than starched muslin' for babies' dresses and robes (*Our Baby*). Mrs Ballin, inspired by Dr Jaeger's *Rational Clothing Reform*, dismissed the 'long clothes system' as 'little better than the old barbarous swaddling'. She provided a complete set of patterns for her own version of rational clothing. A layette was simply four fine binders, to be worn until twelve months, four little woollen vests, made perhaps from father's wear-softened cast-offs, four flannel 'blankets' (sleeveless robes with a buttoned lower edge), four robes of flannel or cashmere, two day gowns, four pilches, two head flannels, and four dozen Turkey towelling nappies. As soon as the child began to 'feel his feet', the dresses could be turned up, thus making two complete sets of clothes unnecessary.

It is striking that even in a 'rational' wardrobe, binders were still included. These were a last relic of swaddling, still supposed to be essential for warmth, for their bracing effect upon the navel, and neatening of the infant silhouette. 'Customs, however foolish, die hard, and there still seems to be a legion of nurses who implicitly believe in the necessity of bandaging up the body of an infant like a mummy, and securing the roll of flannel after being pulled tight with a row of stitches,' complained Henry Ashby. By 1921, the roll of flannel was outmoded—baby's tummy only had to suffer a little woollen belt, a mere gesture to tradition. Similarly stays for little girls lost their bones to become 'corded', and eventually changed to 'liberty bodices'. Hence the description 'liberty': these stiff little vests were only a release from what had gone before.

A move was set afoot to exchange the traditional long cloak, a heavy and elaborate status symbol often accused of strangling babies by its weight, for a cosy shawl, but the stigma attached to shawls was hard to overcome. 'Few mothers have the moral courage to give up the cloak,' lamented Sophia Jex-Blake. But by 1896 even as conservative a writer as Mrs Panton declared against them:

That mother is wise who simply buys a charming shawl and sends out her baby wrapped in that. It does sound horrid, and is horrid, I know, for naturally one recollects with a shudder the people and babies one often sees in connection with these garments, but Liberty sells such charming white soft shawls, that I think if an effort in the right direction were made, it would not be so dreadful after all. (*The Way They Should Go*)

Clothes for the toddler were to be loose, warm, and comfortable. An overall of grey gingham with long sleeves would protect 'pitty frocks' while gardening or making mudpies. Four layers remained average—a little girl in winter had to be in warm woollen stockings, thick-soled boots right up her legs, a chemise of stout longcloth, drawers like knickerbockers, a scarlet flannel petticoat with one or two tucks buttoned on to scarlet homemade stays, an upper petticoat with sleeves, of fine cloth or flannel, and a warm dress with detachable sleeves—these were an odd eighteenth-century hangover. Boys wore just the same until they were three or four, when they took 'their degree in knickerbockers' (*Sylvia*).

Mrs Ballin and Mrs Panton agreed that the nicest thing for little girls were 'carters' smock dresses, tucked at hem and sleeve'. With less thought than *Sylvia* for mudpies, Mrs Panton suggested a much more elaborate style of pinafore with embroidered neck and Liberty sash at the waist. On boys' clothes, the pundits disagreed. Mrs Ballin put her little graduates into serge sailor suits with trousers—Scotch dresses, she felt, were not to be recommended, as they 'exposed the legs'. Mrs Panton was determined to remain exclusive. 'Kilts can never become common like those odious little sailor suits, as they are so dear to buy.'

Shoes could be approached in the proper scientific spirit once Daniel Neal introduced his revolutionary 'Phatpheet' range. 'No infant is too young or too small for Mr Neal to devote his personal attention to it' (*Our Baby*). Expertise went far beyond the simple advice of Dr Allbutt to ensure that shoes had a left and right foot, and an instep strap. Ashby included X-ray photographs and diagrams of distorted feet, and insisted on frequent, careful fittings. Instead of tightly buttoned boots, sandals were acceptable for everyday wear. Holden's 'natureform' shoes were advertised in the end-papers of *Our Baby*.

Brand-names were nowhere more in evidence than in children's clothes. Harrington's Hygienic Squares, Wolsey, Chilprufe's and Jaeger's underclothes, Weldon's and But-terick's paper patterns—the commercialization of baby-hood was well under way. Readymade clothes were achieving 'a high pitch of perfection,' thought Mary Gardner, and she feared that 'sweating' (labour, rather than hot babies) was going on somewhere. It probably was—but the key to the new quality and the low prices was the sewing machine. Invented in the 1850s, by the turn of the century it was treadle or electrically powered. 'Our grandmothers would have considered it sacrilege to have had recourse to machines in making baby-clothes,' Gardner reflected, but added philosophically, 'machines were not in use then.'

The consideration shown to babies at table and in the bath also extended to clothing them. 'Should a child have a preference or distaste for a certain style or colour, that child should be humoured in any way possible,' declared Mrs Panton, and reminded mothers of the agonies suffered by children who felt wrongly dressed. Seaside holidays were a case in point. A generation before, children could scarcely dip their toes in the water without immodesty. They had had to promenade stiffly behind their parents, and suffer the indignity of the bathing machine with its nightmarish professional attendant, who had hurled them into the water for a medicinal swim. Now special beach kit was provided— seaman's jerseys, and serge skirts or knickerbockers. 'Those india-rubber boots which can only be purchased at Scarborough,' even made paddling a possibility.

For a few peaceful decades, nothing much had been said about toilet training. Nurses and mothers had been using the newly available macintosh wrappings to stop everything getting wet. The new scientific and sanitary approach to babyhood allowed no such sloppiness. Nappies were to be changed whenever wet, and the waterproof pilch was dismissed as particularly objectionable. It kept baby's tender skin in 'a state of perpetual poultice'. Moreover, it was believed that if the baby had a wet nappy so rarely that it found dampness a discomfort, this helped early training.

There was more specific information than ever before on how to dispense with what Ashby saw as the 'necessary evil' of nappies, by training at a very early age. Infant chambers were thoughtfully provided with a little flannel jacket for baby's greater comfort by Dr Brockbank, but other autho-

rities preferred the Pavlovian stimulus of the cold china rim.
Training started at birth.

> With very young babies, the nurse should let the baby lie
> on its back, her right thigh being lower than the left, on
> which the baby will chiefly rest . . . After the second month,
> the baby can be held more in a sitting position, with some
> weight on the chamber. The baby will very soon begin to
> relieve itself in this way, especially when encouraged by the
> nurse. It should be put on the chamber before, during and
> after each meal, to teach it to pass water at regular times,
> and control of the bladder develops if this is done properly.
> At the end of a few months, with a healthy child, only six or
> eight diapers ought to be wet. (Brockbank, *Children, Their
> Care and Management*)

This makes one pause for thought. My totally untrained
babies never had their nappies changed more than six times a
day, if that. Clearly, standards of hygiene were being set very
high if the target of training was to reduce the number of
nappies worn to 'six or eight'. In recommending a 'small pad
of Gamgee tissue in the fork of the body for the first few weeks
of life', Brockbank said the number of nappies could be cut
down from the 'normal two dozen a day'. Mrs Ballin had
included four dozen nappies in her layette. It is likely that
fungal nappy rashes were common in pre-Napisan days, and
so more changing was necessary. No advice on sterilizing had
yet appeared, although washing methods of the time included
a spell of boiling. The crudeness of laundry methods, improved though they now were by simple wooden rotary-
motion washing-machines, must have given mothers a great
incentive to train their babies early.

To return to 'encouragement by the nurse'—how exactly
did one encourage? The manuals became more specific. 'At
first,' wrote Holt, 'there may be some local irritation, like that
produced by tickling the anus, or introducing just inside the
rectum a small cone of oiled paper, or a piece of soap, as a
suggestion of the purpose for which the infant is placed on the
chamber.' A standard purgative method, then, was being
recommended for frequent daily use. Many optimists hoped

to dispense with nappies altogether at seven or eight months, except at night, and the columns of the baby magazines were punctuated by the latest record or method for 'clean and dry'ness.

Interest in the baby's stools was not limited to when and where it delivered them. Regularity had always been a worry to mothers, and the purgative methods available have already been noted. Now quality became a major issue as, in the early years of the twentieth century, 'divination by stool' seized the imaginations of the paediatricians. In the Boston Floating Hospital, 'more attention was paid to the stool than the infant', recalled Alton Goldblom, once an intern there.

> The professor carried a wooden spatula in his breast pocket which was used to smear the specimen of stool, to note its consistency, to search for curds—soap and beans; with never a look at the infant, but only from this meticulous examination, on which he would expatiate lengthily and eruditely, he would finally offer suggestions for the next day's food.

'The stools of the infant', wrote Ashby, 'should always be carefully watched by the mother, as important information with regard to digestion may be gathered from careful and continuous examination.' The baby's motions were classified, and cures provided for every variation from the norm. Castor oil and 'grey powders' were now discouraged. Baby could have milk-sugar, medicinal paraffin, cod-liver or olive oil, or just a spoonful of honey. The *Glaxo Baby Book* also dealt with breast-fed babies—the mother was instructed to take oatmeal, salad oil, fruit—and plenty of Glaxo.

An issue related to early potty training, and again one rarely openly referred to in the older manuals, was masturbation. Perhaps there was more need for it now that babies and small children were no longer allowed the comfort of their mother's or nurse's bed. 'Self-abuse', as Mrs Ballin called it, 'must always be looked for in little children, especially in little girls in the early years of life.' It could be caused by local irritation, which, as the child rubbed it, resulted in a 'pleasurable sensation'. One reason often given for getting baby trained so early was to avoid this; possibly the frenetic nappy-changing was also done with it in mind. In other cases the origin of the habit was traced to 'wicked nurses', who when a baby cried 'have been known to tickle it in this improper way to stop the crying'. (What, incidentally, was the effect of the standard encouragement to early bowel-training?)

Whatever the cause, Mrs Ballin felt that mothers could not be sufficiently watchful in this respect, as the habit 'constitutes a danger which is very far reaching, and may lead to ruining the child, body and mind, for life'. Stern measures had to be taken. 'When the habit is discovered, it must in young children be put a stop to by such means as tying the hands, strapping the knees together with a pad between them, or some mechanical plan.' Many of the 'mechanical plans' resembled instruments of torture—one, for boys, was constructed on 'iron maiden' lines. Mrs Ballin was convinced of the merits of circumcision 'to avoid moral backsliding'. Helen Campbell made children sleep in combinations fastened at the back, with thick woolly gloves on their hands. Once they were four years old, she felt that the immorality of the practice could be discussed with them.

Other 'bad habits' which now came under the arc-lights were thumbsucking, nailbiting, nose-picking and dirt-eating. I have not just ignored earlier references to these familiar childhood traits. Either they did not exist in former times (which seems unlikely, although it is possible that babies' anxieties were on the increase), or it suddenly became important that they be stopped. They didn't fit in well with the image of the walking, talking, well-adjusted clockwork baby. In this sphere as in almost all aspects of baby-care, intrusion and interference, tinkering about with the works, was getting more marked.

Sucking was said by Holt to lead to a misshapen mouth or fingers. It was to be corrected by applying pasteboard splints to the elbows, or putting the baby into mittens. There are still maternity wards today that provide baby-gowns with neatly rounded sewn-up sleeves to prevent thumbsucking. Comforters were dirty things—a ceremonious burning in the child's presence discouraged their use. Nailbiting could be stopped by painting the fingertips with bitter aloes, or by making the child wear gloves. Some mothers put mustard powder in the fingertips, Brockbank remarked neutrally. For his own part, he thought 'the present of a pair of nail-clippers with a taking spring mechanism' more attractive. Dirt-eating was more serious—'a morbid craving seldom seen in a normal child', thought Holt, who told mothers to take medical advice for this and for masturbation.

It is worth remembering in trying to understand these extreme attitudes that the force of habit—which will be discussed in a later section—was regarded at this time as ineradicably powerful. Today we think in terms of stages through which children pass. Then the brain was believed to be permanently seared by the habits established in infancy.

Moulding the Clay

Small children began to spend less of their time in the nursery. Walks in all weathers were the rule, and the windows of the nursery were to be kept open as much as possible. If the nurse complained, said Mrs Pepler firmly, she should be told to wear an overcoat in the nursery. Holt estimated that a child would spend a quarter of its day in the nursery, whereas Combe's estimate in 1840 had been 11/12ths. Exercise and fresh air were rigorously pursued, and in the process physical contact between baby and caretaker was cut down more and more.

Mothers were told not to dandle their babies up and down, in case they injured their spine or brain. Instead the baby was left to kick on a sofa turned against the wall or a rug on the floor for fifteen to twenty minutes a day. The play-pen, convenient prison, made its first appearance: 'A nursery fence two feet high, made to surround a mattress', wrote Holt, 'makes an excellent box stall for the young animal.' Carrying babies about became suspect. 'To keep infants constantly in arms cramps their heads and bodies, stops the free circulation of their blood, and often makes them weak in standing,' claimed *Sylvia*. So off went the babies in their perambulators and the newly fashionable mailcarts.

139

Mailcarts were fantastical elaborations on the simple two-handed carts which postmen had used since Rowland Hill established the penny post. Mrs Ballin did not think them at all suitable for the under-twos—'it is a pitiful sight to see, as one does every day, infants strapped into these vehicles, sitting all in a heap, with their spines and legs bent, their chests contracted, and the strap pressing against their stomachs'. What would she have made of baby-buggies? Mailcarts were popular because they were cheaper and lighter than prams—easy to manoeuvre and very dashingly designed. Once they were upholstered, with attachments across the handles to allow babies to lie full length, even Mrs Ballin found them acceptable.

Perambulators proper became more and more grand. The carriage-built models of the 1900s are the star attraction of baby-carriage collections. Double hoods meant that two children could be housed with ease in all weathers. Carriage lanterns on the mudguards allowed walks to extend far into the twilight or the fog. Perhaps as a result of their elegance, perhaps as a cause, mothers were occasionally to be seen wheeling their own prams. Marion Harland advised:

> If you have only one servant, who is unwilling to leave her work early in the morning, and so catch the best of the day for baby, then take an early breakfast yourself, and arrayed in lawn, percale, or modest gingham, brave public opinion by tending your darling in person. To wheel a perambulator is a crucial test of your moral courage and innate ladyhood.

The nursemaidless future was being rehearsed via the obsession with fresh air.

The remoteness forced on babies by the exile into play-pens and prams was increased by the determination of most manual writers to end the promiscuous kissing of babies. Holt told mothers 'the less kissing the better'—if kisses had to be given, then only on cheek or forehead. Brockbank dealt with the subject in a chapter titled 'Spreading Infection' (it also covered schools and children's parties). Mrs Ballin was perhaps the most explicit:

140

Many a horrible case of disease has arisen through the indiscriminate kissing of babies by men in the park, who are paying attention to the nursemaid, and I know one dreadful incident in which such a man took up the baby's bottle and sucked it, thus transmitting a loathsome disease to the infant in whose mouth it was next placed.

It took a more human observer to put the issue into a perspective that we find normal today.

Are there not very many scientific wiseacres who say that kissing is extremely bad for children, and a most unhealthy practice? I wonder—supposing a child is absolutely and entirely healthy because it has never once been kissed, whether that miraculous health may not have been gained at the expense of its poor little heart! Would not an unkissed, rigidly hygienic baby have a very cold little soul? Would it not miss the tenderness? And how could it ever be loving and tender to anyone itself if it had never been fondled and fussed over? (Burrell, *The Little Foxes*)

The nursery itself improved. The *Glaxo Baby Book* even suggested that the best room in the house—the drawing-room—should be used as a nursery if there was no alternative. 'Nothing is too good for His Majesty the Baby.' Ideally, there were to be two nurseries, one for night and one for day. Three thermometers were needed—one for the air inside, one for outside, and one for the bath-water. The fumes from closed stoves or gas fires were declared to be a deadly threat to health—rumour even suggested that unscrupulous nurses lulled their charges off by putting their head beside the unlit gas-fire. So, with much sentimental harking back to the joys of the twilight hour, open fires were re-installed.

The increased interest in the child and its position in the family was reflected by a change in the name of its home. The distancing term 'nursery' was replaced for some writers by 'playroom'; others used the even more optimistic 'family room'. How much less of a second-class citizen the child was could be seen in the amazing range of purpose-built furniture available. Mary Gardner itemized the delights 'in artistic

141

shapes and the newest designs, which can be obtained from firms that specially cater for the modern nursery needs, such as Messrs Heal and Son, Messrs Waring and Messrs Whitely'. The bright colours and scrap screens suggested by earlier optimists were now available commercially as nursery friezes, designed by well-known artists such as Christopher Hassall, Cecil Aldin and Walter Crane.

Behind all this interest in the child's surroundings was a consciousness of the effect of environment on character. 'Do not choose pictures of sad and depressing incidents, such as a child weeping over its mother's grave, or a faithful dog dying on a gory battlefield. Morbid subjects attract children's attention and do their nerves much harm' (Gardner, *Nursery Management*). Honnor Morten agreed. 'The child's earliest impressions should be of brightness and sunshine, and a sort of indefinable homeness in the atmosphere of its special room.' Creamy yellow walls, a sunny aspect with short cretonned curtains, and a stained floor with rugs would make a 'thoroughly comfortable and artistic playroom'. Although linoleum was available, it was criticized as cold and cheerless by several authorities—its heyday would come in the 1920s. Brockbank suggested brightening up the floor with a rug 'made of white flannel, backed with red turkey twill calico, and with various animals cut out of the red cloth stitched onto it. With button eyes, they afford much enjoyment to babies in the quadruped stage.'

Play in the up-to-date nursery was a serious business. 'It is the apprenticeship for the work of life,' wrote Drummond. 'It has favoured the growth of intelligence and thereby permitted man not only to choose, but to some extent to make his environment, and thereby to assist at his own evolution.' Again a speeded-up evolutionary scenario was assumed, and child-rearing methods made racially crucial. To Honnor Morten the vital lessons that a child learnt through play were developed imagination and a respect of law and order. There had to be strict rules in children's games 'so that the love for these laws enters into their soul' (a conscious Platonism). There was little need to encourage imagination in children, as it was second nature to them. But parents had to be careful not to stamp it out by a too strict regard for truth:

1 The 'voluptuous fondness' of eighteenth-century husbands forced mothers not to breast-feed, but to offer the risky alternatives of a wet-nurse or starchy paps and panadas

2 The new-style, post-Rousseau mother was told to abandon herself to Nature and the needs of her children: swaddling clothes were abandoned and breast-feeding became all the rage

3 'Hence ye doating train / Of midwives and of nurses ignorant.' In manuals like this 1811 *Female Instructor* doctors took it upon themselves to spread enlightenment to mothers and to make baby-care the province of 'Men of Sense'

4 If breast-feeding was impossible, putting the baby to the udder of a goat or ass could provide a safe alternative. Leroy's methods at Aix in 1775 were still in use in French foundling hospitals late in the nineteenth century

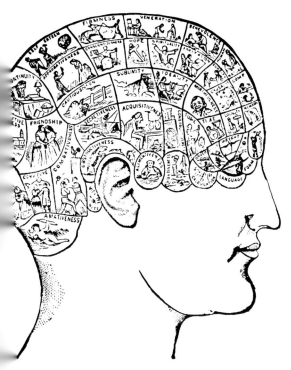

5 Elaborate domestic medicine chests show the responsibilities of the mid-nineteenth-century mother, who was free to give her baby dangerous drugs. Later manuals stopped providing dosages, and advised calling in a doctor more often: the mother's status was eroded, but infant lives were saved

6 Phrenology offered parents a theory of the brain which increased interest in infant thought processes. Learning had to wait until the appropriate faculty developed: observation, curiosity, imagination and memory could all be exercised at the right time

7–10 No infant found the statutory cold bath fun, but the upbringing recommended in the manuals of the 1850s and 1860s caused no traumas over early toilet training, showed much interest in novelties like Mr Tuttle's 'Infant Gymnasium', and allowed mothers to remain in command of early learning processes

11–12 Marion Harland criticized the growing distance between the fashionable mother and her baby. She felt that nannies were growing too powerful, and recommended English and American mothers not to be ashamed to follow the French custom of the 'promenade en famille' – with the *bonne* well in the background

13 The 'Renaissance of Motherhood' in 1900 brought mothers
back to their baby's side with a flush of sentimental
enthusiasm. Newton Shepard's illustration to Carl Ewald's
My Little Boy (1908) was captioned, 'A mother is a watch-
dog, a lioness, an idiot'

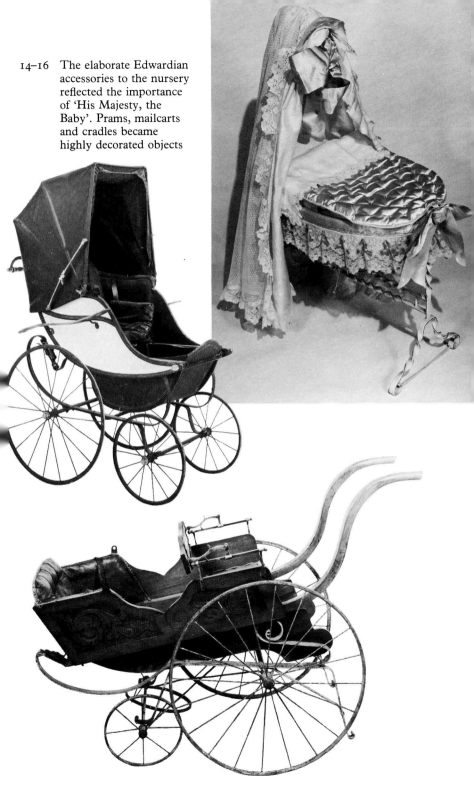

14–16 The elaborate Edwardian accessories to the nursery reflected the importance of 'His Majesty, the Baby'. Prams, mailcarts and cradles became highly decorated objects

17 Demoralized by well-informed educationalists, mothers abandoned their three-year-olds to the song and dance of kindergarten learning

18–19 The distance between this mother and her bottle-fed baby conveys the foreignness of 'formula feeding', while the barren order in the Van Houten nursery foreshadows military interest in the 'hopes of the future'

The **'Allenburys' Foods.**

MOTHER AND CHILD.
Baby, 6½ months of age. Fed from birth on the Allenburys' Foods.

A Pamphlet on Infant Feeding and Management
(48 pages) free on request.

The **'Allenburys' Foods.**

The "Allenburys'" Milk Food No. 1 consists of fresh cow's milk scientifically modified so as to closely resemble human milk in composition. The excess of casein (indigestible curd) in the cow's milk has been removed, and the deficiency of fat and milk-sugar made good. The method of manufacture pasteurises the milk and absolutely precludes all risk of contamination with noxious germs. Thus a perfect substitute for the natural food of the child is obtained and vigorous growth and health is promoted.

The "Allenburys'" Foods are : like suitable for the robust and delicate, and children thrive upon them as on no other diet.

No starchy or farinaceous food should be given to an infant under six months of age, it is not only useless, for the young infant cannot digest starch, but is a frequent cause of illness and rickets.

MILK FOOD No. 1.	MILK FOOD No. 2.	MALTED FOOD No. 3.
From birth to 3 months.	From 3 to 6 months.	From 6 months upwards.

ALLEN & HANBURYS Ltd., Lombard Street, LONDON.

United States: Niagara Falls, N.Y.   Canada: 68, Gerrard St. East, Toronto.
Australasia: 7, Spring St., Sydney.   South Africa : 39, Castle St., Cape Town.

The Nursery.

The Nursery is the training ground of the future generation. Whether the manhood and womanhood of the next decade will be physically and mentally healthy and vigorous depends largely upon the manner in which the children are fed. Mothers should therefore remember that there is no beverage equal to Van Houten's Cocoa for promoting health, strength and good digestion. It is rich in food value, easily digested and most economical in use. Its exquisite natural flavor makes it the favourite beverage for old and young alike.

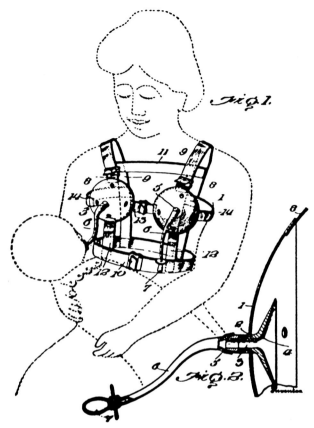

20 An 'anti-embarrassment device' patented in 1910 allowed mothers who still had the nerve to breast-feed their babies at least to appear not to

21 'An excellent box stall for the young animal': playpens became popular once mothers were told that too much carrying could harm their babies

22 Well-intentioned lady volunteers heralded the official state-paid health visitors of the early twentieth century. They brought the latest theories on hygiene and infant care into the backstreet slums – and were advised to sprinkle disinfectant powder around wherever possible

23 Madame Montessori made a huge impact with teaching methods that encouraged toddlers to learn order much earlier than had been thought possible. This suited the mood of the new century: children were to grow up while bothering adults as little as possible

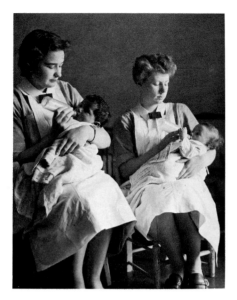

24–6 The Mothercraft Movement re-established breast-feeding in a scientific context. Trained nurses showed mothers how to 'top up' their babies professionally. Tender closeness between mother and child was approved by the romantic frontispiece to Truby King's *Natural Feeding of Infants* – but it had to be meted out 'by the clock – not by guesswork'

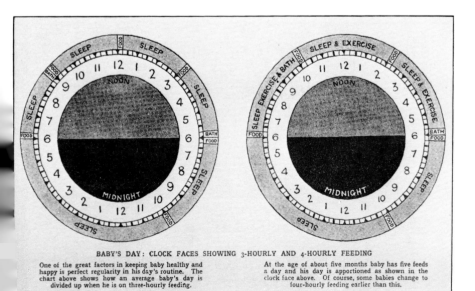

BABY'S DAY: CLOCK FACES SHOWING 3-HOURLY AND 4-HOURLY FEEDING

One of the great factors in keeping baby healthy and happy is perfect regularity in his day's routine. The chart above shows how an average baby's day is divided up when he is on three-hourly feeding.

At the age of about five months baby has five feeds a day and his day is apportioned as shown in the clock face above. Of course, some babies change to four-hourly feeding earlier than this.

Daddy can be a great help with tricycle rides

27   Behaviourism distanced parents – especially fathers –
     from their children. Affection had to be severely
     rationed – pats on the head instead of kissing good
     night, occasional trike rides instead of trauma-inducing
     rough and tumbles

28–30 Post-Freudian manuals felt they ought to face up to the facts of life, but only indirectly – as Eileen Elias's coy chapter head indicates. Fresh-air fetishism tried to blow the nasty thoughts away. Balcony cots were the answer for city babies, but only the elite could afford a Dunkley Pramotor (1922)

THE CHILD AND SEX

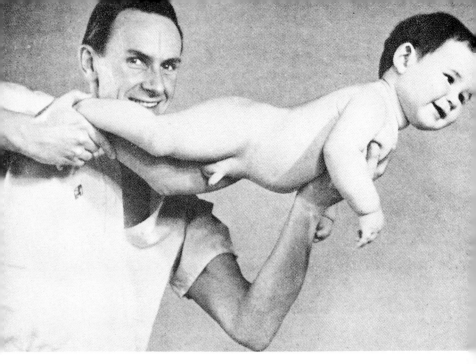

31 'This is a job you will enjoy': Dr John Gibben himself showed fathers how to give their babies 'directed development' exercises

32 Sunshine was as important as exercise, but had to be taken in careful doses. 'Janice takes a sunbath' in bonnet, with sunshade and (inexplicably) a small pumpkin

33 Pint-sized world: the Wendy House and the pedal car allowed children to imitate the adult world from which they were excluded; they also established sex roles which would prove difficult to escape from

34 A living legend: the first edition of Dr Spock's *Baby and Child Care* (1946) was only outsold by the Bible. Its cover offers a fine illustration of his 'any time can be funtime' philosophy

35–6 The Piaget-dominated present: parents with a smattering of developmental psychology 'interact' with their babies.
Above A mother establishes an 'emotional ritual' with her baby by chanting, 'Rub a dub dub / Thanks for the grub / Yeah yeah yeah'.
Below An optimist is teaching her nine-month-old twins how to count by Glenn Doman's 'build a better baby' method

Never drag a child back too quickly from its land of play. How well I remember a drawing-room at Richmond, and a lot of idle women sitting around a teatable, and you heard the perambulator come into the hall. Then the door burst open, and in rushed a little fellow of four, and began, 'Oh Muver, we wented into the Park, and out came a Great Big Black Bear!', and the mother with a cuff hurled the small romanticist out of the room, saying, 'You naughty little boy! Go up to the nursery and don't tell any more lies; there are no bears in Richmond Park.' And I heard the tearful protest, 'But, Muver, I *fort* it was true.' It needed little sympathy with childhood to recognize how the child had enlivened a dull walk beside the baby in the pram with a play of imagination probably founded on last Sunday's Bible lesson about Elijah. (*Child Nurture*)

Although manuals continued to tend to the austere on the subject of toys ('let us burn all the absurd ones', offered Pepler shortly, as yet undistracted by children of her own), concessions were made to the magnificent range of toys then available. Charlotte Yonge criticized the Edgeworths for 'their want of poetry, and failure to perceive the way in which toys deal with the imaginative, the tender, and the aesthetic sides of children's minds, as well as the intelligent and mechanical ones'.

Opinion differed, however, on how the imagination was to be stimulated. Holt, predictably, first of all reminded mothers that toys must be smooth, easily washable, and unswallowable (as if any really good toy fulfilled all those criteria). He went on to say that toys helped children to develop imagination and concentration, and trained them in habits of order, neatness and regularity—and future sex roles: blocks, toy soldiers, balls, engines and cars were suitable for small boys; girls should be given dolls and housekeeping sets.

Kate Douglas Wiggin, high-priestess of the cult of the toy, took quite a different attitude.

Choose his toys wisely and then leave him alone to them. Leave him to the throng of emotional impressions they will call into being. Remember that they speak to his feelings when his mind is not yet open to reason. The toy at this period is surrounded with a halo of poetry and mystery, and lays hold of the imagination and the heart without awakening vulgar curiosity. Thrice happy age when one can hug one's white woolly lamb to one's bibbed breast, kiss its pink bead eyes in irrational ecstasy, and manipulate the squeak in the foreground without desire to explore the cause thereof. (*Children's Rights*)

Complicated mechanical toys reached a peak of complexity, especially in America. Wiggin described with fascinated horror an improvement on the recently invented electric talking doll—this was in 1892. The original version could only say Papa and Mamma, but this

superb new *altruistic* doll was fitted to the needs of the present decade. You are to press a judiciously-located button, and ask her the test question, which is, if she would like some candy; whereupon with an angelic detached movement smile (located in the left cheek), she is to answer, 'Give brother big piece; give me little piece!' If the thing gets out of order, (and I devoutly hope it will) it will doubtless return to the state of nature, and horrify bystanders by remarking, 'Give me *big* piece! Give brother *little* piece!'

Parents, then as now, were thrilled by such novelties, but in a classic piece of child's-eye-view writing, R. H. Bretherton warned that their children might not be.

It was a weird toy. The parents wound it up, and it ran across the floor towards the child. There was something almost diabolical in its noisy gesticulations, so that the child shrank from it as it hastened drunkenly in her direction. It came close to one of her feet, and she could have almost shrieked with terror, but ere it reached her, it fell over on its side in attempting the figure eight, and groaned out the last few minutes of its brief life. The mother pounced on it, and having resuscitated it with a key, set it off to the other side of the room. It suffered, however,

144

from locomotor ataxy, and failed to reach the father by many feet. It went wide to the right, and staggered against the skirting. For a moment it hammered and kicked at the board, and then fell down, buzzing like an entrapped bee. The parents laughed hysterically, but the child sat solemnly in the centre of her nursery floor, and did not even smile. Though she was glad that her parents were so happy, the ingenuity of the toy frightened her. She was too young as yet to understand how and why the thing moved and ran and shook its arms. For her there was an appalling reality in its movements, and then the angry buzzing against the skirting board at length ceased, she heaved a big sigh of relief. (*The Child Mind*)

Nationalism, rampant everywhere, entered the toy-box. Wiggin was interested in the idiosyncrasies revealed by the Universal Exhibition held at Vienna in the early 1890s. Did the absence of any dolls on the Turkish, Arabian and Persian stands reflect their fear of idol worship, she wondered. The 'sober and meek demeanour' of Chinese dolls contrasted with Japanese ones 'in gold and gaudy colours, absolutely saucy' She felt that 'the application of natural and mechanical forces in Japanese toys cannot fail to determine the taste of the next generation towards physical sciences'—time certainly proved her right.

The French toy represents the versatility of the nation touching every topic, grave or grotesque ... From Berlin come long trains of artillery, regiments of lead horse and foot on moving tramways ... The American toys ... refer the mind and habits of the child to home economy and husbandry and mechanical labour; and their very material is durable, mainly wood and iron ... So let this Republic make the toys that will raise the moral and artistic character of her children.

Kate Douglas Wiggin was of course American, the author of best-selling children's books like *Rebecca of Sunnybrook Farm*. Children's imagination was to be promoted by books as thoroughly as by toys. Enthusiasm for fairytales made light of the old objections that they were immoral—what mattered were the colourful images, deeply rooted in folk culture, which they projected. Mrs Ewing, Mrs Molesworth, and that classic stand-by of the goodygoody, Mrs Sherwood's *Fairchild Family*, were contemptuously dismissed by the new-wave writers. Morbid books should go the same way as morbid pictures, said Gardner, and Mrs Panton had never 'found a child who cares for such authors'. She prescribed *Alice in Wonderland*, *The Hunting of the Snark* and Andrew Lang's many books of fairytales.

Drummond agreed that, until the age of ten, fairytales and folklore were more appropriate to extend the imagination. He was wary, however, of the 'enormous growth of a special literature for children in recent years'. Although a boon in some ways, it made it difficult for the child to form any permanent friendships among books. 'A child who is wantonly supplied with books, all carefully written down to his level, can have little chance of gaining any natural appreciation of style, or of overcoming the initial effort required to read books which have a place among the classics.' He thought that parents ought to read demanding books aloud to their children, explaining anything too difficult for them to understand.

The fantastical quality of the drawings of Rackham, Dulac, Charles Robinson, and the many other superb artists who illustrated children's books at this time, confirms the premium put on stimulating the imagination. Nevertheless, Honnor Morten had enough sense—and showed the same sensitivity to the child's own feelings that advocacy of small furniture and comfortable clothes did—to point out that a child's taste in literature might not coincide with the ideals of its parents and the age:

Some children are very backward in a love of reading, which may mean merely that their own vivid imagination is enough for them, and that they tell themselves stories far more brilliant and congenial than any ever written or printed. Other children fall victim to the magic words, and love Hiawatha or the Psalms; whilst a third class care only for stories about little boys called Bobby and little girls called Margery.

The strange mixture of science and sentimentality which characterizes these decades is perhaps exemplified best in the widespread enthusiasm for Froebel's kindergarten schools. Such schools were not new. They had been flourishing in Germany and other European countries since Froebel founded his own in the 1830s. Charles Dickens's *Household Words* mentioned the 'infant gardens' in 1855. However, they did not become fashionable in England and America until the 1870s, when the Swann-Sonnenschein press started to publish English translations of Froebel's *Mother-songs and Plays*, and other handbooks on method.

The basic idea of the kindergarten was that children should be allowed to discover things for themselves. Froebel developed a series of 'gifts' ranging from a simple wooden ball to complicated mathematical puzzles. These were presented in a logical sequence to the child, and it was able to deduce certain basic physical laws and mathematical facts from them. The child started the course at about three, and would graduate to paper-folding, weaving, threading beads and clay modelling. Modern primary schools owe a great deal to Froebel's vision.

But besides teaching manual dexterity and physical concepts, the kindergarten had a strong moral and social purpose. Froebel was a rather woolly deist, who aimed to put across his religion of love and unity to the tiny tots by giving the make-believe play natural to their age cosmic significance. Whether they were baby swallows sheltering under their kindergartener mother's wing, or bees and butterflies buzzing around the sheltering and sustaining branches of their teacher-cum-tree, words, music and gestures were calculated to send messages to the soul via the body.

Kate Douglas Wiggin's kindergarten, in a socially deprived part of the city, was, she hoped, a powerful tool for extending tolerance and understanding. In one interesting passage it is clear that she was trying to break down the traditional divorce between girls' and boys' playthings which Holt had accepted so lightly. She managed to get a little boy to rock the cradle of the kindergarten doll during a song—'the radical nature, the full enormity of the proposition did not strike Josephus . . . my heart sang with triumph.' After this, ' "fathers" as well as "mothers" took part in all the kindergarten games, and this mighty and much needed reform had been worked through the magic of a fascinating plaything'.

Since the very early formal schooling of the eighteenth century had been dropped in favour of 'fireside education' by the enlightened nineteenth-century parent, there was considerable uncertainty about what education before the seventh year should amount to. Busy parents turned with relief to an institution which appeared to be prepared to do their job for them. It also suited many 'redundant' women well to enter this major new profession. Just as many agnostic parents today send their children along to Sunday School in the pious hope that they will be improved as well as amused, so parents shunted their offspring along to the new kindergartens. Dressed in consciously traditional Kate Greenaway frocks, they could 'mince up the lawn with elderly kindergarteners of affected sprightliness' (Morten, *Child Nurture*) and sing songs of imaginary days of yore.

Approaches to discipline mellowed towards the end of the century. 'The ideal of Nursery Gardening has in these days certainly changed—twig-bending is much less fashionable,' wrote Lady Magnus, in an article, 'About Training', for the first number of *Baby* magazine, in 1887. Her own ideal was an even older one—John Locke's 'teach them betimes to be good-natured'. But mothers, or rather, the experts who advised them, would not be satisfied with this for long. Children had evolved a little. They were now seen as little animals, puppies rather than plants. Pavlov's experiments with nervous stimuli appealed strongly to child psychologists convinced by Darwin of the oneness of all creation. Moral training, it was now thought, was inextricably linked with physical. It was generally felt that the easy-going freedom typical of the last two decades had not succeeded—perhaps the combination of new-fangled parents and old-fashioned nannies was at the root of the failure. Parents took control of the reins with enthusiasm in the 1900s, and the secret of their success was to be the formation of habits from earliest youth. This was not a new idea. 'Train up a child in the way he

should go: and when he is old, he will not depart from it'
(Proverbs 22:6) had been a favourite introductory quotation
in baby-care books from their genesis. What was new was to
base training on a structure derived from neurology and
psychology rather than the old one of physiology and religion.
It took a lot of the heat out of nurture once original sin was
replaced by inherited weakness. Parents could hardly blame
their children for faults they had passed down to them
themselves. There was similarly less fear of corruption,
which the parallel Blakeian view of the child as originally
innocent had once implied. Sinfulness was just a tendency to
wrongdoing which might or might not be inherited, and
which careful training—habit formation—could eradicate.

As Bernard Perez, one of the most popular child psychologists of the day, put it, 'the business of psychological
educators is much more concerned with the habits which
children may acquire, and with their wills, which are also
developed by habitual practice, than with their moral conscience. The latter is the blossom which will be followed by
fruit, but the former are the roots and branches.' This
practical neglect of the moral conscience, in favour of training
the will, was perhaps the greatest revolution in approaches to
child-rearing that these decades witnessed. It demanded a
totally different view of the child from the moment that it was
born. Perez's shift in emphasis lies behind the neutrality and
consideration with which we treat children today.

Perez also considered that small children were 'egoists'.
Understanding their actions and directing their wills required that this be borne in mind. Drummond also accepted
that 'phases of contrary suggestion' needed careful handling.
When a child refused to do anything suggested by its parent it
was simply discovering its own personality, learning that it
could obey or disobey. Patience and the example of older
children would soon lead the child to see that voluntary
obedience was the price of its own happiness—a remarkable
revival of the utilitarian argument. If it was really troublesome, it should be *made* to have its own way—left behind if
not dressed to go out, breakfastless if slow to eat.

Recognizing worthy and enduring habits, and feeling the
relative moral value of different courses of action were

matters of experience, and had to be the work of time, Drummond believed.

Such ideals are part of the heritage of the race, but they are not transmitted as such to the child. They must be acquired by each generation afresh. This is the function of training. To train a child to feel and recognise the higher motives of conduct is an important part of moral education. To train him to subordinate to such motives the promptings of the lower appetites and impulses is the most important aspect of training the will. (*The Child: His Nature and Nurture*)

Here again one can see clearly the effect of the known facts of heredity and genetics on moral education. Training was to become so important that the perceptions of the psychologists on subtler aspects of the child mind (egotism, phases of contrary suggestion, and many others) were overshadowed by a general enthusiasm for habit-formation. 'It is never too early to discipline the small body,' warned Pepler. 'The baby will very soon become a tyrant if the mother gives in to it.'

Darwin had said that the most important years of the child were the first three. 'In these early years, the brain is capable of receiving impressions, which, although retained unconsciously, the memory of them having totally disappeared, will be *automatically* rendered active.' Freud was to examine the abuse of this capacity of the brain with some interest—his contemporaries were more concerned with exploiting it to the full. The atmosphere surrounding the baby had to be carefully monitored for suitability. Everyone near Mrs Pepler's child had to have the right attitude. 'Beautiful thoughts are the right true ones,' she insisted. 'A sweet word or a harsh word, a good desire or an evil desire, all leave their minute impression on the unconscious child brain ... We know that a bad temper is more catching than measles, and we would absent ourselves from baby when the illhumour approaches until we may return with a clear smile' (*His Majesty*).

How did these attitudes affect some of the basic problems of child management—temper tantrums, for example? Harland had described one 'ingenious mother' who 'cured her five-year-old daughter of fits so passionate as to threaten convulsions by throwing a handful of cold water in her face whenever she began to scream. The child, whose infirmity had been pronounced incorrigible, would suspend operations with ludicrous suddenness when her mother moved towards the washstand.'

This Pavlovian handling was not universal. Perez told mothers that they must understand that anger was a legitimate animal instinct, a self-preservative mechanism, the sign of a strong character. (Already the mother could feel removed from the child, a little superior, less personally threatened.) The cause of anger had to be looked into. Passion was usually due to 'a poisoning of the sources of health and happiness', thought Morten. Consistent and calm management avoided the worst outbursts of temper, and particular care had to be taken when the child was waking from a nap, when the nerves were inclined to protest at having to resume their functions so quickly.

Lying, a deadly sin formerly, was now called fantasy in very small children, and thought to be a positively good thing, a sign of imagination. Alternatively, it could be due to fear—some mistake on the part of the parent or nurse might have led the child to be deceitful through fear of the consequence of telling the truth. The parent was told to be gentle in such cases: 'Laugh away the untruth, and steadily give an example of openmindedness and honesty.'

Punishment? The experts sighed. In an ideal world there would be no need for punishment. It should certainly not be corporal—whippings were totally out of fashion. '*Never* shake, slap or smack a child,' commanded Gardner. She believed in fitting the punishment to the crime. If a child stuck pins into other children, it should receive 'very mild correction in the same form, with a clean pointed needle'. It was important to avoid rewards and bribes. The child should be rewarded by feeling the essential virtue of its act, or if that was too far-fetched, of enjoying its parents' approval.

Bending over backwards to understand the child led to a curious tendency to tolerate naughtiness—it was almost welcomed, certainly respected and found natural. It was seen as a sign of developing consciousness of the difference between right and wrong. 'Chronic good behaviour is the most deadly of children's diseases,' declared Cunnington. Attractive traits of mind such as strength of character, or artistic sensibility, might develop from the 'naughty' obstinacy or forgetfulness of youth. The profound confusion in the child's mind that could arise when wickedness was understood rather than punished was foreseen by one journalist when he lamented that 'the age of naughtiness has gone. That of the educationalists, kindergartenists, and anticorporal punishment men has succeeded it, and the glory of the nursery is extinguished for ever. Vice itself has lost half its charms by losing all its danger' (G. W. Stevens, *Daily Mail*, 1 Nov. 1897).

Where did this leave Christian nurture? To substitute scientific explanations of the nervous system for either original sin or original innocence was to undermine the role of Christianity in baby-care. Germs rather than Providence were responsible for babies dying. The doctor rather than the priest was the man to pin your faith on. The punctuation of Mrs Gaskell's *My Diary* with prayers had no parallel in the new journals of babyhood. Although many of the tenets of the kindergarten were in origin religious, Froebel's semi-mystical approach to God was too vague to be directly applied. Instead, the kindergarten message of togetherness and co-operation was emphasized. It was a tool for social reform rather than evangelism.

Lip service was certainly still paid to Christianity. Drummond attempted to bridge the gap between nineteenth-century religion and twentieth-century science. His explanation of child behaviour was a purely scientific one—habits were caused by the actual impact of an action on the 'sensation-action-circuit' of the brain. Every time the circuit was traversed, the path was made deeper, and the action more readily repeated. But his description of the perfect method of habit formation was based on the writings of the profoundly religious Horace Bushnell, author of *Views on Christian Nurture*.

The Sabbath twilight talk, the simple prayers, the religious life that it was hoped a nurse would lead: all were nodded to, but in asides, rather than as preoccupations. Leave the child's religious feelings alone, advised Charlotte Yonge. Avoid making Sunday 'a hateful day of disagreeable cramming of collects and bible verses', wrote *Sylvia*. Don't tell a fearful child that God is near it and will look after it, Mrs Panton warned—'so he may be, but many children are more afraid of God than they are of the dark'. The later baby-care manuals simply had no heading under which religion fitted. Moral training was merely a tail on chapters on habit formation of every kind. Most of their pages were devoted to feeding, tables of weights and measures, details of clothes and doses of exercise. God was no longer among their terms of reference.

Charlotte Mason, more concerned with older children than babies, put her finger on the dilemma of many parents. 'The traditions of our elders have been tried and found wanting; it will be long before the axioms of the new schools pass into common currency, and in the meantime parents are thrown on their own resources, and must absolutely weigh principles and adopt a method of education for themselves.' Her solution was to found the Parents' National Education Union, an independent body of parents who chose to educate their children themselves, outside the state system. God remained in Mason's books. Through him she felt she could find the unifying principle, the definite aim, the philosophy of education which the 'national system of psychology' lacked. The PNEU was a particularly interesting development (it still exists) because it reflected the resentment felt by independent-minded parents at state interference in the bringing up of children. Most mothers, it has to be admitted, would fall as lambs to the slaughter under the cannonade of hygienic and disciplinary advice offered on every side— numbed to their destruction, perhaps, by the wartime propaganda of conformity to military discipline.

Bringing up babies was at a peak of interesting complexity in the 1900s. The austerity of the following decades has veiled the sensitivity and perception of many of its baby-care experts, who succeeded in preserving an awareness of the many shadings and vagaries among babies which should preclude any dogmatism on the subject. The division of opinion between the women who thought babies should fit in with their lives and the 'octopus' mothers was clearly drawn up. Harland and Hogan stood at opposite poles. But the poles were not exactly the same as those which separated the wildly scientific and theoretical parents from the down-to-earth traditionalists, nostalgic for the free-and-easy ways of their own youth. The Child Study Movement, psychology, and kindergartens were all effectively debunked by Harker in her account of a visit from a Froebel student:

While expressing her very deepest interest in 'childhood', for her, children had no separate identities: they were 'types' or 'results' of divers kinds of training. She belonged to one of those dreadful societies that 'studied' children as if they were 'ologies' and whenever she found a parent polite or meek enough to listen, gave forth her views.

'With children one should be educating all the time,' she said to mother, and we hated her forthwith; 'they should be watched and guided in their play quite as much as in their studies, that every faculty may be developed equally. There is even a material register of our educational labour made in the very substance of the child's brain.' The Giant shuddered. 'Organised games are so necessary because they afford opportunity for insight into character and self-discipline. How profoundly right, therefore, is Froebel in his games, where every action corresponds to some observed impression.'

'But don't you think,' the Giant interrupted, 'that more insight into character, and certainly an equal amount of give and take, and therefore self-discipline of the best sort, is provided by the games that children invent for themselves?'

'No,' answered Eleanor, 'no doubt some good purpose is served by the games children invent for themselves, but the games taught by Froebel's system correspond to facts, and advance the observation and knowledge of such things as should be familiar to everybody.'

'I fear you are sadly lacking in imagination,' said Fiammetta gravely. (*A Romance of the Nursery*)

Science won, of course. The shadows of the bracing years to

come grew longer. Ennis Richmond deplored the over-indulgence of little children, the way adults reduced themselves to the position of slaves waiting on their child's every whim, and the ridiculous fashion for considering the children's point of view as if 'they were not just immature beings, but of value in themselves'. For her own part, she could 'only stand an hour or two of being on all fours, rumpled and dragged at, and deafened' (*Mind of a Child*).

John Masefield took a venomous lunge at the cult of the mother in his novel, *The Street Today*, and epitomized the masculine austerity of the future:

> I would make it a criminal offence for mothers to attempt to impose their personality on their children. Certain things have been proved to be of use in this world. Hardness. Truth. Keenness and quickness of mind. Indifference to pleasure. Honesty and energy in work. Hatred of dirt in all its forms. Belief in the power of man to perfect life. These things can be taught and should be taught. I believe they can best be taught by men. You can't get them from the average mother. They aren't in her. The world has gone steadily downhill in all manly qualities since the 'mother's personality' became what is called a 'factor in education'.

Nobody rose to challenge the offensive assertions of this passage. Women were too busy fighting for their rights as real, enfranchised people, able to stand beside men in time of war, to defend their position as mothers. The billowy Renaissance of Motherhood deflated into the man-directed Mothercraft of Dr Truby King.

155

4
Growing Superior
Children
1920–46

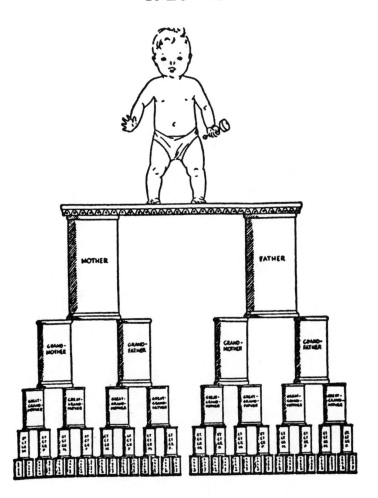

Pillars of the State

'It needed the impetus of the Great War to make the country realise the value and importance of infant life,' recorded Gwen St Aubyn in her encyclopaedic *Family Book* (1935). 'The neglected toddler in everyone's way is the material which becomes the disgruntled agitator, while the happy contented child is the pillar of the State.' The wartime habits of obedience to authority extended into the shaky years of peace that followed. Depression reinforced the need for firm leadership, and the build up to a second 'war to end all wars' left parents as resigned to following bulletins of approved infant-care practice as they were to coping with ration books and national service.

In 1918 maternity and infant welfare legislation provided for centres where parents could learn the newest methods of child-care, and where routine inspection of mothers before and after pregnancy, and of children from birth to the age of five, could take place. Health visitors were now a universal hazard. Even the comfortably off were invited to join 'Babies' Clubs for Educated Mothers of the Professional Class'. At the cost of a subscription, these improved on the infant welfare clinics by giving mothers an appointment with the doctor, rather than leaving them like a herd of disconsolate cows to be summoned at the whim of a distant oracle. Child welfare had a dramatic effect on the infant mortality rate. In England and Wales it dropped from a 1901 peak of 161 per 1,000 births to 66 per 1,000 in 1928–31.

The American equivalent of such legislation was the Sheppard-Towner Act, passed in 1921. The opposition to it, although hysterical in many details, is interesting because it could see, perhaps more clearly than we can today, the implications of such laws. 'The basic idea of this bill', declared Senator Reed of Kansas, 'is that the American people do not know how to take care of themselves; that the State must force its official nose into the private homes of the people; that a system of espionage must be established over every woman about to give birth to a child, and over the child at least until it reaches school age.' His speech rose to a spectacular climax in the defence of maternal instinct—it was a lonely voice:

> I care not how estimable the office-holding spinster may be, or how her heart may throb for the dream children she does not possess, her yearnings cannot be substituted for a mother's experience. Mother love! The golden cord that stretches from the throne of God, uniting all animate creation to divinity. Its light gleams down the path of time from barbarous ages, when savage women held their babes to almost famished breasts and died that they might live . . . The wild beasts hear its voice and answer to its call. A tigress finding her cubs slaughtered, pauses to lick her wounds, and then with raging heart seeks out their murderer. A she-wolf standing at the mouth of her den, with gleaming fangs and blood-red tongue, dies in defence of her whelps. Tiger's cub or wolf's whelp, I would rather feel the rough caresses of the hairy paws of my savage mother, I would rather have her care and protection than that of an official animal trainer. (Bremner)

More likely to appeal to his contemporaries than such eighteenth-century-style romanticism was Reed's next argument—that the idea that the state should take charge of individual citizens smacked of Bolshevism—'that noxious plan reached its highest degree in Russia'. There, every child was looked upon as a ward of the state, motherhood and birth control were established by law, and children were taken from their mother's arms and turned over to public officers.

The examples offered by Germany and Russia's theories of child-care were of acute interest to thinkers in the 1920s and 1930s. Not until they were disenchanted by Stalin and at war with Germany did sympathy with the plans of the totalitarian governments for creating 'master-races' cease. The behaviourist, B. F. Skinner, wrote a utopian novel, *Walden Two* (1948) which floated the idea of bringing children up independently, without their parents, imbued with a sense of community and acceptance of authority; it had much in common with the first revolutionary scenario of the Bolshevists. J. B. Watson wrote in the preface to the book he hoped would become the standard guide to infant management in America:

It is a serious question in my mind whether there should be individual homes for children—or even whether children should know their own parents at all. There are undoubtedly much more scientific ways of bringing-up children, which will probably mean finer and happier children. I suppose parents *want* their children to be happy, efficient, and well-adjusted to life. (*Psychological Care of the Infant and Child*)

In order to tell whether mothers were keeping their babies up to scratch, clinics used norms of infant behaviour established, outstandingly, by the Arnold Gesell, Frances Ilg, and Louise B. Ames team. Gesell Institutes in America translated their findings into facts simple enough for the manuals to summarize. A typical chart was that drawn up by Mabel Liddiard (*Mothercraft Manual*, 1948 edn). 'Milestones' mapped the correct points at which the baby smiled, kicked, sat and walked. It included little clocks indicating shifting sleeping patterns, weight increases, and when nappies could be dispensed with. These were only the most basic norms. Other advisers added remarkable anecdotes of their own children's progress, or thumbnail sketches of what well-known geniuses had achieved—Catherine Cox wrote *Early Mental Traits of 300 Geniuses* in 1926.

Milestones of development have several dangers. One is the demoralization of parents whose children score below average; another the exaggerated expectations of parents whose children score above average. (Most children do one or the other.) Although books usually included a comforting aside on 'late developers', the message in general was that the earlier development took place, the better. The third—and most insidious—threat of the apotheosis of the 'normal child' was indicated by Grace Abbott:

161

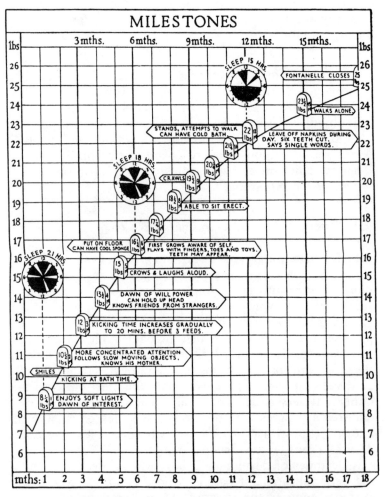

Fig. 1 Mabel Liddiard's arbitrary 'Milestones' of development added the spectre of the norm to parents' anxieties about their children

Parents are asking why their child has temper tantrums, why they must be coaxed to eat, why they are jealous, why they are afraid, why they have not learnt physical control. They want to know what is normal behaviour and what are the signs that indicate that their children need the help of a specialist in mental health. (Preface to D. Thom, *Everyday Problems of the Everyday Child*)

Milestones were mental as well as physical. Moreover, parents were even less fitted to judge the state of their children's minds than to cope unassisted with their bodies. Douglas Thom pointed out gleefully that the apparently normal child could be considerably more peculiar than the obviously problematic one. The quiet, self-reliant child, who disapproved of his peers' frivolities and played by himself, was more likely to be 'emotionally unhealthy' than the hyperactive, over-curious, inattentive pre-school child who more commonly caused his parents concern.

If only an expert could reassure parents that their child was normal, then visits to welfare clinics had to be supplemented by visits to the mental health centres, or mental hygiene clinics, as they were called in America. Thom's Habit Clinics were set up to deal with pre-school children who were developing 'undesirable' methods of solving the daily problems with which they were confronted (the view of life as a series of problems to be solved was an interesting innovation, and was to become the standard approach). Bad habits and 'unhealthy methods of reaction' could be analysed, and by 'proper training and treatment' the clinics could further 'the formation of habits that will tend toward the proper development of the child and its best interest'.

The implications of handing over the child's mind and body to professionals were made startlingly clear in an address at a White House Conference in 1930, 'We Want Our Future Men and Women to be Self-Starters'. Ray Lyman Wilbur, president of Stamford University, declared: 'We want to see our children develop into adult citizens with wholesome bodies and prepared minds, both under the control of the developed will operating in the atmosphere of what we call character.' Wholesome bodies meant that Freud need not apply; one falters at the implication of prepared minds. 'The emotional element in mankind must be harnessed by the intellectual, or individual and mass decisions will be too variable for either individual happiness or mass safety,' Wilbur continued.

Parental responsibility for the child had to move outwards, to become a community responsibility. Society was a complicated affair now that the old, normal relationships of mother and child, child and family, family and neighbourhood, had changed. Giving as an example the number of factors on which the safety of the child brought up on prepared milk depended, Wilbur pointed out: 'We have substituted a whole series of organized services between the mother and her child, and have replaced much of the home training of the child with these activities. We have brought in kindergartens, playgrounds, and schools under government auspices, where the time of the child is spent, and where proper training is essential.' Inevitably, in this situation, 'it is probably true that it is beyond the capacity of the individual parent to train her child to fit into the intricate, interwoven and interdependent social and economic system we have developed'. So expert guidance always had to be on tap to instruct the inadequate parent.

I think the general tone of the manuals between the World Wars is only explicable if this background of state arrogance and individual defeatism is understood. Certainly, as always, there were exceptions—confident parents, sympathetic manual writers. The outstandingly sympathetic popular author of the time was Mrs Frankenburg, a Somerville graduate who wrote *Common Sense in the Nursery* at a time when it seemed to her that there was absolutely nothing worth reading on the subject around. Her American contemporaries were still in thrall to Holt, and shortly to fall prey to Watson and Gesell. Mrs Frankenburg unashamedly regarded her best qualifications as her own experiences in handling four children, and the good things that still endure in her books are certainly due to these rather than the philosophies to which she inevitably paid lip-service. Where else could you discover that pretending to blow out a candle with its nose teaches a child how to use a handkerchief? *Common Sense* ran through several editions between 1922 and 1954, remaining ruggedly individualist, and opposed to government interference. 'The Gentleman in Whitehall does not always know best ... It is the parent's business to train children in healthy and active interests; to influence their taste so that they prefer occupations of a high standard, and grow up to like that which is good.' But Mrs Frankenburg's balance and good sense were far from being the hallmarks of these sadly distorted decades.

The two powerful personalities who dominated infant-care theory in the 1920s, Frederick Truby King and John B. Watson, both came to the study of children from the study of animals, and their debts to it are all too obvious. Between them, Truby King and Watson projected a relentless physical and psychological programme of infant development which largely ignored individual differences between babies. Both had a gift for publicity unrivalled in baby-care since Rousseau. Both were dedicated to the rights of their own theories and impatient of the wrongs of other people's. They complemented each other: King approached via the stomach, Watson via the brain. They further resembled each other in suffering discredit in their own lifetimes, and dying disappointed men. But their influence, discredited or not, still lives on underground, like ground elder. It remains in the basic assumptions of grandmothers, it probably lingers uneasily in the earliest impressions of many of today's mothers.

Behaviourism Triumphant

Superficially, there is little evidence in popular baby-care manuals before the 1940s that much notice was taken of the implications of psychoanalytical thought for infant care. The behaviourists' approach suited the domestic and social mood much better, and most of this part of the book will be taken up with an examination of their thinking. But Freud's theories did make themselves felt—they were in the academic and intellectual, if not the nursery, air. Watson, the arch-behaviourist, was very interested in Freud, although he disagreed with him on many issues. And a careful study of the manuals shows that writers began to recommend measures designed to forestall Freudian-style traumas, although they refused to recognize Freud openly.

Sudden caveats appeared concerning early toilet training, and masturbation was treated a little more sensitively, although the 'Essay on Infant Sexuality' was explicitly dismissed as disgusting (Marie C. Stopes referred to 'the aberrant mind of Freud') or not mentioned at all. Its influence could be further deduced from the quite novel concern that children should be told the facts of life from the moment they spotted the difference between males and females, presumably to prevent castration anxieties. How superficial a grasp popular thinkers had of Freud will become clear a little later on. In general their approach was based on the idea that all such problems could be avoided by removing love and affection, and all that they implied, from children's lives altogether—'we want our children to be self-starters'.

Freudian concepts other than sexual ones were integrated into the 'mental hygiene' now recommended for babies. Freud's trinity of personality is well known. The id is concerned with the immediate discharge of energy and tension. The ego regulates the interaction of the person with his environment, and so governs the id. The superego is the repository of the social norms acquired by the child from its parents and environment, the judiciary to which the ego refers for moral guidance. When things go wrong with the mind, the balance of these elements has been upset, so it would be logical to attempt to prevent things going wrong by ensuring that an individual is well-adjusted and self-controlled enough to keep his personality in balance. An extraordinarily pervasive theme of these decades was the emphasis on self-control and self-reliance. Ideally, a child learnt to stand on his own feet without any help from his parents, and was well-integrated—although on no account emotionally involved—with a peer group. 'Self-control governed by conscience is our object,' wrote Mrs Frankenburg, summarizing succinctly, albeit unwittingly, how id, ego and super-ego ought to be interacting.

Freud divided the instincts that provided energy for the id into two groups—life-giving ones and death-seeking ones.

The first produced the energy known as libido, the second the urges that tended to aggression, suicide, masochism and sadism. Again, there was no direct reference to Freud, but in almost every manual written after the 1920s a paragraph or two was inserted on 'destructive instincts' and how to cope with them. Destructiveness was attributed to many things—a wish for power, a curiosity about how things were made, or to 'deep-seated mental conflicts'—and it is certainly not an exclusively Freudian concept. Nevertheless, its general currency in the context of child-care was remarkable, and new.

Perhaps the best known of Freud's psychological constructs concerned the family, and the internal jealousies known as the Oedipus complex. Sexual impulses in a son towards his mother led to jealousy of the father, a suppressed wish to kill him, and a fear that his father would punish him by castration. Little girls had their parallel problems described as the Electra complex. Moreover, competition between siblings for their parents' affection led to jealousy and feuding. One would expect that if these ideas were current the manuals would show fresh interest in the position of the child in the family, and, sure enough, writers treated the problems of jealousy and relations between parents and children with new seriousness.

Len Chaloner considered the possibility of sibling rivalry in *Modern Babies and Nurseries*, advising parents to prepare children for the shock of a new brother and sister by 'keeping them independent from the start'. It was then less of a blow to have to share their kingdom. *The Motherhood Book* described jealousy as 'chiefly derived from sex love' but gave many other causes—egoism, moral indignation, class distinction or envy. In a passage well aware of Freud, it pointed out that 'in a family where a little boy feels that he possesses his mother's love, he may well be wildly jealous of his father or his brother'. The answer was for the mother not to 'keep the child psychologically too close to her'. In a large family, the book went on, 'jealousy is not so likely to be found; there is a larger herd, less possession of the parents by one child, a healthier atmosphere'. (I think this is a very interesting point, easier for people living at a time when two-child families were not the norm to appreciate.) Watson hotly denied Freud's assump-

tion of jealousy between siblings, and made careful observations of his own son's reactions to the birth of a new baby
brother to prove his point. Like Mrs Frankenburg, he
believed that jealousy was only a consequence of tactless
management, and in no way innate.

Susan Isaacs, who will be more fully considered as an
educationalist, was one of the few writers who put Freud's
ideas to positive use. She stood out against the general
tendency to isolate and effectively neglect the child, especially
in the early months. She also sketched all the possible
tendencies in the family—hate, love and acute jealousy—and
explained how the child coped by using playtime fantasies to
work out his feelings for his parents, since they lay too deep
for words. 'They come to him in wordless longings for
caresses, in desires to remove and destroy, in fears of rejection
and retaliation' (*The Nursery Years*).

Freud was by no means the only psychoanalyst whose
influence can be detected in the manuals. Alfred Adler broke
away from Freud's ideas in *The Neurotic Constitution*, in
which he assigned all adult neurosis—and all normal adult
activity, for that matter—to the feeling of inevitable inferiority as the godlike baby was forced to come to grips with
the reality of his position. He had to grow up surrounded by
people far bigger and cleverer than himself, who didn't
hesitate to command, interrupt, criticize and punish him—
rather like living in heaven and perpetually having to justify
your position to God and his angels. Adler's conclusion was
that enormous care should be taken not to discriminate
between one child and another, and that independence
should be encouraged and over-protection avoided. The
thwarted will to power was a refreshingly different basis for
human action. Craving for dominance was much more
acceptable than throbbing with sexual desire. It was correspondingly more openly accepted as a spring of childish
conduct.

Ethel Brereton gave a version of Adler in *The Happy
Nursery*, a conservative but fair-minded book, written in
1927. 'The modern child is as much burdened with a sense of
sin as the Victorian child, but now we call it an inferiority
complex.' She thoughtfully explained in a footnote that a

complex was 'the whole tangle of thoughts and feelings connected with some unpleasant event, either past or forgotten by the child, or present and still a cause of unhappiness'. Of all the complexes, inferiority complexes were 'the most common and easily dealt with'. The boastful, self-assertive child commonly set down as conceited, was often the child who had not got a 'sufficiently good conceit' of itself. It was absolutely harmful to stint it of praise, or to snub it. The nursery's 'Ugly Duckling', once at the root of all trouble, had only to be praised and life would be 'as smooth as a millpond in the best of all possible—nurseries'.

Brereton's optimism was not shared by Douglas Thom, founder of the Habit Clinics, and author of an extremely unnerving manual, *Everyday Problems of the Everyday Child*. The 'so-called "inferiority complex" is a much abused term ... carelessly used by laymen'. It was far from easy to dismiss it with a little morale-boosting, and it was still suffered at all times by children. 'Parents constantly impress upon a child his immaturity, size and inexperience as a means of keeping him in his place. Servants and other adults all adopt a superior attitude to the child or ignore it.' The only way for parents to create 'an individual who was adequately equipped, physically and mentally, to compete in the world at large with his fellows, who need not be continually asking for favours, nor be haunted by the fear of failure' was to 'push the child away psychologically, so that he can stand on his own feet'. Psychoanalysts were asking that a special world should be constructed around the child, that the impact of society on him should be featherbedded, which required that the adults caring for the child played parts. Rather than pursuing their own ends in life, they were to manoeuvre, pretend, and manipulate so that the child would become 'well-adjusted'. This scenario, although congenial to the enthusiasts of the Child Study Movement, was not generally acted on until Dr Spock became required baby-care reading in the late 1940s.

Instead, behaviourism was adopted. It tailored the baby to fit into the world he was born into, manipulating him along predictable patterns of stimulus and response. Animal psychology lay behind many of its theories—hence the old chestnut distinguishing behaviourist psychologists from magicians as men who pull habits out of rats. A touching willingness among the public to regard themselves as at one with the animal kingdom made the reactions of baby monkeys to surrogate mothers, or the evasive actions of pregnant rats, matters of consuming human interest. Brisk training rather than wallowing sensitivity was the watchword of the new age—the quickest way to get the atmosphere of the average manual between the wars is to leaf through a modern book on training household pets.

The parallel was frequently made explicit. 'We demand toilet-training in our cats and dogs,' wrote Watson, 'yet feel no shame when our two- or three-year-old children go wet around the house.' Mrs Frankenburg emphasized the need for parental consistency by saying: 'Ask any keeper whether he would expect to train a retriever if he occasionally let it eat partridges for a treat.' Pleading for less sloppy handling, Watson pointed out that, 'if you expected a dog to grow up and be useful for anything except as a lap-dog, you wouldn't dare treat it as you do a child'. All in all, the tone of the time was that of a team of handlers trying to convert an unruly pack of puppies into dignified, self-reliant, unemotional cats.

John B. Watson's background goes some way towards explaining the genesis of *Psychological Care of the Infant and Child* (1928), the manual designed to be the New Testament to Holt's best-selling 'infant bible of the nation'. Watson was born in South Carolina, to a devout Baptist mother and a drunken father, who left home to live with two Indian women when his son was thirteen. Watson became something of a hoodlum, and was arrested twice, but by the time he was sixteen had turned over a new leaf. He was accepted to read natural sciences and philosophy at the local university, and from there went to study at Chicago under the famous educational philosopher, John Dewey. Dewey was interested in functionalism—the extension of the study of mind to the study of its practical effect in guiding behaviour. Watson went on to jettison the mind entirely, and to define psychology as the study of behaviour pure and simple. There was no need for introspection, or theories about mysterious mind-stuff. All psychologists needed to consider were the tangible manifestations of mind—the responses to stimuli, the conditioning by repetition, the problem-solving function of thought.

Watson started work as an animal psychologist, following in the footsteps of Pavlov by studying the mechanics of how rats learn mazes. He continued to study homing birds and monkeys, and decided that there was no reason why human beings should not be studied similarly. His campaign for 'behaviourism' opened with a lecture in 1913, and a plea that human beings should be studied both in laboratories and 'in the field'. Many of his contemporaries were hesitant, but bright young things were enthusiastic, and Watson, Professor of Psychology at Johns Hopkins University from 1908 onwards, continued to push his 'science of real life'.

In 1915 he began a long-term study of how children develop. Using the waifs and strays in the city hospitals, as well as a few babies in home settings, he observed what they could do from birth, tested their reactions, made films of their movements, and sat in a specially built observation room in a Washington hospital watching how mothers and babies interacted from birth on. He found he could make a newborn child terrified of a rabbit by banging loudly near its head whenever the rabbit was put near it. To his triumph, he found that he could reverse this conditioned response by reintroducing the rabbit gradually and at a distance, under more soothing circumstances. The seeds of 'behaviour therapy'— still a respectable mental 'cure'—were thus sown.

A hiccup in Watson's career came when, because of a scandal arising from his affair with a student, and consequent divorce from his wife, he was sacked from Johns Hopkins. Left out in the academic cold, Watson put his psychological expertise to lucrative use in the J. Walter Thompson advertising agency. He quickly rose to a vice-presidency on the strength of his selling techniques. He perceived that people bought products not for what they were, but for how they made them feel. So he might announce: 'Caring mothers use J ... and J ... talcum powder for their babies.' Not to do so implied neglect. Mothers toed the line and bought the talcum.

Watson's slick salesmanship, with its psychological needling, was evident in *Psychological Care of the Infant and Child*, which was the culmination of his studies in infant behaviour. It was dedicated in challenging copywriter's fashion 'To the first mother who brings up a happy child'. Nobody, Watson claimed, knew enough to raise a child. 'The world would be considerably better off if we were to stop having children for twenty years (except for experimental purposes) and were then to start again with enough facts to do the job with some degree of skill and accuracy.' Unlike most of his contemporaries, who were deploring the plummeting birth-rate, Watson thought fewer, better brought-up babies preferable to saddling the world with so many crippled personalities. His dream baby was an interesting new model, perfectly suited to an age when there were not enough nursemaids to go round, and when more and more women were trying to find fulfilling jobs away from the domestic treadmill. This child would hardly notice if his parents were around or not:

> The happy child? A child who never cries unless actually stuck with a pin, illustratively speaking; who loses himself in work and play; who quickly learns to overcome the small difficulties in his environment without running to mother, father, nurse, or some other adult; who builds up a wealth of habits that tides him over dark and rainy days; who puts on such habits of politeness and neatness and cleanness that adults are willing to be around him, at least part of the day; a child who is willing to be around adults without fighting incessantly for notice; who eats what is set before him and 'asks no questions for conscience's sake'; who sleeps and rests when put to bed for sleep and rest; who puts away two-year-old habits when the third year has to be faced; who passes into adolescence so well-equipped that adolescence is just a stretch of fertile years, and who finally enters manhood so bulwarked with stable work and emotional habits that no adversity can quite overwhelm him.

Watson had reacted right away from the child-centred, turn-of-the-century world, with its conspicuous consumption in the nursery, and happy neglect of the adult *now* in nostalgia for the childhood *past*. How was such a convenient infant to be constructed? Watson's research into tiny babies had told him that only three responses were innate: fear of sudden noises, fear of falling, and rage at being prevented from moving head or limbs. Love was not innate—like all other emotions it was a conditioned response, evoked in the baby by stroking and fondling.

A social renaissance was necessary, Watson announced, once mothers faced up to the implications of his research. 'Am I not almost wholly responsible for the way my child grows up?' a mother should ask herself. 'Isn't it just possible that almost nothing is given by heredity and that practically the whole course of development of the child is due to the way I raise it?' If, on shouldering this burden, she staggered under the load, she was bound to ask: 'Where shall I find the light to guide my footsteps?' The answer was in the behaviourists' mapping out of 'infant culture'. The mother who mastered the essentials of behaviourism became 'a professional, not a sentimentalist masquerading under the name of Mother'. She could follow the Watson blueprint and produce the ideal child, 'a problem-solving child', for 'we believe that a problem-solving technique (which can be trained) plus a boundless absorption in activity (which can also be trained) are behavioural factors which have worked well in the past, and will continue to work well in the future'. The ideal child would also be 'a socially competent being, as free as possible from sensitivities to other people', and, almost from birth, 'relatively free of the family situation'.

Several of these objectives will strike the modern reader as odd—the obsession that the child be concerned with how rather than why, the desire to play down the emotional side of life and to discourage sensitivity to other people, the de-termined programming towards scientific objectivity. When one finds out how Watson intended to rear such children, the whole scheme becomes even odder. But *Psychological Care* sold more than 100,000 copies, *Parents' Magazine* declared that a copy ought to stand 'on every intelligent mother's shelf', and the *Atlantic Monthly* described it as 'a godsend to parents'. Watson's ideal lurks on, moreover, perniciously but tenaciously, even today.

Watson felt that the key to success in bringing up a better baby was not to over-stimulate the love-response by too

173

much stroking. 'There are rocks ahead for the over-kissed child.' Mothers and nurses had discovered by trial and error the efficacy of caressing the child's lips, ears, back of neck and sex organs in order to quiet it. They had now given up the tyranny of rocking babies to sleep—not because Holt had told them not to, but because they needed the time thus saved for 'household duties, gossip, bridge, and shopping' (Watson was no feminist at the best of times). Unfortunately, petting and caressing took very little time, and so mothers continued 'to indulge in it'. The end result of this treatment was 'invalidism in adulthood'. Marriages often broke down because the wife failed to cosset her husband in the way his mother had done.

The sign of a child overconditioned in love was that it dropped what it was doing when its mother came in and insisted on being cuddled. If the mother attempted to go away, it was heartbroken—'many mothers often sneak from home the back way to avoid a tearful, wailing, parting'. Watson felt that a child could not have too little affection:

> Just to the extent that you devote your time to petting and coddling the child—and I have seen almost all a child's waking hours spent on it—just to that extent do you rob that child of the time which he should be devoting to the manipulation of his universe, acquiring a technique with fingers, hands and arms. He must have time to pull his universe apart and put it together again.

Watson further revealed to mothers that their motives in fondling their babies were not unmixed—besides aiming to make the child happy, a sex-seeking response was involved. Starved of love and devotion herself (was Watson recalling his own father's desertion?), the mother aimed to instil 'nest habits' which were really pernicious evils. They resulted in the 'mother's boy syndrome, likely to wreck all chance of marital and vocational happiness, and end in insanity or even suicide'. Watson's answer to the complications identified by Freud was to bypass them altogether—to eliminate the love factor.

The sensible way to bring up children is to treat them as young adults. Dress them, bathe them with care and circumspection. Let your behaviour always be objective and kindly firm. Never hug and kiss them. Never let them sit in your lap. If you must, kiss them once on the forehead when they say goodnight. Shake hands with them in the morning. Give them a pat on the head if they have made an extremely good job of a difficult task. Try it out. In a week's time you will find how easy it is to be perfectly objective with your child and at the same time kindly. You will be ashamed of the mawkish, sentimental way you have been handling it.

Since love conditioning tended to grow up 'even if scrupulously guarded against' while feeding and bathing, it was the mother's duty to keep away from her child for a large part of each day. Watson envisaged a community of homes that could circulate nurses among themselves, thus even preventing the babies becoming attached to one nurse. 'I sometimes wish', he added, only half-jokingly, 'that it was responsible to rotate the mothers too, occasionally!' If a mother didn't have a nurse, and so couldn't give her child the benefit of her complete absence, positive psychological use could be made of the current fashion for an outdoor life.

Put the child out in the backyard a large part of the time. Build a fence round the yard, so that it can come to no harm. Do this from the time that it is born. When the child can crawl, give it a sandpile, and be sure to dig some holes in the yard, so it has to crawl in and out of them. Let it learn to overcome difficulties almost from the moment of birth ... away from your watchful eye. If your heart is too tender, and you must watch the child, make yourself a peephole, so that you can see without being seen, or use a periscope.

Watson confounded tender-hearted critics by bringing up two little boys by behaviourist methods, with the help of his second wife, Rosalie. Neither child could ever remember any demonstration of affection from their father, although their mother could not resist occasionally kissing and hugging 'her two little pieces of protoplasm'. She admitted that she was 'not the perfect behaviourist wife'. The diaries that the Watsons kept to describe the details of Billy and Jimmy's upbringing are full of small failures over nailbiting, 'a very bad symptom in a behaviourist's family', as well as major successes over sibling rivalry (none in evidence because of careful conditioning, and the sacking of a nurse who attempted to control Billy by crude preference for the baby). Newspapers photographed Billy and Jimmy as model children, 'happy children, free from fear and temper tantrums'. The little boys never obliged hopeful psychoanalysts by going ape—according to Cohen's biography of Watson, they apparently remained 'well-built, healthy, bright, and good advertisements for behaviourism'.

The Well-adjusted Baby

The habit training of the 1920s and 1930s differed in its psychological subtlety and its ruthlessness from earlier, more tentative efforts. As more and more springs of human behaviour were laid bare, the stimulus–response conditioning technique could be applied with increasing effect. It pervaded all aspects of infant care, physical and mental. If Watson was the guardian of the mind, Frederick Truby King was the director of the body. Truby King advocated a forceful approach to feeding, and improved methods of coping with crying, sleeping and other nursery problems, but before examining his theories we need to know more about the man whose 'Mothercraft' typified the age.

Having studied medicine at Edinburgh, Truby King became superintendent of the Seacliff Lunatic Asylum at Dunedin, New Zealand. It was an important teaching hospital for students of psychology, and he lectured on the subject to students of Otago University. Truby King became very interested in the scientific rearing of animals and plants—Seacliff was well-equipped with farms and gardens as occupational therapy for patients. Struck by the high death rate among bucket-fed calves at Seacliff from 'scouring', a disease akin to gastro-enteritis in babies, he invented a 'scientific system' of feeding, which ended all deaths from this cause. He was convinced, he announced, in a paper on the subject delivered to the New Zealand Farmers' Union, that a human life a day could be saved if human mothers fed their babies in a similarly scientific and rational way.

In 1907 the Truby King movement started in earnest in New Zealand, where the Plunket Society was formed to put his theories into practice. Within five years, the infant death rate there had dropped by 1,000 a year—not one, but three lives a day were being saved. At his week-end cottage at Karitane, Truby King installed thirteen of the worst cases of unwanted babies that he could find, and proved that with skilled attention to their care and feeding, they could be brought up to be 'normal, useful citizens'. The Mothercraft movement developed so rapidly in New Zealand that 80 per cent of mothers were soon being visited by Plunket Society nurses, and infant mortality was halved. The nurses encouraged breast-feeding ardently, guarded against overfeeding by rigid attention to clockbound mealtimes, taught a modified form of the complicated percentage feeding involving cow's milk and two Truby King patent additives, kariol and karilac, and instructed mothers in the orderly mothercraft which would produce a Truby King baby. His adopted daughter Mary described this paragon, recognizably the small sibling of the Watson child, in her handbook for mothers, *Mothercraft*:

A real Truby King baby is completely breast-fed till the ninth month, and then slowly weaned onto humanised milk, with a gradual introduction to solid foods ... Truby King babies are fed four-hourly from birth, with few exceptions, and they do not have any night feeds. A Truby King baby has as much fresh air and sunshine as possible, and the right amount of sleep. His education begins from the very first week, good habits being established which remain all his life.

A real Truby King baby is not too fat—every bit of his flesh is firm and clear, his eyes are bright and one only has to hold him for a moment to appreciate his muscular tone. He is not treated as a plaything, made to laugh and crow and 'show off' to every visitor to please his parents' vanity; yet he is the happiest thing alive, gambolling with his natural playthings, his own hands and toes; he is interested in the new and wonderful things which come within the range of his vision and touch, and is as full of abounding vitality as the puppy playing in the yard.

He sleeps and kicks out of doors as much as the weather allows, and sleeps at night in the airiest bedroom, or on an open veranda or porch, being carefully protected by a screen to keep him from draughts. After he has gone through his regular morning performance of bathing and being 'held out', and has had breakfast, he sleeps all morning. If he wakes a little before his 2 p.m. meal, all that one knows about it is a suddenly glimpsed chubby little leg or foot waved energetically from his cot for inspection, or a vigorous jerking of his pram.

Altogether, he is a joy from morning to night, to himself and all the household—a perfectly happy and beautiful Truby King baby. The mother of such a baby is not over-worked or worried, simply because she knows that by following the laws of nature, combined with common sense, baby will not do otherwise than thrive.

Like Watson's vision of independence, Truby King's as-tonishingly idealized and simplified projection of babyhood still lives as an ideal in many parents' minds, particularly for the grandmothers to whom the definition of a 'good' baby is one which prefers solitary confinement to human intercourse. With such a picture of perfection in the back of one's mind, the reality of children or grandchildren can only be a disappointment. Notice, too, that the Truby King objective is the independent 'puppy playing in the yard', soon to be Watson's 'useful dog' or Mrs Frankenburg's trained retrie-ver.

Truby King first came to spread the word in Britain in 1913, not particularly successfully. He visited eminent Ger-man paediatricians, and then went on to New York, where his crusading style was better received. 'Breast-fed is Best-fed' became a popular slogan. A more successful visit to wartime Britain in 1917 led to the establishment of a Mothercraft School in Highgate. For the next thirty years, the 'Truby King Baby' became the ambition of Britain's mothers. Undeniably, the movement successfully revived breast-feeding at a time when the scientific finesse of artificial feeding was a source of wonder—no mean achievement. It also established hygienic standards of mothercraft which probably saved more little bodies than it lost little souls—who can say but that it was the best approach for the time?

Since Truby King claimed to 'follow the laws of nature and common sense' (like many others before him), it was odd that a man so interested in nature should have become so obsessed by hard and fast rules on quantities and times of eating. He certainly failed to allow for difficult feeding cases adequately, and later critics felt that his emphasis on the evils of overfeeding led to a generation or two of hungry, thwarted babies, convinced of their essential unimportance during the long, hungry night-time sessions of 'crying it out'. On his third visit to England, near the end of his life, Sir Frederick Truby King was rambling, senile, and more dogmatic than ever, and the cause suffered some discredit in informed circles. It remained bedrock practice for many mothers, however, even after the *cognoscenti* had turned to Spock and freedom.

How did the Truby King approach to feeding work in detail? He believed that 95 per cent of all mothers could breast-feed—spirits, not flesh, were weak—but they had to learn how. 'Just as the whole subject of Mothercraft does not come by instinct to a woman the moment she becomes a mother, but has to be studied, so does breast-feeding require thoughtful study and competent management if it is to be a success' (*Feeding and Care of Baby*). He gave a plethora of reasons for breast-feeding. Breasts were made by God to function, just as the lungs and the stomach were—it was implicit blasphemy not to make use of them. Cow's milk was for calves, not for humans. Death rates were higher among artificially fed babies, and breast-milk conferred immunity to diseases. The exercise at the breast was good for baby—'not only are the jaws, tongue and mouth stimulated, *but the whole*

Fig. 2   This poster, in support of Truby King's 'Breast is Best' campaign, showed the 'Long Haul' that cow's milk travelled to get to the baby.

body. You may have noticed the same sort of happy, natural energy in the tail-wagging of lambs and other young mammals while suckling.' Moreover, the mother would regain her health sooner, and avoid the 'more or less consistent pelvic congestion' likely to dog the mother who didn't breast-feed. Breast-milk was germfree and cheap—and finally the motive that would be put first fifty years later: 'You and your baby are drawn nearer together on account of your dependence on each other.' Watson would have disapproved—but Watson never mentioned breast-feeding.

Baby had to be fed by the clock—not by guesswork—not when he thought he needed food, but when his mother knew he needed food because her book told her so. Clear intervals of three and a half hours were to be established between the end of one nursing period and the beginning of the next one (it is quite an achievement to feed and change, let alone mother a baby in half an hour). These intervals, plus eight hours unbroken sleep at night, gave the mother plenty of time for sleep, rest, housework, outings, exercise and recreation. Moreover, the baby's stomach then got a chance to rest. 'A clean-swept stomach effectively scotches microbes which might otherwise cause fermentation, indigestion, diarrhoea, etc. Babies fed only five times a day will sleep more soundly, run less risk of overfeeding, and have fewer dirty nappies—in itself an important item.'

Truby King found it extraordinarily difficult to get mothers to admit all this. They became absurdly distressed by the sound of a mere hour or so's crying. The great virtue of a trained nurse was that she could override all maternal objections (instincts?) and make sure that the baby was kept on a routine until it despaired of anything better. Of course, if men could produce milk, there would be none of this shilly-shallying:

Were the secretion of milk and the feeding of the baby the functions of men and not women, no man—inside or outside the medical profession—would nurse his baby more often than five times in the twentyfour hours, if he knew that the baby would do as well or better with only five feedings. Why should it be otherwise with women? Mothers have too much to do in any case: why should they throw away time and leisure by frequent useless nursings? (*Feeding and Care of Baby*)

A note of rebellion made itself heard in the 1930s. The attribution of all babyhood ills to overfeeding was questioned once Arnold Gesell's work on how varied infant intake could be was publicized. Marie C. Stopes queried the opinion of Eric Pritchard that a gain of more than seven ounces a week was excessive.

If you are lucky enough to be the mother of a prince among men . . . you are to check this growth, interfere with the rhythmic response between your flow of breast milk and his happy and lusty development, and instead you are to rear a child, wantonly and wickedly *cut down to pattern* so that he, who might have been a big-boned, strong, glowing, six-foot Apollo with perfect teeth, is to be starved into matching the ill-begotten and ill-nourished 'average' with whom 'trained' nurses and 'doctors' in their disease-infested lives are accustomed to meet. (*Your Baby's First Year*)

Marie Stopes was one of the great originals, and her manual was full of confident rebellion against the 'sterilizing and petrifying pundits'.

Weaning was generally agreed to be best effected at around eight or nine months, taken slowly and naturally over three to four weeks. Few babies could compete with Marie Stopes's child, who, soon after eight months of breast-feeding, 'pushed away the breast and looked around intelligently, making a gurgling sound very like "Bokkle"'. Goat's milk was Stopes's preference, since she could show, by tables breaking down different milks into their proportions of proteins, fats, sugars and minerals, that it approximated most closely to human milk. Once one forayed into the field of prepared cow's milk, the same alarming range of choice and opinion that had confused mothers influenced by Holt and Pritchard was maintained. Advice ranged from the simple 'body weight × 2½ ounces' recipe to pages of complicated formulae on sliding scales.

The new excitement of the age was the discovery of 'vitamines', as they were originally called. These 'very subtle and complicated organic molecules' were 'growth-controllers', and essential in a healthy diet. Orange juice began to be given to babies as a matter of course, since boiling or pasteurizing milk was known to destroy vitamin C content. Marie Stopes pointed out that all the vitamins were naturally found in raw pure foods, and she recalled that 'years before the word "vitamin" was coined or the idea had penetrated the research blockheads' her father had taught her all the up-to-date essentials then known. She criticized the 'glib talk' of vitamins, and the way government 'supinely allowed "big business" to make profit out of destroying our pure milk, and selling expensive vitamin-containing foods to make up for it'. Country cooks and housewives' good sense should be better trusted—'but the lesson is not learnt by the "experts", who continue to sneer at the accumulated wisdom of countless generations of mothers, and to ask the nation blindly to trust their "expert" knowledge'. Most writers were less sanguine, although admitting that vitamins existed naturally in fresh food. Victoria Bennett and Susan Isaacs's *Health and Education in the Nursery* described vitamins from A to P, detailed the many diseases deficiency could cause, and listed foods or substitutes calculated to ensure adequate vitamin content.

The effect, as Thom pointed out, of the 'attempts to standardize the weight and height of children, much the fashion nowadays', and the crucial importance given to vitamins, was to make mothers 'over-solicitous, especially in relation to eating properly'. Children were quick to sense an 'indefinable something . . . doubt, weakness, or misgiving on the mother's part, and to attempt to assert themselves to a position of power'. Although the sensitivity to personal taste was still paid lip-service to—*The Motherhood Book* admitted that 'preferences and dislike must be taken seriously'—the knowledge that certain foods were vital for growth meant that the same book added that 'the last things that we should be prepared to give up are those very greenstuffs for which the average child often *has* a distaste . . . they are of enormous importance to the blood and the system generally, and the mother must try to surmount the dislike'. Good habits at mealtimes would lead to less faddiness. The toddler should be encouraged to lay his own place, to sit quietly for a reasonable length of time, and 'should not be served out of turn, treated as a favoured guest, or have his plate watched with anxiety'. Mealtimes, it concluded, 'are a wonderful opportunity for character training'.

The second great opportunity for achieving 'health, happiness and efficiency' was the sound establishment of good sleeping habits. Kugelmass, author of the ambitiously titled *Growing Superior Children*, produced an interesting theory about sleep. He saw it as a refuge, a return to the foetal situation when the 'baffling stimuli that overcame a baby in daytime' became too much. This gave him room to explain night-time waking because of the baby's ability to cope comfortably with the relatively few stimuli that assailed him in the dark. His conclusion was not, however, cosy night-time chats with mum and dad.

> Baby must be educated to sleep and taught not to cry. Born into a social organization where nocturnal sleep is universal, he must be trained to pass through an unbroken night's sleep. Continuity of sleep comes gradually. It is a development from periods of sleep interspersed with periods of activity, which is the sleeping habit which characterizes the newborn as it does most animals.

Knowledge of the facts of infant behaviour was not allowed to influence Kugelmass's advice. The socially undesirable phenomenon of napping had to be programmed away. If life began with a crash training course, the baby could be expected to sleep for nineteen hours a day. Firmness at night was vital. The baby was to be settled into his cot alone, avoiding any excitement after the six o'clock feed. Solitariness would 'give him control of his environment. He thus learns to sleep in the dark. Fear of the dark is really fear of anything. It is a fear which becomes worse if the feared object cannot be seen.' Early practice, it was hoped, would lead to general fearlessness later on. 'If he awakens, he should be left to cry it out, provided he really is well.'

184

Marie Stopes distinguished between shallow sleep and the truly restful sleep which allowed cells to clear away any minute particles of waste matter, and the nerves and brain to rest.

When a baby wakes out of a long deep sleep he should be ready to laugh. But if he has been disturbed and waked before these processes have been completed, he will be fretful and inclined to whimper. This is a reflex from the vague feeling of misery caused by the incomplete natural cleansing of all the dirt accumulation of his system.

She held that it was a crime to wake a sleeping baby for any reason whatever—except of course for 'routine feeding by the clock'. Anne Medley agreed that sleep deprivation was sinful—her baby slept all the time except when being 'fed and attended to' until three months, and still slept for eighteen hours a day at six months. 'Every additional waking hour is at the expense of the delicate nervous system' (*Your First Baby*).

Babies were clearly expected to sleep for very long periods. Stopes's sleep table was:

Age	Hours a day
first month	22
second month	$21\frac{1}{2}$
second to third months	21
third to fifth months	20
fifth to seventh months	19
seventh to twelfth months	18

To get matters into perspective, and to show how abnormal a pattern this was, here is a table of the average number of hours a day that young babies were observed to spend in sleep:

Age	Average sleeping time
3 weeks	14·9 hours
3 months	14·9 hours
6 months	13·7 hours
12 months	13·6 hours
2 years	13.0 hours
5 years	11.5 hours

(from J. and E. Newsom, *Infant Care*, 1963)

These facts are somewhat surprising, if you believe what you can still read in baby-care books. The Newsoms also pointed out that the averages concealed enormous individual variation. Some babies did indeed sleep for eighteen hours out of the twenty-four—about the same number slept for only nine. But the baby books were united in finding fault with parent, environment, or baby, if the allotted hours were not slept away.

Watson's recipe for an 'orderly bedtime' for the toddler began after supper, 'a light meal of your physician's choosing'. Quiet play, with pencil and paper, was best. 'I find that children, when allowed to romp, are loath to leave exciting play. They whine, and bad discipline results.' This was a good time for father's half-hour. 'It keeps the children used to male society. They have a chance to ply him with questions'—presumably those that their ignorant mother failed to answer during the day.

Although taking a toy to bed was 'a sloppy habit, easy to get into, yet very hard to break', there was one argument in favour of it—'the child is less tempted to explore his own body'. Once the child had been placed on the toilet, and given a drink of water, he could be tucked up ('hands outside the covers if not a thumbsucker, inside if he is') with a chamber under his bed and a flashlight under the pillow. 'Then a pat on the head; a quiet goodnight; lights out and door closed. If he howls, let him howl.'

If a child did develop a fear of the dark, Watson suggested lighting the room gently, and then by degrees making it darker until the child accepted complete dark again. Chaloner and Frankenburg were quick to offer a nightlight to a frightened child, although Frankenburg pointed out that the waving shadows it produced could be even more scary than the dark. Better was a little light at the head of the bed which the child could switch on himself if he woke up and was frightened. Unlike most of the manuals, Mrs Frankenburg went to some trouble to explain the possible fears of loss of mother, or throwback fears 'akin to those of our ancestors in the primeval forests' which might be aroused by chance remarks or frightening stories—or even by prayers full of alarming ideas. The filtering through of psychological sensitivity to childhood fears was clear in the more temperate approach of some later manuals to sleep problems, although the majority continued to ignore them.

The increased space devoted to the subject of sleep, whether at night, or in daytime naps, reflected the reduction of nursing staff in many homes. When a mother had to deal with her baby's sleep problems personally, it became more important that children slept long and well. The right precautions made getting up at night as little trouble as possible. Very small babies were even allowed back into the mother's bedroom, in small cots placed across the foot of the bed, so that she would not even have to get her feet cold. A supply of dill-water, a thermos of boiled water, and clean napkins to hand meant that baby could be coped with rapidly if it did wake up. Night feeds were still out of the question, but prompt attention might settle the infant with the minimum of disturbance.

After six months, however, baby was out on his ear, because of the 'grave psychological difficulties' which could arise. 'An enormous number of bad nights and subsequent night terrors for children would be avoided if this ruling were strictly adhered to,' Chaloner believed. 'We are told by psychologists that strong emotions felt by other people may affect his emotional life unfavourably,' wrote Frankenburg. 'Avoid taking the child into your own bed for company if father is away,' she advised; jealousy could easily arise. Oedipus lurked under the bed instead of bears. American manuals added that children should not sleep with their siblings, especially if they were of different sexes.

Insisting that small children and babies sleep alone, often out of earshot of their parents, is one twentieth-century Western custom which the Victorians would have found as odd as many contemporary non-Western cultures do. Lonely cot-deaths match thoughtless overlaying for horror. The reassuring snores of the nanny were replaced by silence and emptiness, peopled only by nightmares that psychologists would enjoy analysing.

Inevitably, getting baby into good habits and used to its routine involved a great deal of crying. The first cry in reaction to the stimulus of the obstetrician's spank conditioned baby to cry for what it wanted—in that case, the end of the pain of spanking. But crying then had to be conditioned out of it by *not* giving it what it wanted when it cried. Crying was no longer to be 'nature's voice'.

Crying, it had to be admitted, could mean that there was something wrong. The baby had to be checked over for wet nappy, uncomfortable pin, cold feet, or the like. A different position sometimes helped. Could it be wind? These were the years when wind was discovered in a big way. Babies left lying flat on their backs in approved Watson/King style probably did get more wind than babies nestled semi-upright in a nurse's arms had done. Winding became a fine art. The back had to be patted at exactly the right point—just below the stomach. Dill-water (a gentle soporific recently revealed to have addictive properties—some mothers consume several bottles a day) could be given as a digestive. Failing this, a succession of warm flannels could be wrung out and applied to baby's tummy. As a last resort, a warm enema would help to pass wind from the bowel. It is comforting to reflect that babies must have come by a good deal of unofficial mothering while they were being winded—the classic head-on-shoulder enfolded position, and gentle patting, was very similar to the outlawed soothing and walking of restless smalls.

Once it was established that there was nothing wrong with baby, it had to be turned over and tucked up tightly. A sure sign of 'naughtiness' was the baby who stopped crying the moment it saw or was picked up by its mother. This young imp could be safely left to 'cry it out', although mother had to visit every ten minutes to mop up tears, turn the wet pillow, and tell it that it was bad. Mrs Frankenburg assured mothers: 'The tiniest baby soon learns that you mean what you say.'

Crying was once again regarded as 'absolutely essential exercise' by most writers at this time. Thus Frankenburg in *Common Sense in the Nursery*:

The lungs do not expand to their full extent unless they are exercised every day. The infant cannot sing or shout, and therefore he has to cry. If Nature is regularly thwarted by some well-meaning person who picks up the baby and distracts his attention after the first squeak, there is a risk of the lungs remaining almost unexpanded. A case is recorded of a baby who died of pneumonia at eight months, and because he had never been allowed to cry at all.

Baby's 'naughty time' was thus to be interpreted as 'a wise dispensation of Nature'. Marie Stopes agreed that 'a couple of minutes good bawl between the time he is waked for his feed and the time he has the nipple of his mother's breast in his mouth' was necessary exercise, but she warned against overdoing things.

> I heard with amazement from a friend of mine that her trained nurse regularly woke the child and tormented him for a whole half-hour a day so as to make him cry, as 'crying was good for him'. The psychological evil wrought by this ignorant piece of wanton cruelty is to be added to the indigestion and nervousness it generated.

Full-scale temper tantrums in toddlers ought not to arise if routine had been planned 'so that they fall comfortably into it from babyhood'. If they did occur, the parent had to ensure that the child got no 'fun' from losing self-control. It could be shut up in a room, or ignored. Afterwards, the mother could explain what a sight it had looked, or how it had disgraced itself—but 'he should not be made to feel that he has done something irreparable' (*The Motherhood Book*). The traditional cold-water shock treatment was still recommended for extreme cases.

It was a little hard on British babies that fresh-air fetishism in its ultimate form should be introduced by a New Zealander, whose home country offered a considerably more attractive climate for open-air life. The substitute of the garden for the second nursery was domestically most convenient, particularly in the smaller homes built after the First World War for Mr and Mrs Average and their two children. Although fresh air had been highly prized from William Buchan's *Domestic Medicine* onwards, and the pram had enabled longer walks to be taken in worse weather, nothing like the total approach of the 1920s had occurred before. Mrs Frankenburg described the previous half-hearted attitude scornfully:

The old-fashioned nurse likes, especially in cold weather, to dress her children by a roaring fire in the nursery, and to give them their breakfast there. They probably play by the fire until 10 or 11, and then go out until 12.30, when they 'come in to get ready' for 1 o'clock dinner. Then, when they have had their dinner, and played by the fire while nurse sips her tea, they are got ready to go out, and at 2.30 or 3.00 they start. At four they come back for good. Of course, the days on which they have 'streaming colds', they do not go out at all.

This would not do at all. She contrasted it with Truby King's description of Karitane, where:

The babies live out of doors all day, and a broad stream of pure cold air flows through the sleeping rooms all night long; tiny delicate babies, after a week or more of gradual habitation, sleep well, grow and flourish in rooms where the temperature may sometimes fall almost to freezing point.

Marie Stopes and Mrs Frankenburg were among the most enthusiastic advocates of the outdoor baby. A few days after birth in summer, or a few weeks if the weather was very cold, baby took to outdoor life. Everything could happen out of doors, particularly if the garden was equipped with a revolving shelter. Feeds, changes of nappy, sleeps and playtime could be open-air events. 'Infants should hardly be indoors at all between 8 in the morning and 5 at night in the winter, and from 7 a.m. to 10 p.m. in the summer,' thought Mrs Frankenburg, although she allowed that breast-feeds were indoor affairs. Marie Stopes's own baby 'was particularly fortunate, perhaps, for, starting his outdoor life in April, he never had even meals indoors for the first two years. There were various sunny corners and verandas which offered shelter whatever the weather, even in January.' A decent-spirited nurse would not object to 'this gypsy life', but the mother had to be prepared to do the same when nurse had her day off. 'Any nurse who feeds a baby out-of-doors in cold weather would feel resentment against a mother who, when it was her turn to feed him, did so selfishly by the fire.'

It is to be doubted whether mothers were united in going to these lengths for the good of their babies, despite the promised advantages of rosy cheeks and a complete absence of colds. A note of conservative rebellion was sounded by Ethel Brereton:

> My personal opinion is that 'fresh air', the catchword of the day, has become an absolute fetish with the careful modern mother. In the summer, I agree, it is worse than a crime—it is a blunder!—to be indoors for one unnecessary minute from getting-up time to going-to-bedtime, but in winter—no thank you! The healthy child only needs about three hours a day in the open air, as long as the day and night nursery windows are always open.
>
> The Eskimos are, I believe, a particularly healthy people (though plain), but I have never heard that the children of their wealthier classes are sent out with lamps fastened on their sledges during the darker hours of what one might call their indoor season. (*The Happy Nursery*)

The pram itself 'evolved almost as wonderfully as the motorcar', thought Len Chaloner. After the old-fashioned perched-up models from which an active child was all too easily capsized (shades of the Lost Boys), an 'opposite mistake developed'—bodies were so deep and low that baby hardly gained any fresh air at all. The happy medium reached by 1930 was a deep pram, with a device to raise or lower the bed inside, depending on the weather. It sported small-ish wheels, cushion-tyred and mud-guarded, and rolled smoothly along on ballbearings. Few manuals mentioned the extraordinary sport invented by the doomed firm of Dunkley's—a motorized pram with a small platform on which the nursemaid stood. In its final, totally enclosed form, it would have been anathema to the breezy.

Even hoods were criticized by Truby King: 'One of the most pitiable and exasperating sights of modern babyhood is the spectacle of an unfortunate infant sweltering and sweating under an American leather pram hood' (*Feeding and Care of Baby*). He recommended the ventilating canopy designed by Lady Plunket, or the even airier wicker hood. Ideally, baby was put in the garden in a light wickerwork crib, so that as much sun and air as possible could reach it. A little later on, it could be left to play on a rug under the trees, then, once mobile, in a play-pen to keep it out of mischief while unsuperintended. Failing a garden, balcony life was suggested. A special cage could be attached to an ordinary window by a friendly builder, so that cot, pram or play pen could be pushed out to greet the elements, even in a high-rise flat.

The experts felt increasingly that it was better for baby to be left alone, motionless, than wheeled about town in its pram. Walks jarred its spine, worried its brain with too many uncensored impressions, and might well threaten its health if the nurse chose to wander among shops and slums. If it had to be wheeled to the park, then once there it should be taken out and put on a rug to kick. Garden-life alone, while the routine household tasks were undertaken, meant that the baby was even further removed from human contact than when taken for sociable excursions in its pram. Convenient domestically, this also suited the psychologists' emphasis on the virtues of self-reliance and independence.

Enthusiasm for the outdoor life was partly caused by the discovery of the beneficial vitamin D-giving properties of sunbathing. Artificial ultra-violet lights were suggested for nurseries in cold climates, or a special 'Vita-glass', said to allow ultra-violet light from the sun to pass into the nursery, could be fitted in windows. When the weather allowed, the baby was to be stripped off outside, or by an open window, and given sunbaths. Dosages of sun were measured out as carefully as medicines, gradually increased by a minute or so a day until the baby could roll in sunshine with impunity. Heads had to be shaded, but the new simple way of dress allowed toddlers to wear virtually nothing while they enjoyed their outdoor life.

Exercise became a less casual affair than before. Kugelmass, a Watsonian, believed in directed development. After the first month, the baby was to be put on a padded table for exercise. Laps encouraged curvature of the spine. The mother had to initiate exercises, encouraging the baby to imitate her. Single-knee bending, double-knee bending, knee-circling and abdominal kneading (excellent for constipation) strengthened abdominal muscles. Arm-bending and stretching, chest expansion and swimming stroke strengthened trunk muscles. Toe-gripping and foot-pulling strengthened feet. Mrs Hewer described a deep-breathing exercise which was initiated by splashing baby's chest with icy water. 'He will gasp and take some deep breaths, but if the game is kept up he will soon appreciate the fun.' In *Care of Young Babies* John Gibbens recommended 'the many little books of babies' exercises on the market' to fathers, assuring them that 'this is a job that you will enjoy', and illustrating his point with a photograph of himself proudly spread-eagling a baby on the palm of his hand.

If trends in exercises reflected the current interest in railroading babies along the right habitual lines, fashions in clothes were designed to encourage independence. They were meant to be easy for the toddler to take on and off itself. Dresses buttoned up the front, knitted jerseys could be pulled over the head. Only sleeping suits continued to be inaccessibly closed at the back. Two, rather than four layers, were now all that was felt to be necessary indoors. Crawling suits, or rompers, became popular, and knitted jackets and leggings began to replace baby's long skirts. Even the cut of sleeves and yokes was reconsidered. Raglan sleeves and magyar yokes, or simple shoulder tucking, fitted more easily around little arms than the old-fashioned square yokes with their set-in sleeves. Nighties lost their belts, and pilches their drawstrings. Coatees were knitted, or in soft flannel; excessive lace frilling was replaced by simple bindings or rickrack braids. Knitted binders and infant stays, the last hints of swaddling, disappeared altogether.

The wool versus cotton question remained unresolved. Truby Kingites favoured Aertex next to the skin; more traditional chilly souls preferred the reliable insurance of a thin woollen vest. Great emphasis was laid on not allowing the baby to become overheated—again an Antipodean rather than British hazard. Two or three manuals even wistfully reminded mothers of the endurance shown by Spartan babies, although they hastened to deny the modern usefulness of the practice. Perhaps their admiration for the hardy little survivors could be used to point the difference in attitude between then and now—today we would be far more concerned about preserving the doomed weaklings.

Sanitary Sexuality

Watson sighed. The problem of elimination 'obtrudes itself almost from birth. No-one likes to see wet children, and yet that seems to be their chronic state. Somehow nothing seems to make us take this problem seriously.' A Watson baby was held out regularly after breakfast. After he was eight months old, he was strapped into a special toilet seat and left alone in the bathroom, with the door closed and with no toys to distract him. Within twenty minutes Watson felt that a bowel movement should occur. If the door was left open, or the mother or nurse stayed, it would lead to 'dawdling, loud conversation, and generally unsocial and delinquent behaviour'.

Most of the manuals continued to recommend the familiar rigmarole of 'holding out' at regular times of day. But it was noticeable that such advice was qualified by warnings that no displeasure should be expressed at any failure to perform. In a magnificently defensive piece of writing by Marie Stopes, the secret of the new hesitancy was revealed:

> When a baby has responded to the touch of the chamber and passed either water or a motion, he should be rewarded by an expression of pleasure by nurse or mother. 'Good baby. That's right. Good baby,' will be understood long before an inexperienced mother thinks it possible. Though the words mean nothing, yet the baby tends to respond. Well-born babies *like* to be good and to be thought good, contrary to the ideas of some nasty-minded and vocative adults.
>
> On the other hand, it is a cruel mistake to show signs of displeasure or annoyance about wet or soiled nappies. There should not be a hint of displeasure connected with them, and they must just be taken as a matter of course.

194

A sense of guilt or dirtiness associated by adult disapproval with these natural events tends to create an artificial nervousness which may be latent and show itself later on in dirty-mindedness or bed-wetting at school age. Then it is extremely hard to put matters right.

Babies, loved properly and well-bred, do not like to be soiled, and do not take that perverted pleasure in ordure which the aberrant mind of Freud has smeared on the social consciousness. (*Your Baby's First Year*)

Stopes was reacting against the 'permissive' approach of such popular infant psychology books as Mrs Gasquoine Hartley's *Mother and Son*, which spelt out the implications of Freud far too frankly for the ears of motherhood in general:

In the baby's life, everything that concerns himself is exceedingly important and delightful. The action of the bowels and the bladder, connected as they are with vivid sensations of pleasure and also of pain, are certainly enjoyable acts to the child. 'Acts of creation', Dr Constance Long has said they seem to the child . . .

Of course the child has to be taught to control and sublimate these primitive cravings and must be taught not to void promiscuously. But to achieve this result without permanent harm to the character requires the greatest patience and much more knowledge than the usual mother or nurse possess. Repression is often disastrous. Conflicts are started which are determinative over the whole after-life—anal eroticism, and its immense significance in character formation, is one of the subjects we are beginning to understand.

Clearly there was a body of opinion among parents as early as the 1920s which hesitated to take much decisive action over 'elimination', and it was this sector that Watson shook his head over, willing them to make their young conform at least as well as their pets did. But they were in the minority, to judge by the general run of the manuals. Kugelmass, for example, believed that 'with maternal diligence' proper bowel control could be achieved by the end of the third month, and that intensive bladder training need only take a week or two, if the potty was offered every twenty minutes.

By the 1940s new editions of popular manuals (such as Liddiard's *Mothercraft*) inserted paragraphs warning of the possible 'psychological difficulties'. Len Chaloner told parents not to 'make a fetish' of this type of cleanliness.'If some little responsibility is desirable, then the little one may be shown how to remove the traces of the accident from the floor with a cloth. Adult weaknesses in this subject have often been traced to early fears.' Clean-cut John Gibbens, whose *Care of Young Babies* was perhaps the most popular new British manual of the early 1940s, suggested postponing the whole business until weaning or beyond.

> Regularity can be overstressed. Some authorities emphasise the importance of developing regular habits at an early age. Mothers as a rule are most loyal in carrying out these instructions, and if things do not turn out according to plan, they feel it must mean that the child is abnormal or that they themselves are to blame. They will keep the child on the chamber for half to three-quarters of an hour, they will appeal to him, they will scold him, and if all this is in vain, both mother and child will become exasperated and despairing.

This passage is not only interesting on the subject of training. It also reveals the confusion caused by the plethora of manuals offering anxious mothers contradictory advice. If things did not go according to the Truby King plan, the Watson plan, or the Gesell developmental schedule, mothers felt that they had done something wrong, or that their child was abnormal. It was hardly surprising that they should consider themselves at fault. Most of the manuals—excepting the sympathetic Stopes/Frankenburg school—made it clear that they were likely to be so.

The idea of abnormality on the slenderest of evidence could only arise once accepted norms of child development in every direction had been laid down. Although most books were careful to say that their developmental charts and baby milestones were only rough guides, it was impossible to resist checking one's child up against them, and difficult not to be disappointed if it appeared to be backward in some respect.

Another aspect of 'norms of development' was the competition they fostered between mothers. Coupled with the immense range of received opinion on how babies ought to be brought up, they contributed to making mothers feel more inadequate than ever. Mothers were isolated both from their mother's generation (who failed to understand their obsession with mental hygiene) and their own (who seemed to have much better developed/disciplined/socially competent children than they did). Anne Medley reflected the extent of competition in toilet training when she wrote:

> Do not be disappointed if other young mothers with children of the same age tell you that their baby is 'asking' to be held out, and dry all day long. Strangely enough, there is no point on which there is more boasting and exaggeration than this. If you happen to come into the home of such a lucky mother at an unlucky hour, you will, as likely as not, find a dozen nappies on the line to dry. (*Your First Baby*)

Babies' bodies were to be as immaculate as their bottoms. The opportunity behaviourists offered of conditioning infants to lifelong habits of cleanliness was not lost. Consciousness of germs led to more thorough and intrusive cleansing techniques. The bath became, according to Watson, 'a serious, but not gloomy, occasion'. Its aim was to get the child clean, not to entertain him.

> Many mothers fill the tub full of celluloid toys and prolong the bath to a degree that is useless and foolish. The child cries when he gets out, and gets so interested in his water games that he never heeds your instructions in the art of washing and caring for himself. Give the baby a washcloth at a year, and make sure that he is completely proficient at dealing with himself by about $3\frac{1}{2}$.

Kugelmass aimed to 'ingrain' habits of cleanliness into the baby. Eyes, ears, nose, mouth and teeth were all ritually attended to. Mineral oil was used to cleanse 'local debris' from the private parts, 'but with the minimum of handling'. It became fashionable among the uncircumcised to teach the child to retract the foreskin of the penis for cleansing, but doubts existed—would it lead to 'bad habits'? Circumcision became increasingly popular as a means of avoiding the issue altogether.

Baby was now equipped with a toothbrush, although some writers felt that it was not strictly necessary until he was one year old. He had to be taught how to use it himself—altogether, the bath experience was a splendid opportunity to instil the all-important virtues of independence and self-help. Kugelmass suggested that a miniature wash-bowl, cloth-rack, soap-dish holder, and tooth-brush holder be clamped on to the side of the tub. Let the baby be introduced to 'the cleanliness crusade' early, directed Mrs Hewer in *Our Baby*. He could scrub his knees himself to learn the difference between clean and dirty.

When a child can wash his hands, he should gradually extend his activities, and be taught to go over each part systematically—it can be called bath drill—to save dawdling and half measure. Tooth drill, nose drill, nail drill, and hair drill will help make cleanliness amusing, and these good habits, once learnt, will last through life.

Fascination with the potential of conditioned responses led to the return of the cold douches beloved of the 1840s' physiologists, and the revival of the cold bath, to be reached by the same gradual degrees that increased the infant's exposure to sunshine. I think there was more than hygiene to cold, or at best tepid, bathing. Bathing in warm water is a relaxing and undoubtedly sensual experience. It was unlikely that it would be tolerated at a time when bracing character and eliminating the risks of love-conditioning were the experts' primary concern.

Typical of the 1920s pundits' interference was the announcement of a new peril: mouth-breathing. 'Everyone is so delighted to see baby breathing at all for the first day or two, that no one minds how he does it. But soon he must be taught the right way to breathe,' announced Marie Stopes, striking at the last bastion of infant autonomy. How odd it was that at a time when the declared aim was to increase children's independence and self-reliance on every front, practices like these required interfering with babies more than ever before.

Nose-breathing was to be preferred, according to Hewer in 1921, because it was 'a simple preventive of colds'. It warmed and moistened the air before it reached the lungs. Consider, pointed out Marie Stopes, 'the personal and social disadvantages of a mouth-breather. He is always one who snores. Who can endure a snorer as a room-mate? Only one with the same bad habit.' Moreover, breathing through the mouth sent 'streams of germs into direct impact on the delicate skin of the tonsils'. In a later, 1945 edition of *Our Baby*, Mrs Hewer warned that this 'vicious habit' led to ear disease, glandular swellings, and retarded physical and mental development. Mrs Frankenburg asserted that the 'atmospheric pressure' that mouth-breathing produced forced up the arch of the mouth, stretching and shortening the upper lip and crowding together teeth in the lower jaw.

So a new duty was added to motherhood—to creep in while the baby slept and gently push up his jaw to prevent mouth-breathing. If it insisted on dropping open, a roll of blankets could be tucked under the chin. The nostrils were to be kept scrupulously clear by twists of cotton wool dipped in oil or boracic before the child was put down to sleep.

Germ consciousness ruled nursery life. The fresh-air fetish was a means of protecting children from stuffy, germ-laden atmospheres. A potential dilemma arose over the matter of visiting other children. Psychologists encouraged socialization with peers, but they could easily prove to be sources of infection. A compromise was reached by suggesting that parties should only take place in the summer, out of doors, and that whenever possible playmates should be entertained in the garden. Household pets were discouraged once microscopes had revealed the horrific germs they could carry. The small delirious patient was further confused by the white masks worn by all its visitors—sound hospital practice was now imposed on the domestic sickroom. Such hygiene-consciousness was in part a necessary counter to the childhood illnesses that medicine still had no satisfactory cure for, but it is hard not to believe that there was something a little paranoid about this ritual cleansing.

Although the 'aberrant mind of Freud' was rarely referred to in the manuals, it is clear on closer inspection that the serpent of sex had raised its ugly head in conscious as well as unconscious minds. It was hoped that the whole problem could be coped with if children were informed, in the nicest possible way and as early as possible, of the facts of life, so that any potential traumas could be nipped in the bud. One or two manuals actually rejoiced in the opening-up of the psyche in this way. Mrs Gasquoine Hartley's *Mother and Son* opened with a quotation from Schopenhauer: 'Most of us carry in our hearts the Jocasta who begs Oedipus for God's sake not to enquire further, and we give way to her, and that is the reason why Philosophy stands where it does.'

Hartley believed that the 'very early age' at which sex manifested itself had to be accepted—ostrich-like denials were no longer possible. She pleaded for 'less fear, and more openness of understanding to receive and use the new knowledge'. Any mother who tended her child herself had to admit the true nature of the baby's gurgles of delight at realizing its bodily needs.

Many of his activities, such, for instance, as his unconcealed interest in nakedness and in his own and his mother's body, or as his very evident concern and delight in his excretory function, or again as the attraction he finds in suckling and other sensatory pleasures, and also the direction of many of his curiosities, are all of a character which should be recognised as being frankly sexual.

The mother also knows, Hartley continued, that 'it is her task to train the babe almost from the hour of his birth away from this egocentric interest in his own body'. Parents refused to recognize the presence of overt or repressed sex desires in their babies because they did not want to know about them.

We have set up an entirely false conception of the child to which we cling most desperately. We want to see the child as an angel. We cannot easily surrender the picture of childhood as a period of delightful ignorance and happy innocence. Yet the reverse is true. The child is nearer to the savage than to the angel.

The status of the child clearly took a backward step in the 1920s. Having struggled up from child of nature to innocent babe, trailing clouds of glory, and finally to prodigious, much-studied genius in the 'century of the child' epoch, the baby now slid back to unpredictable, coarsely motivated savage.

The boy's rebellion against the authority of his father, his nestling in the protective mother's arms, the little girl's preference for the father; the rivalries and jealousies and quarrels for mastery among brothers and sisters—in these nursery scenes you have expressed in their frankest form, and unchecked by the inhibiting influences of social necessities, the fundamental emotions of love, of hate, of fear, and of jealousy.

Hartley had read and digested Freud on sex, Adler on the inferiority complex, Jung on returning to the womb, and Kempf on the importance of early family relationships. Her conclusions certainly improved on former recipes for civilizing the infant savage, and would be typical of post-Second World War manuals rather than of her contemporaries: she was trying to slow down the blind rush into habit-training, to study the child's development pattern, and to adapt social demands to its potentialities. She felt that an immense strain was placed on the child's emotions during the growing-up process.

Most child-care experts did not face up so frankly to the new psychological theories. Pinning their faith on behaviourism, and the idea that all emotions, including that of love, were related to conditioning, they felt that ever-more efficient habit-training was the answer to the dirty-minded perverts who wanted to take their well-scrubbed angels away from them. In fact, the obsession with scrubbing takes on an interesting new dimension when seen as a physical erasing of possible emotional sin. The desperate effort to make children self-reliant and independent of parents and siblings was an attempt to escape from the problem of unattractive emotional involvement, the Freudian bogey of incest.

Nevertheless, the facts of life were to be made clear to 'the denizens of the nursery' to avoid the traumas that might otherwise arise even in the best-regulated of homes. Did frank, plain speaking now replace the traditional deathly hush, doctor's bag, stork and gooseberry bush (chosen, apparently, because it was too prickly for even the most curious to investigate)? Contemporary taboo on every aspect of the subject was to prove difficult to overcome. The extent of the problem was made evident in a case history provided by Douglas Thom:

> The mother of a youngster of six had just presented him with a little sister. His parents had confided in him, and he had taken part in the preparations and anticipated the event with joy. He had a clear but simple idea of where babies came from, and had no feelings of shame on the subject. One day on the porch with his mother and several of her friends, he said quite clearly, pointing to one of them, 'Mother, don't you think that lady is going to have a baby too, pretty soon?' The group freely showed their consternation and disapproval. To the little boy, this was a humiliating occasion, producing self-consciousness and diffidence with outsiders for some time afterwards.

Ethel Brereton set out bravely in *The Happy Nursery*, a book addressed to nurses rather than parents, to bring 'certain subjects' out of 'the twilight of decent obscurity'. She thought the 'taboos ought to be lifted', although 'in all these subjects there are things offensive to our senses'. Her approach could not have been more delicate. It made no mention of the father's role, but simply explained that the baby lived and grew in the mother, then came out 'like all baby things; like flowers from the ground or eggs from under the hen'. To avoid 'giggling behind doors and goggling at bathtime, let the children see you [the nurse] naked'. Altogether, the chapter which was coyly headed 'Physiology' mystified more than it informed.

How true, it seemed, was Watson's dictum that 'only one mother in four understands sex well enough to talk about it'. His own handling of the situation was as thorough-going as his approach to most things. Two or three times a week, the mother had to have a half-hour 'talking-it out' period, where she kept up to date with the way her child's life was organized. By inviting questions on the weather, clocks, and so on, she could become established as a reliable source of information, and in time the subject of sex would arise. Or she could let the children see her in the bath. Any conversational leads offered were to be followed up. If she was 'blocked' by some inhibition of the child, the subject could be reintroduced at some other appropriate moment. Any information given had to be relentlessly reinforced by repetition as often as possible.

Literally hundreds of books explaining the facts of life in more attractive but impenetrably veiled terms were published at this time to meet the professional insistence on information which parents were still loath to impart. Lavish illustrations of flower fairies, cuckoos, acorns, tadpoles and lace-hung cradles left the child more baffled than ever. Hartley dismissed them wearily as generally inadequate, and defeatedly wondered if it was not after all a subject that children would be better hearing about from their peers rather than from parents or teachers. 'What the parent says is interesting, but it is not intimate, not convincing, often it hardly counts.' The real responsibility of the parent, she concluded, after the hard facts had been made clear, was to make sure that the reality of sex was felt in the family through an emotionally successful relationship between the parents. Parents had to set to, with dutiful pleasure, for the sake of the children.

'Sexual instruction', wrote Thom, 'should be given before unnatural gratifications of this instinct have led to the formation of habits that undermine the moral stamina of the child by developing a degrading sense of inferiority.' Parents were still seriously worried about masturbation, and there was some optimism that teaching children the facts of life early would make them less likely to experiment upon themselves.

Preventive measures were advised. Sliding down banisters, persistent tree-climbing, and dangling astride Daddy's legs were discouraged. Back-buttoned pyjamas were recommended. Once the child was old enough to understand, the Watsonian parent could say: 'That is not for handling, it is to be used now for just one purpose.' If the child answered: 'Why can't I play with it? It's mine,' then he was to be met by the statement: 'Father and Mother do not do this.'

Persistent masturbation could be a sign that a child was getting too much petting and cuddling from its parents, according to Susan Isaacs. It was vital that no feelings of guilt should be incurred, so discouragement had to be indirect. This theory was carried to its extreme by H. C. Cameron in *The Nervous Child*. Having recommended a change of scene—sea-bathing, or collecting sea-shells (according to Freud, a sublimated form of sexual curiosity), as the best means of effecting a cure, he explained that if this failed then 'apparatus of restraint' might become necessary. An iron bar between the thighs, confinement of the hands, or 'at the worst, confinement in poroplastic armour, as for spinal caries, or severe poliomyelitis, may be necessary'. The child was on no account to guess why it had been treated in this way. 'I believe that it is worth taking endless trouble to convince a child that his legs are so crooked or his back is so one-sided that the apparatus must be worn. The desire only passes when the child has forgotten about it.' Similarly, if a little girl's vulva was painted with silver nitrate solution to desensitize it, 'it is well to make a pretence of similarly painting the mouth and ears as well (this time with water) to divert attention from being exclusively directed to the vulva'.

Short shrift continued at first to be given to thumbsuckers, blanket-chewers, and nailbiters. A doctor addressing a tuberculosis conference was quoted by Mrs Frankenburg in 1922 as saying: 'I believe the comforter has killed its tens of thousands of children.' Thumbsucking was a similar evil, as was toesucking (?). If not cured by firm restraint, thumbsucking would lead to nailbiting. All combined to produce the greatest evil of all, mouth-breathing. The 'haze of sentiment' that surrounded thumbsucking should be dispelled, *The Motherhood Book* felt. Making sure that baby was not hungry, and supplying a toy as substitute, should be discouragement enough. Watson was equally convinced that rapid action would condition bad habits away.

However, by the 1930s, a new leniency was making itself felt. Later editions of *Common Sense* saw thumbsucking as an expression of a need rather than delinquency. 'In every case, in order to effect a cure the underlying cause must be investigated.' The actual habits were to be left severely alone, never commented on, and attempts should be made instead to alleviate the boredom or anxiety that might have caused them. Susan Isaacs saw the thumb as a nipple substitute, and told parents to ensure that the infant was satisfying his hunger fully, and not being deprived of 'his legitimate time of pleasurable love play with the nipple before he is put down to sleep'. Freedom was in the air.

Nursery Schooling

In the years between the wars small children were expected to do a great deal for themselves. Maria Montessori rather than Froebel characterized the approach of the growing nursery school movement. Even children who did not go to nursery school were educated to cope with their own lives at a very early age. Time alone in the pram became time alone in large garden pens, in which the toddler mucked about with mud, sand and water. Two- and three-year-old children were expected to wash, dress and feed themselves competently. Today, washing, dressing and feeding children of that age is not only taken for granted as a task, it is seen as a positive reinforcement of mothering. Attempts at independence are remarked upon as endearing, not taken seriously or forcefully pursued. Then, the nursery motto was 'plenty of love [unless you were a dedicated Watsonian] and plenty of wholesome neglect'.

The central idea of the Montessori system was self-education. Carefully constructed as her apparatus was to appeal to the interests of children between the ages of three and six, it was useless educationally, she felt, unless the child chose to work with it. Unlike adult-invented toys, its purpose was to teach the child how to cope more competently with life. Buttoning-frames and lacing cards showed it how to dress itself. In its totality, the Montessori method went further than any of the manuals which nodded their heads at it were prepared to follow. It was a way of life, the practical exploration of living on equal terms with other children while the teacher remained in the background—a sharp contrast to the circle of skipping worshippers around the wheedling kindergartener. Little sentiment was involved. Montessori was not reacting as Froebel had against a world in which children were generally ignored or misused, but against a world in which children's abilities were being severely underrated. She first came into the public eye because the supposedly backward children in her care were getting better results in public examinations than their normal contemporaries. Given the opportunity to establish 'Case dei Bambini' in tenements where juvenile vandalism was rampant, she showed that the young savages could be turned into intelligent, useful individuals by providing the right background and mental stimulus for them. She taught them to read and write at a much earlier age than educationalists had considered advisable, and extended the senses of sight, touch, and hearing by exercises for the 'tactile, thermic, baric, and stereognostic senses'. As an American popularizer of her work, Dorothy Canfield Fisher, put it, she gave children all the freedom and opportunity for discovery that they longed to exert in the 'forbidden but fascinating province of the kitchen'.

Montessori's intellectual achievements were regarded with even greater interest once Alfred Binet's work on intelligence testing was made public. Binet was concerned, like Montessori, with improving the education of subnormal children, and he realized the need for a method of classifying inferior states of intelligence. He developed the concept of 'mental age'. This challenging idea set a vast amount of psychological activity and publication into motion. The mentality of the entire United States army was tested and measured. Lewis

Terman improved and extended Binet's scale, and added to the mental-age formula that of the intelligence quotient, or IQ, which became an accepted measurement among educational psychologists. It expresses the ratio between mental age and chronological age, measuring between 0 and 200. Binet never liked the IQ, because he doubted whether intellectual qualities were measurable to that extent. The popular mind, however, simply grasped the fact that ability to perform the appropriate mental tricks made their children clever, and thinking parents set about getting their children taught them.

More important for the parents of pre-school children than the IQ was an understanding of the stages of development which Arnold Gesell recorded in children from birth to five or six years. His detailed, month-by-month comparisons of the skills and social responses of babies were at the root of the dramatic changes in attitudes to small babies which occurred in the 1940s. Forward-looking writers like Susan Isaacs referred to Gesell in the 1930s, but at this point the exciting lesson to be learnt from his observations was how independent and capable the small child was. At last the old confusion between precocity and nervousness was sorted out—clever children no longer had to be tucked up in bed:

> Many intelligent children are nervous, but that is not a result of their intelligence. Many ordinary or dull children are 'highly-strung' too; and a great many exceptionally intelligent children are stable and healthy. The 'nervousness' is a function of other conditions, either within the child's emotional life or outside in the environment—or both. (Susan Isaacs, *The Nursery Years*)

Although parents were told that heredity governed the intelligence of their children more than environment, the improvement exhibited in children bright or dull who were allowed to develop in an exciting, stimulating environment like a Montessori school, made early education—by trained teachers—newly desirable. Sending small children to nursery school became the fashion.

Nursery schools were sharply divided between those set up

by official bodies to redeem the children of the poor, and the private schools run for the benefit of middle-class mothers. In discussing the desirability of nursery schools, no mention seems to have been made of the question of maternal deprivation until what was delicately described as 'the New Psychology' made itself familiar to forward-looking thinkers in the 1930s. Until then, the work of Margaret Macmillan and the Nursery School Association brought 'a rapidly growing section of the population to realize that nursery life is necessary and desirable for all children over two or three years of age, quite irrespective of what their home conditions are like'. Beatrix Tudor Hart's *Play and Toys in the Nursery Years* appeared in two editions—in 1938 and 1945, so it bridged the absorption of new psychological thinking very neatly. The first edition was committed totally to the benefits of nursery schooling. It pressed the advantages a nursery-school teacher had over a mother—her premises were planned and arranged exclusively for the use of children aged between two and five, and 'she herself had only one job to do—to look after the children'. The earlier children went to nursery school the better—two-year-olds were still 'individualists' who would at first play alone among the crowd, then effortlessly learn social skills of co-operation. The 'possessive instinct' would probably never develop. If a child started at a later age, it would take it much longer to adjust. Children could do much more for themselves in the child-scale world of the nursery school. They were expected to lay tables, and clear them away, and even to wash the dishes. They kept toys and apparatus tidily on shelves, putting away playthings as soon as they were finished with. Under supervision they could use dangerous tools and attempt dangerous physical feats—climbing ladders or walls—and so become increasingly self-confident.

After the wartime experience, the 1945 edition of Tudor Hart was considerably amended. The need for female labour had led to the opening of more and more nurseries, to cater for children of all ages whose mothers were doing warwork. Not all were run by the ideal nursery teacher envisaged in earlier manuals, and clearly not all were happy places. Tudor Hart inserted a long section explaining why nursery schools were not at all well fitted for the needs of babies under two, who needed security both of environment and of caretaker. The sentence introducing the first edition's chapter on 'Birth to Two Years' was changed from:

> so long as the baby can be safely left in a cot or per-
> ambulator sleeping or kicking the problem of toys and
> play material does not arise; mothers are still free to
> concentrate their thoughts and worries on such things as
> food, clothing, fresh air and hours of sleep.

to

> I have heard it said, by persons who should know better,
> that children under two years of age do not require any
> occupation ... Anyone who has had any intimate contact
> with babies knows just how soon it becomes impossible to
> put him in his cot or pram to sleep for hours on end while
> mother busies herself with other things.

Nevertheless, nursery schools remained inescapably pop-ular because, as St Aubyn's *Family Book* made clear, they were replacing nannies. Some form of help, it felt, was always necessary with small children. 'In practice, this is universally recognised in the institution of children's nurses, ranging from one little nursemaid for a whole family, to at least one nurse for each child. The conviction is steadily growing, however, that the best form of outside help is the nursery school.' The advantage of using a nursery school rather than having a nurse was that 'the mother is in closer contact with her children at the beginning and end of the day' than she would be if she had a nurse, and that when the children were at school, 'the mother is absolutely free, can follow her other duties and occupations without interruption, and return to her children with renewed vitality when their hours at nursery school are over'.

Repeated insistence on the importance of the toddler's peer group was due in part to the shrinking families which too often left children unused to company, and in part to theories of personality development which required that children measure themselves up to the challenge of their contemporaries from the word go. As Thom put it: 'The earlier the child is given an opportunity of working, playing, and competing with other children, the more likely he will be to formulate habits which will aid him in the process of social adjustment.' The phrase 'emotional stability' or the word 'emotions' peppered new editions of manuals in the 1930s. What might be involved in establishing sound emotional development was still ducked away from; self-reliance in a crowd of strangers continued to be the aim.

The most marked legacy of the nursery-school mentality was the belief that the child required a purpose-built world of its own. While this was provided in nursery schools, such an assertion could be accepted easily enough. Once nursery schools were challenged as depriving very small children of necessary mothering, conscientious parents were left to provide this child-sized world for their children themselves, or to feel inadequate if they didn't. It didn't occur to many that a child's own home might be the best place for it to grow up just because it was different from any other place. Ethel Brereton, however, while praising the 'wonderful system of Madame Montessori', and finding it 'good for dull, backward children, who need goading on and enlivening', warned that kindergarten material could be 'intensely boring for clever children stimulated by and developed by the society of cultivated parents'. Such children 'leap and strain like eager dogs held on the leash towards learning of all sorts'. It was 'simply a waste of time', she felt, to teach such children the names of colours with little balls and coloured beads, or to rub their fingers up and down a cardboard letter.

> They will either pick up such things themselves or do jolly well without them. You are simply overlaying their originality with rubbish when you bustle up to them with your little scraps of information, only sullying their powers of observation, and teaching them to depend on you for information secondhand rather than by the use of their own senses. (*The Happy Nursery*)

Discipline was faced up to squarely by the behaviourists.

Watson kept his child 'in a positive environment where he can't get up to much mischief'. He was conditioned not to do socially unacceptable things by a sharp rap over the fingers with a pencil just as the act was taking place. 'This is not a punishment but an objective experimental procedure . . . Forbidden objects will gradually lose their stimulating value.'

Mary Scharlieb made use of the child's suggestibility. Instead of telling it not to go out thinly dressed, she recommended saying: 'Now that the weather is cold and bright you will be able to have your new overcoat with the beautiful naval buttons!' And she warned that suggesting to a child that it was always faddy, or always taking cold, would make it be so. Suggestions had to be positive—as in: 'Now we're going to have a really good night!' rather than: 'I hope we won't have a bad night again.' Press the right button and the correct action would result. Self-discipline was important too—'the tonic of unselfish work for others'. A cancelled treat was 'a very palpable and valuable piece of moral education', and accustomed children to the 'discipline of circumstances'. Clearly children were not only expected to do more for themselves than they are today; they were also expected to be considerably more resilient in character.

Although Mrs Frankenburg aimed at 'self-control, rather than Prussian discipline', she saw instant obedience as absolutely essential. This did not mean breaking the child's will, or suppressing its initiative—her metaphor was a military one, but more subtle than most: parents 'might well take a lesson from the discipline of the British Army and Navy, where, while instant obedience is the first duty, the most junior ranks are expected as a matter of course to take command in any emergency'. Even Madame Montessori, 'so often quoted as the apostle of freedom', said that there are unpleasant things in children of which they must be cured. Children could not be allowed to indulge in anti-social behaviour. She quoted Kipling's spine-chilling story, *Rikki-Tikki-Tavi*, as an instance of how only absolute obedience—'Sit still, Teddy, you mustn't move'—saved the child from certain death.

Mrs Frankenburg's disciplinary methods were unique. She invented tooth fairies, useful all-round home-helps.

211

Besides helping the child to clean their houses, they are very fond of dancing, and can only dance when he is biting his food. They are dreadfully disappointed when he swallows it whole ... They don't like him to drink at mealtimes much, as it makes their dancefrocks wet. Between meals they have time to put up their waterproofs. If he coughs without putting his hand up, they might be jerked right out of his mouth.

These and a squadron of other fairytale characters, secret societies, and other ploys, spun her children through their world on a roundabout of humour and good sense. What emerges from her books, my own chosen reading ever since I discovered her, is a sense of enthusiasm and loyalty towards her own children, and a grasp of the realities of a life spent bringing them up. Moreover, she seemed to combine life with children with a life of her own, neglecting neither, to an enviably successful extent.

Spanking was generally condemned. To take Solomon's advice, not to spare the rod and spoil the child, was no longer fashionable. Look what happened to Solomon's own children—Rehoboam, for example (1 Kings 12:14). 'There is no doubt that violent punishment is a great relief to the grown-up's nerves,' admitted Mrs Frankenburg, 'but most of us prefer to manage our children without the emotional stimulus of execution and reconciliation.' Moreover, as Rousseau had revealed, spanking 'aroused definitely sexual emotions even in a very young child'.

One of the reasons that discipline could be more carefully considered, and dealt with in terms inspired by new findings in psychology, was that the nanny's exclusive charge of the baby was becoming a thing of the past. Earlier manuals had often recommended a nurse because she could be consistent and firm in situations in which a mother would knuckle under to her child. Once mothers, through necessity or inclination, took more command in the management of their children, they looked for a girl whom they could train up themselves to bring up their babies as they—the mothers—thought right. Both Marie Stopes and Mrs Frankenburg emphasized the advantages of doing this, rather than leaving their children to the tender mercies of a 'trained nurse' who, they felt, could well have been trained to do things they disapproved of.

Reflecting the decline of the separate nursery establishment was the movement for 'parenthood'—an attempt to bring fathers on to the stage. A. S. Neill attacked *The Problem Parent* rather than the problem child in 1932 (unfortunately his attractively iconoclastic book deals more with school children than babies, so I can't linger on it here). Titles increasingly reflected the inclusion of father as well as mother in the manuals' vision of the order of things, but their advice for fathers remained disappointing. Their role was limited to John Gibbens's offer to let them exercise baby, or to indulge in the occasional rough and tumble. It was assumed that for the most part fathers would not be around while the baby was awake. Fathers' opinions were limited to the wider sphere— theirs were the decisions to limit their family, to decide which school the child would go to, to deal with the older children's more profound questions. The mother's outlook was limited to the nursery, according to Mary Scharlieb; the father's 'wider vision' was needed when 'matters of unusual difficulty' arose. So, although the prescriptions for the running of the nursery were uniquely masculine in inspiration in the 1920s and 1930s, fathers in practical terms were offered less responsibility for or companionship with their babies than the nostalgic or psychologically minded fathers of the pre-war years.

Throughout these two decades, which I have characterized as dominated by the behaviourists, there were voices of dissent—psychoanalysts, independent-minded mothers, 'Bohemians', who never toed the military line of the 'well-ordered nursery'; but the dominant mode was the brisk and breezy Mothercraft of Truby King. Suddenly, in 1938, the worms turned (arguably far too far) and Anderson and Mary Aldrich's *Babies are Human Beings* became the most talked-about book on babies of the year. As the inspiration of Dr Spock's world-famous baby-care manual, it deserves a section to itself.

Coda—Babies are Human Beings

The first impact of *Babies are Human Beings* was a little lost on a Britain marshalling itself for war, but its publication in the United States caused a stir of interest and relief. Its strength lay in combining well-informed scientific observation with a set of conclusions which most mothers found naturally attractive. They were not told to build better babies for a brighter world or to mould citizens for the empire. They were not warned that they and their husbands were probably providing a dangerously contaminated environment for their child. Instead they were encouraged to enjoy their babies—albeit 'in an intelligent way'.

The Aldrichs looked at babies developing, and accepted that inevitably they had to come into conflict with their environment as they grew up. Nevertheless, 'by the time he is two, this entirely self-centred barbarian does take his place as a responsive member of society'. The parents' task was to ease this adjustment by taking cues from the known facts of his development (as revealed by Gesell and Ilg), and not to urge ideal standards on to him before he could physiologically accept them. Too much conventional baby-care advice dictated how the baby should act, rather than responding to his inbuilt 'developmental plan'. Newborn babies were not 'static bundles of flannel' but 'active, hardworking members of society'. Fun was the new essential. The baby quickly changed 'from a serious, uncompromising barbarian to a responsive, jovial member of the family, eager to exercise his lighter side'. Pleasure received new status, became a philosophy: 'To those interested in the philosophy of fun, the fact that the ability to have a good time is almost the first accomplishment initiated by our rigid developmental schedule should be of great significance.'

The Aldrichs rejected the hospital ideal of baby-care. They pointed out that the majority of the under-twos studied by baby-care experts had been in institutional care, and that the available evidence was too inadequate for any 'universal foundation' of theory to be set out—except, perhaps, that all babies were different. 'If they were alike, we could use the mass-production methods of the chick industry, and bring them up in huge infant incubators.' Some babies were obliging from the start—they let their legs be pumped up and down. Others *always* refused. Some were hair-trigger reactors—sparklers. 'When handled with respect the sparkler becomes highly responsive and fairly sparkles with the zest of living. When placed under a rigid and unsympathetic regime, however, he becomes a typical spoiled child, screaming or whining until his desires are appeased, an unhappy member of the family.'

Parents often kidded themselves that they had 'trained' their baby in good behaviour when all that had happened was that the baby had 'grown up a little'. There was no point in forcing through projects against the will of the child—too many parents felt ashamed to admit defeat at the hands of a mere baby. But the baby was not inferior: 'He is merely younger, and in reality well able to baffle those who care for him.' Mental hygiene and habit-training needed reappraisal—above all, they had to be approached in the context of warmly affectionate physical care.

To give the baby all the warmth, comfort, and cuddling that he seems to need; to meet his wishes in the matter of satisfying and appropriate food; to adjust our habit-training to his individual rhythm; and to see that he has an opportunity to exercise each new accomplishment as it emerges; these are the beginnings of a forward-looking programme in mental hygiene.

The Aldrichs deliberately chose what Douglas Thom, founder of the pre-school mental hygiene movement, had called 'the three most vital habits'—eating, sleeping and eliminating—to examine and reapproach in the light of 'the reality of development'. 'If we should find any of our family standing over the baby trying to regulate the number of times a minute he breathed, or showing him a better way of using his muscles, we might question his sanity.' Similarly, the Aldrichs believed, a baby should be allowed to feed when and how he liked. Dr Clara Davis's experiments (see p. 262) on self-selected diets had shown that babies chose the right amount of food for their needs, if left entirely to themselves. From his very first days, a baby felt a pain in his stomach when hungry which made him cry out for food. But modern management ignored this one ability—the hunger cry. Following 'Baby's Way of Eating' (note the carefully sympathetic phraseology) meant that 'in order to help this pain–food–relief sequence, we supply food when we hear the hunger cry'. Routine feeding, by the clock, destroyed the efficiency of these internal sensations.

The process of feeding should be comfortable—he was to be cuddled rather than left lying on his back with a bottle on a hard table. How much to give him could be safely left to baby—'respect your baby's appetite'. Babies often cut down on food a few days before an illness erupted, so it was a mistake to demand that the same amount be eaten every day. His food preferences should be taken into account, to encourage the development of taste. New foods should be introduced very gradually and should certainly not be forced down. At this time, because of the enthusiasm for vitamins, some paediatricians advised giving babies vegetables in the first month, but, following the 'developmental plan', the Aldrichs preferred to wait until the teeth erupted. If one substitutes Cadogan's 'unerring nature' for the Aldrichs' 'developmental plan' one sees more clearly how akin they were to the eighteenth-century physician, to his direct response to what observation of babies taught him, and to his rejection of the 'very wild conceits' of former days.

But the baby remained a patient, needing professional care from the start. Although natural foods should be provided, and the baby allowed a free choice, 'foods offered will be regulated by the physician who will remove anything undesirable overindulged in'. The rein was free only within limits, albeit humanized ones: 'Babies are like the rest of us—they like the things that are not supposed to be good for them.' Moreover, the Aldrichs dealt only with bottle-feeding, and with method rather than content. They assumed that the baby's doctor would have constructed a formula from his knowledge of the 'peculiar requirements of his patient', and they congratulated nutritionists on having brought the science of formula feeding to such a fine art that their skilful adjustment was 'a prominent fact in making the child's first few months of life a gratifying experience'.

Just as babies could be trusted to feed themselves, so they could be left to take as much sleep as they needed. In fact, the parents' task was not to educate the baby to sleep, but to encourage him to spend less and less time in bed, to enjoy being awake. At first, the Aldrichs pointed out, baby only surfaced for feeding and bathing. Then smiling, talking, and using his hands kept him happy and alert for longer periods. Ultimately sleep was only of value 'as it freshened him up between the thrills of experience'. A baby's sleep was not unbroken—it was more like a series of little naps. Kugelmass had noted this research finding only two years earlier, but his conclusion had been quite different—babies had to be taught to take the long sleep periods that suited their parents.

If a baby cried in his cot, he was genuinely in distress, uncomfortable in some way or other. He might have a wet nappy, or be hungry, or be suffering from 'three-month colic'. The Aldrichs were as mystified by this phenomenon as most of their contemporaries, hazarding a guess that it was due to 'an over-active intestine'. Boredom was not yet offered as a possible cause for crying, but it was not far away once parents were encouraged to long for their babies to wake up rather than told to make every effort to get them off to sleep.

They pointed out that the rapid development of the baby meant that his sleep habits would change surprisingly quickly. At first, he would always wake in the early hours for a night-feed (yes, a night-feed), but at around six weeks this would be dropped naturally. The cast-iron, no-night-feeders were dismissed with curled lip: 'Unfortunately our routines of training do not give baby free rein, but often attempt to make him do without this meal before his stomach agrees to sleep all through the night.' They observed that a three-hour schedule often suited babies better than a four-hour one, and that 7, 11, 3, 7, 11, 3 could be more attractive than the classic 6, 10, 2, 6, 10, 2. The baby 'should not be allowed to lie awake screaming in the small hours', and mothers were warned that 'attempts at super-efficiency' led to 'many a superfluous struggle'. It was no good being in a hurry to establish habits.

217

The parent who, book in hand, tries to make her ready-to-go offspring sleep out his allotted hours does not understand what she is up against. Rooms may be darkened, older children hushed, but the fresh and unwearied baby remains full of interest and unaware that the book says that he is doing the wrong thing. There are even people who have such faith in the printed word that they will give sedatives to keep their children asleep the required number of hours. They seem to lose sight of the function of sleep as a freshener, and take it for granted that unconsciousness is a virtue.

Here, very clearly spelt out, was the new child-centred world. From an adult's point of view, unconsciousness certainly was a virtue. But once the experts decided to follow, rather than lead, the baby into the world he was discovering around himself, such considerations became unacceptable.

'The astonishing preoccupation of our civilization with elimination' was 'a sure sign that our management of eliminative functions has failed'. The Aldrichs saw the 'baby's physiological plan' as the clue to successful potty training. As the bowel filled and pressure built up, a 'mass movement' naturally took place. It was an absurdly arbitrary decision to condition a child to react to a pot being placed against his rectum, first with the aid of suppositories, and then just as a conditioned reflex. The natural internal mechanism was a far more efficient one. Moreover, when the shift from potty to lavatory seat was made, the baby's artificial stimulus changed and he had nothing to go by. 'His innate mechanism has been educated out of him, and the new situation is so different as to be unrecognised or unacceptable. Pleasant reaction gives way to confusion, and we say he is constipated.'

Their answer was to wait for the 'mass movement', to establish its usual time of arriving, and try, if possible, to pop the baby on the pot. 'When placed on the seat at his right time, he automatically develops the necessary association between the mass movement, toilet seat, and his own satisfying effort. Thus real, permanent training becomes a fact, even though the diaper washing is prolonged for a few weeks.' A few weeks—they were still very much more sanguine than modern mothers would be about early success in training.

Getting the baby dry should wait until he was walking. Then he could be left without a nappy, and offered the pot frequently for two or three days. 'If he is disinclined, put the nappy back on and wait until he is older. Every child eventually becomes trained.' The Aldrichs were against lifting at night, as this shifted responsibility on to the mother, and delayed the child's assumption of a more mature attitude. Timing, they emphasized, was more important than technique: follow the developmental plan written into the baby since his conception. Follow, don't lead.

Babies are Human Beings toppled the totems and taboos of baby-care to left and right. The baby was not to be washed until nine or ten days after birth, as the natural 'vernix caseosa' was a guard against rashes and infections. His nose, mouth and ears were to remain unexplored by twists of cotton wool. Thumbsucking was a 'prenatal sport', a rehearsal for suckling, which would be discontinued once more interesting pastimes were provided. A sense of sex was natural in infancy—there was no hurry in training baby gently towards adult conventions. The special exercises for training baby's muscles with which books and the radio bombarded parents were quite unnecessary. Woollen undies were too hot in modern homes. And cuddling, *bête noire* of the Watson era, became not just acceptable but essential. 'Conscientious mothers often ask doctors if it is alright to fondle their baby. Their vague feeling is that it is wrong for babies to be mothered, loved, or rocked, and that it is their forlorn duty to raise their children in splendid isolation, untouched by human hand.' This attitude, declared the Aldrichs, was abhorrent—'particularly at variance with the developmental plan'. The fundamental need of every human being for caressing was 'nowhere as demonstrable as in young babies', and they remarked on the numbers of physically and mentally retarded babies in institutions where care was only 'efficient'. Again, it is clear that the hospital image, the quiet, clean, clockwork baby, was at last being rejected.

Finally, the Aldrichs pointed a questioning finger at the

over-organized character of children's lives, a regret reminiscent of Harker's nostalgia for shrubberies at sunset on chill October days. They were left with so little time for spontaneity, either in play or work; with so little time to develop their own initiative. The 'ancient Puritan fear' of spoiling children by giving them their own way was still 'very much alive'. Of course, what the Aldrichs were in fact criticizing was the massive comeback of discipline after the First World War. Now the pendulum was swinging again.

5
Baby Rules, O.K.?
1946–81

Fun Morality

More books have been written and sold on baby-care since 1945 than before. Dr Benjamin Spock's *Common Sense Book of Baby and Child Care* is a bestseller only outsold by the Bible. Watson's psychological New Testament had been popular enough, selling 100,000 copies in its first few years, but Spock's world sales run into tens of millions. Moreover he is not alone. His books are merely the Panzer divisions of an army of information and advice on infant care which has been marching to relieve demoralized parents since the Second World War.

One reason that a huge number of books have been produced and read was the radical change in the advice the new generation of experts offered. Following the Aldrichs, they told mothers to reject the carefully scientific procedures of the Watson/King/Gesell era, and to respond to their babies in an instinctive, 'natural' way. The self-controlled, emotionless infant, hygienic in mind and body, was thrown out with its icy bath-water. The new model baby was warmly affectionate, impulsive, dependent, and (preferably) scintillatingly intelligent. Spock talked about the 'daily stimulation from loving parents' which was necessary if 'emotional depth and a keen intelligence' were to be fostered, Jerome Kagan identified the 'two critical concerns of American parents' as 'attachment to mother and rate of cognitive development'. Similarly Martin Richards in England recognized the modern parent's 'preoccupation with children's education and emotional growth'.

Completely new and up-to-date instruction manuals were necessary for mothers who were self-consciously cutting themselves off from the examples of their own mothers. Spock was neither the first nor the only paediatrician to hold the new views—but *Common Sense* was easily the longest and most comprehensive book of its type. Its brilliant index allowed a mother to look up everything from temper tantrums

223

to itchy toes, and its simple formula—either 'don't worry, this is common-place' or 'ask your doctor'—covered every eventuality. Moreover, Spock had, and retains, the knack of putting across complex information in the simplest terms. Until recently most other books on baby-care confined themselves to sniping at the fringes of Spock, accepting that there would be a copy—paperback rather than hardback—in almost every house. At the same time, which is oddly anachronistic now, the British Medical Association continues to hand out to new mothers through clinics and hospitals pamphlets recognizably based on pre-war conceptions of routines, hygiene, and regularity. Baby-care theory has become an indecisive graveyard of brief enthusiasms, overshadowed by the indelible influences of an upbringing with which we are now at war. A close reading of the several editions of Spock— roughly every decade he reassessed his position—gives a very clear picture of the ups and downs that plague the would-be informed parent. Before I trace how Spock and his contemporaries correct and recorrect their positions, I want to go back to explaining the basis for those two modern touchstones—'emotional depth and keen intelligence'.

Two thinkers who conveniently epitomize these concerns are Sigmund Freud and Jean Piaget. Both were born in the nineteenth century, and had been offering their insights on children's behaviour to the world for some thirty years before they found their way into the popular manuals. Why the delay? Certainly, neither were accessible to mothers in their original form; what they had to say needed considerable premastication. That few writers on baby-care chewed it over for mothers before the 1940s was a reflection of the political, social and economic climate of those decades. As we have seen, the behaviourist approach had been well suited to a world recovering from but still apprehensive of war, which saw its children as a generation with a military purpose. Honed down to robot efficiency, they were to be tailored to fit the new world. Once the child-rearing principles of the Third Reich and Stalin's Russia became threats to freedom rather than models of egalitarianism, a reaction set in, a determination grew to allow the children of the free world to be more free than children had ever been. After the

Cold War, a war about ways of life, became established between the West and the Soviet Union, much political capital was made out of contrasting stereotypes of domestic life. Subordinating the individual to the good of the whole therefore became dramatically unfashionable in the West. The vacuum left by the receding tide of patriotic fervour was filled—perhaps inadequately—by what one social anthropologist described as 'fun morality'.

Martha Wolfenstein, who read all the official US Bulletins on baby-care from 1914 to the 1950s, observed a shift in attitudes. In 1914 the baby was a 'depraved soul' requiring thorough training into sociability. By the 1950s she observed a 'neutral stand' on moral issues, and a concentration on enjoying life with baby. The boundaries between work and play were broken down—what was pleasant for baby was by definition good for him. Feeding—on demand of course—was enjoyable for baby 'and usually his mother'. The introduction of solid foods was 'fun and amusing'. At bathtime the baby 'delighted' his parents. Parents were to be beware lest toilet training became 'a hateful bore'.

Although some of Wolfenstein's generalizations seem suspect after a wider reading in child-care manuals, particularly the 'depraved soul' view of the turn-of-the-century decades, the concept of 'fun morality' certainly rings true. Most manuals, from then on, presented the same assumption of the baby's pleasure being the highest good. Dr Dorothy Hudson's *Modern Parenthood* (1959) was subtitled *Keeping Your Children Well and Happy*. Rudolf Dreikurs's *Happy Children* (1964) was subtitled *A Challenge to Parents*. Closer to our own time, Dr Hugh Jolly's *Book of Child Care* (1981 edn) aimed 'to help you enjoy your children more and have fewer anxieties about their health. If you enjoy them, you are helping them enjoy life too.' Penelope Leach (*Baby and Child*, 1977) likewise declared: 'This whole book is orientated towards you and your child as a unit of mutual pleasure-giving. Fun for her is fun for you. Fun for you creates more for her, and the more fun you all have, the fewer will be your problems.' Undoubtedly, as will become apparent, there were psychological justifications for fun morality—but society needed to be in the right mood to take it up. Reaction from austerity, military discipline and sudden death made parents peculiarly inclined to indulge the new generation.

Political suitability needed the support of economic feasibility. The prosperity of the 1950s and 1960s—the 'You've never had it so good' decades—enabled parents to give time and money to their children in unprecedented quantities. Between the wars, middle-class mothers had had to get used to doing without much domestic help. Children's books of the Ameliaranne Stiggins variety (her mother took in washing and coped with six little Stigginses) betrayed a new curiosity about how on earth these things were done. The brisk, clockwork regime of regular feeds and much 'time alone' had solved domestic logistics as well as meeting current psychological fashion. Freud could not have been allowed free rein in the 1950s if domestic-appliance technology had been less sophisticated. One can plausibly track permissiveness in feeding, playing and toilet training down the income levels in company with modern cooking appliances, vacuum cleaners and washing machines. Being a constant reassuring presence, considering one's child's every need, creating a stimulating environment exactly suited to its current developmental stage—all these take up a great deal of time. Only with two children and a modernized home can the demands of modern child-care theorists be comfortably met.

The rejection of eugenics and patriotic orderliness left a gap in the family's concept of itself not entirely filled by the feeling that everyone should just have a good time. A marked interest began to be shown in how other societies (non-Communist, of course) organized themselves domestically. In an effort to resurrect submerged maternal instincts, the popularizers cited Trobriand islanders or Samoan adolescents as possible models. 'New' ideas on bringing up babies have included slinging babies on parents' backs or fronts, premasticating first solids, family beds, prolonged breastfeeding, and even, recently, swaddling. A parallel with the eighteenth-century doctors' respect for Buffon arises when one looks at the *Reader's Digest Mothercare Book*. Its photographs deliberately juxtapose assorted tribal practices with today's parents relaxing with their children. The parent, once gardener, later animal trainer, has reached the status of anthropologist. He plays an informed, watchful role, but is fundamentally alienated by his self-consciousness. Children are no longer plants or puppies but small savages—Golding's *Lord of the Flies* was written in 1954.

Few baby books since the Second World War have attempted to face up to the wider moral setting of child-rearing practices—there will be no section on religion in the modern part of this book because it is no longer a matter of course to place child-rearing in such a context. In a latish edition of *Common Sense* (1968) Spock made some attempt to do so, as if, after reflection, the resounding silence on the subject seemed odd. In a completely new section called 'What Are Your Aims in Raising a Child?' he wrote:

> The rearing of children is more and more puzzling for parents in the twentieth century because we've lost a lot of our old-fashioned convictions about what kinds of morals and ambitions and characters we want them to have. We've even lost our convictions about the purpose of human existence. Instead we have come to depend on psychological concepts. They've been helpful in solving many of the smaller problems, but they are of little use in answering the major questions.

His answer was not a satisfactory one—it reflected the disillusion after twenty years of 'permissive' upbringing of the man who considered himself partly responsible for it. Criticizing the 'child-centred' nature of modern American culture, he recommended that children should be brought up 'with the feeling that they are in this world not for their own satisfaction but primarily to serve others'. He pointed out that 'human beings behave better, feel more purposeful, have better mental health during wartime, when they have a common purpose'. Although Spock was right to feel troubled, and put his finger very nicely on the odd nature of the child-centred point-of-view, his solution, with its overtones of Baden-Powell and nostalgia for the *bonhomie* of the Blitz, was inadequate to the new horizons being opened up by the research of the developmental psychologists.

227

With interest in the child-rearing practices of other cultures came a powerful move towards equality of opportunity for all children. Because the desirability of this had been accepted in the physical sphere of good health and hygiene, it seemed unexceptional, once good physical conditions in nurseries had largely been established, to extend philanthropic interference into the emotional and intellectual aspects of the baby. Accustomed to being reproached for their failures to achieve babies of 'normal' weight, feeding patterns and sleeping routines, mothers accepted that they should listen to the experts' advice on their children's psychological and cognitive development. Extending human potential by giving everyone equal opportunity to succeed gave the illusion of a sense of purpose. The question of what success involved was largely avoided. Freud and Piaget gave plenty of reasons why the experiences of the early years should be seen as of crucial importance for the emotional and intellectual development of the child. Hospital experiments in intensive stimulation of brain-damaged infants immediately after birth suggested that the quality of the baby's environment from the very start could materially affect its intelligence as well as its psychological health. Although more recent research into 'infant stim' has tempered this belief, the legacy of the earlier optimism is still evident even in the most up-to-date baby books. Mothers are instructed to spend most of their time 'interacting' with their babies in the most stimulating way possible.

The sanguine hope that all babies could end up equal led to a reappraisal of the milestones which had parents measuring their children against the elusive average. Vagueness replaced precision. Walking was achieved 'between ten and twenty months' rather than 'at fourteen months'. Conscious that parental attitudes towards their children affect development, the manual writers protested, too much, that apparent backwardness was probably an illusion. In an otherwise excellent book, *Infants and Mothers* (1969), T. Berry Brazelton followed the progress of three very different babies— 'quiet', 'average' and 'active'—to the age of one. With a conjuror's flourish, he revealed that they were all 'equally' developed at that point, despite individual differences in pace earlier on. Moreover, and significantly, all three were declared from the start to be 'above average IQ'—the ideal baby was equally brilliant, not equally ordinary.

In the context of this prosperous and democratic background, baby-care specialists put forward ideas derived from Freud and Piaget which fitted the mood of the time. Whereas Freud dominated the postwar decades, Piaget's prominence is more recent, and to some extent at the expense of Freud. Studying a few of the writers most extremely influenced by their theories will make it clear how much we still rely on what they had to say, whether we think we agree with them or not.

Freud Rampant

The declared aim of the experts of the 1920s and 1930s had been to produce well-behaved, polite children, with regular habits, who could easily be disciplined to fit into the assembly-line culture of the new metropolis. Tiring of the excesses of the Child Study Movement, they had asserted that this was an adult world and that children ought to take a back seat until they were old enough to be independent. As we have seen, the post-Second World War mood was very different. Recognition of the extreme harm that bad early experience could do to the adult personality was generally accepted through the socially diluted Freudianism of Erik Erikson. In *Childhood and Society* (1950), he neatly knitted together interest in anthropology with Freudian theory, flitting from Sioux Indians to Nazi youth, and constructed a schema that put the child straight back on to the centre of the stage. Just as vaccination had eliminated smallpox as a threat to children's physical health, so careful childhood handling, illuminated by an understanding of Freudian insights, could do the same to mental illness. Refusing to come down on one side or the other of the nature/nurture issue, he asserted that every reaction of the organism (the body and its mental apparatus) was due to both heredity and environment. Infancy was the optimum time to mould the child, so parental actions towards it were highly significant. But instead of being concerned with promoting independence and perfecting instrumental skills in the child, parents were now called upon to concentrate on the avoidance of psychological distress. They moved from the offensive to the defensive. Rather than directing the infant, drawing upon the blank tablet, they became its guardians against a host of fears and anxieties which could, it was believed, produce deviant emotional growth and neurotic disorder. As Jerome Kagan put it in 1978:

> rearing a baby was a serious and difficult mission with many shoals to avoid. Each child was a potential phobic, obsessive, depressive, or in the extreme, schizophrenic, and parents were warned against the potential dangers of practices they had regarded as innocuous. The prevention of psychical pathology had replaced earlier worry over physical disease. (*Infancy, and its Place in Human Development*)

Two books which represented the side-by-side constants of the cuddly and the astringent approaches in a Freudian context were Margaret Ribble's *Rights of Infants* (1943—reprinted six times in two years) and Edith Buxbaum's *Your Child Makes Sense* (1951). Buxbaum's book was sharply divided into two halves, physical and psychological (the first half was written by a paediatrician, Florence Swanson), and was introduced by her mentor, Anna Freud. If this little passage from the introduction is contrasted with the Aldrichs' description of the parents' task (p. 214)—the metaphor of the savage is common to both—the tone of the book is easy to grasp:

> From birth onwards, children feel the pressures of urgent body needs and powerful instinctive urges (such as hunger, sex and aggression) which clamour for satisfaction. Soon afterwards, the child encounters demands for restraint, and the prohibition on wish-fulfilment, which comes from the parents, whose task it is to turn their children from unrestrained greedy and cruel little savages into well-behaved, socially-adapted, civilized beings.

Buxbaum's approach was distant and rather condescending, wearily conceding that one had to be patient and permissive with these unattractive little beings as they went through the predictable hoops of infancy, and to gently persuade them into 'bending and curbing their instincts to the demands of society'.

Inevitably, her major preoccupations were oral, anal and phallic. So, on sucking:

> We arrive, after disastrous attempts to stop the infant suckling outside his feeding times, at the conclusion that we had better give in, let the child lead the way in showing us what he needs, and for once admit that the old people were right after all. The only thing we can do is provide the infant with more hygienic means of sucking. We may allow him to nurse longer—provided he does not pinch the mother. He may play with the nipple on a bottle or with a similarly shaped flexible toy for as long as he likes.

The idea of a baby pinching its mother was a very odd one to introduce arbitrarily, nor was there a hint that breast-feeding might be more than a one-way service. Pinching was soon improved on by a discussion on the potential hazards of biting the mother's nipple—hazardous less for the mother than for the child, who might suffer traumatic rejection anxieties if discouraged too abruptly from doing so. Erikson had spent some time on this issue in his study of the Sioux, surmising that some of that tribe's ferocity could be attributed to the thwarting of their efforts to bite their mothers' breasts.

Children were to be allowed to exercise to the full their urges to mouth objects and to mess their food at the table. Underlying this freedom was Erikson's theory that at this age a basic sense of trust in its parents had to be established in the child, and fulfilment of oral expression was one aspect of this. Buxbaum recommended setting up a 'trusting situation' in one doubtful child by 'encouraging the child to use dirty noises and so recapture the pleasures of being dirty which he seemed to miss'.

The section on excretory functions was largely composed of cautionary tales of frustrated children that Buxbaum had

had to handle—children trained too soon or too strictly. Buxbaum's answer was to allow the child to regress—to soil wherever he liked for a while, and then let him start, undisapproved of, to choose for himself when and where he would defecate. She pointed to the stubborn and stingy nature of constipated people—scarred for life by toilet-training traumas which had made them unable to 'let go'. 'The little boy who kept his stool in his pocket as "ammunition against the enemy" was in later life a great saver, keeping his pockets full of pennies he deposited eventually in the bank just as the stool went into the toilet.'

In considering 'the myth that children have no sexual feelings', Buxbaum was happy to 'upset the concept of the child as the innocent, pure, little angel'. Every time a mother changed a nappy she apparently turned her baby on, and if the baby's genitals were swollen at birth then greater pleasure and earlier sexual awareness would be felt. 'Although masturbation in infants is infrequent, any interference with it is likely to permanently disturb his psychosexual development.' The standard Freudian concepts of penis envy, castration anxiety and oedipal identification were trotted out, complete with possible aberrations. The section on sex was thirty pages long, compared with ten pages on excretion and fifteen on sucking and eating.

In the final part of Buxbaum's book, the child's place in the family was spotlighted. Parents were urged to look at the world through their child's eyes. He created relationships of a sort with everyone he met. The removal of a pet, let alone a grandparent, could be a traumatic experience suggesting his own obliteration one day. New to child-care books was the very long section devoted to considering the father's role in the family—whether he was jealous, effeminate, or frequently absent. Buxbaum emphasized his duty to play an acceptably masculine role. One problem case she recounted (but failed to resolve) was the family in which the father, an injured ballet dancer, ran the house while his wife worked in a factory. The six-year-old son could not be persuaded not to imitate his father, and so pursued the 'feminine' interests of cooking, cleaning, and fashion. The world was clearly not yet ready for equal parenting or role-swapping—although Dorothy Canfield had raised the issue in her excellent novel *The Home-maker* as early as 1924. What makes Buxbaum's book so dispiriting to read is its generous lacing of case histories, which reveal the disastrous errors of parents who have thereby created pathologically sick children. Ironically, considering that their main aim was to protect the child from severe anxieties, the effect of books of this type was to create anxiety in the parent—especially in the mother—to a degree unparalleled in child-care history.

Although Margaret Ribble displayed a thorough grounding in Freud's theories in *Rights of Infants*, she avoided distorting the known facts of infancy into Buxbaum's rigid framework. Instead of using Anna Freud's model of 'powerful instinctive urges which clamour for satisfaction', she described the baby's 'natural resources of life energy' which 'like electricity, water power, or any of the mechanical forces of nature . . . cannot be left free and uncontrolled lest it becomes destructive and distorted'. As the title of her book suggested, she was championing the infant against its parents. 'The natural impulses of an infant cannot be summarily dammed up or snuffled out when their expression becomes inconvenient for adults . . . Parents have to remind themselves constantly that human personality is a continuous development, and healthy emotions as well as a free creative intelligence are rooted in early infant experience.' Here already were the two pillars of modern babyhood—emotional and intellectual well-being. The physical was left to doctors, the spiritual quietly ignored.

Ribble put forward ideas which were remarkably ahead of her time, although her viewpoint was occasionally idiosyncratic. She held, like a good Freudian, that the basic experiences which might dispose an infant to anxiety were weaning and toilet training, but she also interested herself in the effect of the actual birth process on both baby and mother. Ideally, she felt, babies should not be taken from their mothers and sent to the hospital nursery at birth, under the pretext of giving mothers a chance to rest. She reasoned from the known fact that lack of oxygen at birth could damage the brain of the newborn child. She extended this principle to the first few months of life, claiming that the baby needed physical stimulus from the presence of its mother's body to keep it inspiring air as fast as it expired it, and so getting enough oxygen for its still developing brain. Just as earlier babies had sneaked much cuddling under the pretext of 'being winded', so Ribble's babies were kept in their mother's beds to boost their oxygen intake. She derided 'the ancient belief, still current, that babies who sleep with their mother are in danger of suffocation'. The reverse was effectively true. 'Since the contacts and warmth afforded by the human body are a protection rather than a peril to the infant, he sleeps more safely at his mother's side than in the stimulus-free seclusion of the modern nursery.'

Ribble championed close physical contact between mother and child: another of her theories was that the brain substance was incomplete at birth, and so 'the mother must actually function psychologically for the baby for many months'. The first chapter of her book was called 'The Right to a Mother'. She described a disease, 'baffling until recently', known as infant marasmus—literally a wasting away—which she claimed 'was responsible, less than three decades ago, for more than half the deaths in the first year of life'. A special study, undertaken by both medical and social agencies, discovered that:

> babies in the best homes and hospitals, given the most careful attention, often drifted into this condition of slow dying, while infants in the poorest homes, with a good mother, often overcame the handicaps of poverty and unhygienic surroundings and became bouncing babies. It was found that the element lacking in the sterilized lives of the former class . . . was mother-love.

She gave as an example the case of a neglected child who slowly recovered through extra cuddles and a good foster home. But this recovery was not complete. Although physically and intellectually 'Little Bob' (shades of the child angels of the 1840s) was normal by the end of his third year, his 'emotional life' was 'deeply damaged'. With any change in his routine or during a prolonged absence of the foster mother, he went into a state 'quite similar to a depression'. So two crucial issues, the need for mother-love and the irreversible damage done by its absence, were raised. Throughout her book, Ribble recommended traditional practices such as rocking, lullabies, and prolonged breast-feeding because they encouraged contact and stimulation. Security in the relationship with the mother was the basis of good eating and eliminating behaviour. She gave examples of babies whose mothers were absorbed in social, professional or artistic pursuits, or were 'emotionally detached' from their babies. Their children had eating and elimination problems, slept too little, were hyperactive and badly focused, showed exaggerated sexual interest and practised auto-eroticism.

Jumping lightly from branch to branch of a sustained metaphor, Ribble concluded with a splendid cautionary analogy. Mammals, she pointed out, were Nature's most successful breeding experiment since eggs. Some eggs were hatched, and the young then cared for, but:

> sometimes, in the case of the cold-blooded reptiles like the dinosaur, the female laid the eggs in the sand, let the sun do the hatching, and left the infant in the hands of fate. There are some modern parents who seem to think this was a good idea; they do not wish to be burdened with the care of an infant. Particularly has breast-feeding gone out of vogue, and mothers say with spirit that they are not going to be cows. They seem even to prefer to be dinosaurs.
>
> When scientists find the unhatched dinosaur eggs in the sand near a few of the bones of the dinosaur parents they are apt to speculate on what went wrong with the system. After careful study, we can safely assume that one cause of their extinction was a lack of a relationship with their young . . . If in times of war we wonder what has gone wrong with our own system, we may perhaps find the answer in our still inadequate understanding of the mother-infant relationship.

The Second World War certainly had the effect, in Britain at least, of turning thoughts towards children and their mothers. The disastrously clumsy evacuation at the start of the war is remembered with amusement by some of the organizers. It must have shattered the psyche of many of the evacuees, particularly the last to be chosen of the groups of children foisted on half-hearted country matrons. Perhaps the experience of evacuation opened the minds of that generation of mothers to the ideas of the Freudians about 'separation anxiety'. In *The Problem of Anxiety* (1936) Freud wrote that anxiety in adults and older children was analogous to that experienced by the infant separated from or frustrated by its mother; if no anxiety of this sort occurred in infancy, then in later life the child would be more resilient to distress. Erikson extended this more positively, setting the mother's importance in a social matrix, not only as guardian, but as interpreter of the culture:

> Mothers create a sense of trust in their children by that kind of administration which in its quality combines sensitive care of the baby's individual needs and a firm sense of personal trustworthiness within the trusted framework of their culture's lifestyle. This forms the basis in the child for a sense of identity which will later combine a sense of being 'alright', of being oneself, and of becoming what other people trust one will become. (Quoted by Kagan, *Infancy*)

Logically, interest should have been stimulated at this point in establishing mother's 'firm sense of personal trustworthiness', but attention continued to be directed predominantly to Erikson's other requirement, 'sensitive care of the baby's individual needs'. The man most responsible for establishing the concept of 'maternal deprivation' in the popular mind was John Bowlby.

Dr Bowlby was asked by the World Health Organization at the end of the Second World War to study the mental health of 'children who were homeless in their native country'. His original report, *Maternal Care and Mental Health*, was reprinted in abbreviated form, a paperback *Child Care and the Growth of Love* in 1953. From that time on, most important manuals on baby-care mentioned or used his findings. 'Mother-love in infancy is as important for mental health as are proteins and vitamins for physical health,' he wrote. Birds hatched and cared for by human beings will fall in love with human beings in later life. One cannot be sure of the loyalty of a chow unless one has reared it from birth—any attempt to start after a few months would fail. 'These examples are perhaps sufficient to introduce the reader to the basic notion that what occurs in the earliest months and years of life can have deep and long-lasting effects.'

The main purpose of Bowlby's book was to make people look again at the assumptions and methods of institutions looking after homeless children, and to consider the possibility that even a bad parent was better than no parent. But it also had implications for ordinary family life. 'The absolute need of infants and toddlers for the continuous care of their mothers will be borne in on all those who read this book, and some will exclaim, "Can I then never leave my child?" ' Admitting that 'far more knowledge is required before a proper answer can be given', Bowlby advised that 'the holiday whilst granny looks after the baby, which so many mothers and fathers pine for, is best kept to a week or ten days'. Leaving a child under three years of age was 'a major operation, only to be undertaken for good and sufficient reason, and, when undertaken, to be planned with great care'. Moreover, leaving a baby to scream for hours 'because the baby books tell her to do so' was 'a common cause of partial deprivation'.

Maternal deprivation was as positively damaging in the first three years of life as German measles in the first three months of pregnancy. Once the baby's 'psychic tissue' became fixed, no recovery could occur—irreparable scarring remained. The baby might well not recognize its mother on reunion. This could imply a genuine injury to its power of abstract thinking, the loss of the capacity to identify. Or the child might have suffered so much that it was unwilling to give its heart again—it would withdraw and take up a lone-wolf attitude. In later life, its 'affectionless' character would ensure difficulty in forming meaningful relationships, and in all likelihood the child thus deprived would become a 'bad parent' itself.

Bowlby cannot be blamed any more than Freud for the fact that the meat of both men's findings has been borrowed from the world of the abnormal, where they were established, and applied over-enthusiastically to everyday life. Taken literally, these ideas meant that mothers had to devote themselves wholeheartedly to their babies to ensure their inoculation against the danger of emotional hang-ups and unfulfilled intellectual potential in later life. Kagan has summarized the duties of the modern mother as 'physical affection, sacrifice of the self's interests for that of the child, consistency of care, and enjoyment of interaction with the child'. This recalls Wolfenstein's perception of the obligatory nature of the new 'fun morality'. It is hardly plausible, except for the most saintly, to enjoy interacting with one's child while sacrificing one's own interests. But Kagan's analysis is correct—that is what mothers were, and are still, asked to do. Compare Buxbaum with one of the newest baby-care experts, Penelope Leach. In 1951 Buxbaum wrote:

> The young infant is completely dependent on his mother, she is his one means of survival. As soon as he recognises her and looks forward to her smile, to her handling, he is looking to her for the satisfaction of his most fundamental needs. He will be dependent on her love and be willing to do for her what she asks him to do. This relationship of the mother to the child is the very foundation of the child's existence.

Buxbaum's compensation to the mother for her maternal solicitude was infant obedience, 'he will . . . be willing to do for her what she wants him to do'. She made no mention of the two-way emotional satisfaction and reinforcement that more modern theorists have offered. For Penelope Leach love is far more than a means of survival. It is 'the means through which the new-born, wrapped in mystery, unfolds' (*Baby and Child*). Leach is of course a cuddler, a spiritual descendant of Lydia Sigourney. Loving a baby is 'a circular business, a feedback loop. The more you give, the more you get, and the more you get the more you feel like giving' (tiddley pom). She advocates 'sensitively concentrated attention', and admits that:

bringing up a baby in this flexible, thoughtful way takes time and effort. It involves extremely hard work as well as high rewards. But what worthwhile job does not? Bringing up a baby is one of the most creative, most worthwhile and most undervalued of jobs. You are making a new person, helped to be as you believe a person should be.

Although maternal deprivation could take place even if a mother spent all day in the same house as her baby, the crucial practical issue it involved was the question of day care, of mother substitutes, ultimately of whether a mother could have a job outside the home, or whether—as Leach clearly believed —no other job was possible. As the Women's Movement increased in strength and more and more women found the solitude of the servantless household between eight in the morning and six in the evening unbearable, mothers scuttled out of their homes as fast as psychological or financial necessity could carry them. How the manuals have coped with these unalterable facts is the subject of a later section on day care. Here it is enough to recall the standard assumption of earlier manuals that baby would have a nurse. They might have discussed whether to train her or to acquire her trained, how to dress her and how much to pay her, how to ensure she neither gassed the baby at bedtime nor infected it with loathsome diseases while flirting with her boyfriend in the park; but none of them questioned her existence, or the necessity of having help with children. Bowlby's requirement of 'constant attention night and day, seven days a week and 365 days a year' from mother or 'permanent mother substitute—one person who steadily "mothers" him' would have been tossed aside as lunatic. Handed from nursemaid to under-nursemaid, from monthly nurse to permanent nanny to nursery governess—what chance did any such unfortunate child have of growing up with a normal personality?

There have been enthusiasts who have asserted that several upper-class generations went to the emotional dogs because of such treatment. Jonathan Gathorne-Hardy's collection of scurrilous anecdotes about *The British Nanny* left one with little to hope for from them, although it did explain Churchill's excellence as the result of an exceptionally good nanny. Dr Mia Kellmer Pringle clearly believed the same, although she offered no specific evidence, when she wrote:

> In fact, among the upper middle classes in Britain in the nineteenth and early part of the twentieth century, parental involvement with children was quite circumscribed, being delegated first to nannies and then to boarding schools. That this markedly affected emotional and social development is strongly suggested by the available evidence, which however, is mainly biographical and autobiographical. (*The Needs of Children*)

Nor, Pringle continued, did 'the nanny's modern substitute', the au pair girl, make matters any better.'Most are young, and may have little understanding of a small child's needs. Perhaps worst of all, since they usually stay for a few months only, the child suffers the bewildering, if not traumatic experience of being looked after by a succession of such girls who inevitably bring with them the differing expectations and habits of their own national culture.' Mothers were thus left with no alternative but to devote themselves body and soul to their children.

I have dwelt on 'maternal deprivation' at some length, because it seems to be a fundamental issue still, and one which is closely linked to the Freudian assumptions—many of them, as Kagan has pointed out (see p. 278), not proven— underlying recommended child-care practice since the last war. It concerns feeding, sleeping, leaving to cry, and so on. But before attitudes to these are put into focus, the second major influence on baby-care advice must be considered—the work of Jean Piaget and his followers.

Piaget Ascendant

By the late 1940s doubts were being expressed about the accuracy of the psychoanalytic emphasis on nursing, weaning and toilet training, as research failed to follow prediction. These doubts were for the main part reserved for the pages of specialist journals of psychology, although the mood of uncertainty showed itself in the small swing to discipline of the late 1950s and 1960s and in a renewed enthusiasm for behaviourism. Spock's 1958 edition showed this clearly, as did other 'firm' books of the time—Willis Potts's *Your Wonderful Baby*, and Dreikurs's *Happy Children*.

Interest shifted to the work of a Genevan psychologist who had, since the 1920s, been studying how the infant acquired knowledge. Jean Piaget, born in 1896, started work as a biologist, and went on to study psychology at the Sorbonne. He later worked in a mental hospital, where he established his famous 'méthode clinique'. This was a way of asking open-ended questions which, when applied to children, gave quite fresh insights into the extent of their grasp of the world around them. He then tested the reasoning of children in order to standardize items for IQ tests. While doing this, he became interested in why children could not reason logically when they were young, but could solve the same problems easily at a later age. When he became director of the Jean Jacques Rousseau Institute at Geneva, there was a little nursery school attached to it—La Maison des Petits. Here Piaget settled down to construct his theory of cognitive development, the mainspring of modern research on infant minds.

Piaget had been publishing exciting ideas about cognitive development since the 1920s. Why did he take so long to be introduced into the popular manuals? To some extent he was overshadowed by the Gesell school of developmental growth, which provided quick and easy guidelines to both physical and mental growth. Both Gesell and Watson were looking at the phenomenon of the child and describing how it would grow and how it could be controlled. Freud dominated the emotional aspect of its development, setting it firmly in an environmental context. There was no space in the popular mind for a theory which based stages of growth on maturational competences contingent on the development of the central nervous system. Piaget's language and method were of a sufficient complexity to be baffling to many psychologists, let alone parents—he was the expert *par excellence* who needed simplification if his ideas were to be implemented. But once his message had been absorbed a major shift took place in baby-care advice.

Piaget described the first two years of the infant's life as the 'sensory-motor' period: this was subdivided into six stages. From being 'locked in eccentricity', the baby passed to a stage of accidental discoveries. This was followed by intentional behaviour, 'directed groping', and then came the ability to use symbols, first in language, later in imaginative play. From two to seven years old, the child went through the 'pre-operational' period, when he existed on the level of symbolic representation, imitation and memory. His thinking was still egocentric and dominated by a sense of magic competence— he simply could not conceive of the world from anyone else's point of view. Only intuitive discoveries, rather than those produced by logical reasoning, were possible. The next period, that of 'concrete operations' in the over-seven-year-old, only concerns us here in that it contained faculties which had once upon a time certainly been thought of as existing in younger children. The child could then think logically and manipulate symbolically, as in arithmetic. He could reason backwards, put things into series, classify them into groups, and perform other logical operations as well. After the age of twelve, the child could reason logically about abstract mathematical and scientific terms, manipulating variables and coming up with solutions. In order to explain exceptions to his pattern, Piaget used the concept of mental age—so a five year old who could perform concrete operations had a 'mental age' of seven; he had travelled faster through the stages of cognitive development than the average.

This truncated version of Piaget suggests why parents began to be told to 'stimulate' their babies. The Piaget-influenced manuals broke away from the old succession of chapters advising on sleeping, feeding, toilet training, and discipline, and gave instead a detailed month-by-month breakdown of the infant's development—particularly his cognitive development. They suggested ways of talking to, playing with, and encouraging the baby, so that he would grow up to be as clever as he could possibly be. 'Advice to mothers emphasizes rituals and purchase of toys that are supposed to promote the precocious growth of cognitive skills, rather than interventions that might affect co-operativeness, honesty, vitality or empathy.' Kagan saw concern with mental potential as a reflection of the rewards which an industrialized society holds for the technically trained adult. Certainly, now that computers and electronics have begun to suggest a world well beyond the ken of this generation of parents, sales of mathematical toys have begun to rocket. Rubik's cube is grappled with by every toddler. To an unfortunate extent, the concept of an elastic mental age has been taken as a challenge.

Perhaps the most extreme form that this trend has taken is the Better Baby Institute in Philadelphia, where Glenn Doman is attempting to maximize human potential by teaching mothers how to get the most from their children. The children of his 'New Renaissance' can read by the age of two (although they may not be able to tell you they can—it's a matter of faith). They compose music and poetry; their knowledge of maths and astronomy is officially encyclo-paedic. Doman claims that the mind of a young child is like the memory of a computer waiting to be programmed. It needs to be fed with data, and the earlier the input, the easier it is to enter. 'The ability to take in raw facts is an inverse function of age,' Doman is quoted as saying by Marjorie Wallace. Using a brain makes it grow, just as a muscle grows with exercise. Stimulation should begin immediately after birth, by shining bright lights on and off into a baby's eyes, clapping wooden blocks behind his head, and perhaps even putting a little mustard on his tongue. The next stage is to programme him to recognize shapes by holding huge black cards cut into triangles, circles and so on, between the light and his eyes. After he is a few months old, he is ready to learn to read.

Doman's method does not take Piaget's careful plotting of the stages of cognitive development into account in the least. His computer model is probably as distorting as Pritchard's telephone exchange analogy seventy years earlier, a flight of fantasy inspired by a new mechanical invention. But, unlike Piaget, his books are extremely readable. Hundreds of thousands of parents have bought his books, and have presumably tried springing up on their baby with scarlet flash cards. They are likely to emerge from the strange sequence of contortions that Doman recommends with a distinct sense of their own inadequacy as parents. Doman rules that, since all children are potential geniuses (environmentalism run amok, but arguably the spirit of our age), it is the mother's fault if the baby does not learn. The most interesting point about Doman is not whether or not his methods work, or whether they would be desirable if they did work, but that so many people are willing to spend money buying his books and learning kits. It could be seen as part of an attempt by parents to recover an initiative in educating their own children which the state has taken from them wholesale.

Fortunately for the parent who would like to foster his child's intelligence along more orthodox lines, Piaget has been thoroughly digested by manual writers. Brazelton's books, and Penelope Leach's *Baby and Child*, use a Piaget-inspired format. The later editions of Spock have a little cognitive development introduced into them. More open and simple Piaget for parents is given in such books as Mary Ann Spencer Pulaski's little primer *Your Baby's Mind and How it Grows*. This not only explains the baby's development in Piaget's terms, but gives concrete suggestions about ways in which the baby's mind can be stimulated by the appropriate play and toys. The ancient game of peek-a-boo has vital significance as an expression of the baby's sense of object permanence. When your baby is around twelve or eighteen months old:

> you can invent obstacle games. Build a low wall of blocks between the child and his favourite toy and let him knock it down to reach his goal. A sheet of plexiglass or a clear lucite chopping board makes an interesting obstacle. The child sees the toy but can't reach it, and has to figure out an alternative approach. As he gets older, you can make the task harder. Hide a pull toy, but leave the string visible. Put a toy out of reach but give the child a stick or plastic rake with which he can retrieve it. When he goes searching for unseen toys by himself, with a clear and intentional plan of search, you will know that he has achieved object permanence.

Notice the immense amount of effort that the mother is told to put in to encourage the child to learn object permanence. Yet it is not something, such as learning Greek, which the child would not do naturally.

Developmental psychologists spend their working lives bent over babies, observing at what age they can acquire particular skills. Modern manual writers suggest that mothers should imitate these experiments in order to make bringing up their babies more 'interesting'. The impression given in Pulaski's book, as in many other manuals written by psychologists giving a gloss on their own children, is that the baby's setting is less home than laboratory. Pulaski's favourite reference was to her two-year-old grandchild. The most successful toy she gave him, she wrote, was, at the age of one, a two-step kitchen stool, which he could drag all over the house with him, helping to cut out cookies and turn on the electric blender, and which was 'certainly safer than pulling out drawers and using them as steps'. A photograph showing the toddler clambering up his steps to see what was cooking on the stove accompanied these remarks. It seems unlikely that such adventurousness could be allowed without constant observation. We are back to Bowlby's 'constant attention, night and day, seven days a week'. The rationale has changed. Instead of just being emotionally damaging to leave a baby, alternative care could now mean that it loses out on 'infant stim', as the medical textbooks call it, and falls behind in the race for school places, technical careers and success everlasting.

This approach has been taken one step further by Mahler, Pine and Bergman in *The Psychological Birth of the Human Infant*, which sets out Piaget's work in emotional terms. They liken the first three years of the child's life to a slow birth process of the mind (which was exactly Margaret Ribble's analogy back in 1943). The mother is not recognized as a distant individual until the baby is six months old, and it takes two and a half more years before the child is 'a fully separated individual with his own identity'. This thesis implies that the baby's 'attachment'—a sort of ghostly umbilical cord—must on no account be severed by the mother's absence.

Piaget now overshadows Freud as the authority behind baby-care. Freud has not exactly been discredited, he is just very rarely mentioned; although, as we will see in analysing how babies are supposed to be brought up, he lives on. Parents probably feel more comfortable in the benignly scientific role of Piaget-like observer than they did as wicked stepmother or demon king. When we consider what the Freudian-style books had to say in their detailed prescriptions for bringing up babies, it will be clear how much anxiety they communicated. Much of what they had to say has now been relegated into psychologists' manuals of the abnormal. But the bias to Piaget has not made parents relax, although they may be less worried about their secret sexual yearnings. They are now handmaids to intellect instead of emotion.

Everyday Care

Modern manuals are either encyclopaedic or specialist. The strongest contrast that they present with earlier books is their concern with the mind rather than the body. Although advice on clothing may be offered, nobody works themselves up into a state over woolly Jaegers or healthy Aertex. 'Call the doctor' is the simple answer to any illness, and since the development of antibiotics, sickroom skills are rarely in demand. Instead states of mind govern everything—what the baby thinks about its feed, sleep or playtime rather than what it is actually being offered. Theorists offered parents good reasons for being alarmed about their children, and the manuals have made every effort to sustain their anxiety with new chapters on 'Worried Mothers' and 'Father's Role'. So the categories of concern change a little in this summary of advice since the Second World War. In this section the nagging daily problems of sleep, crying, and what to do with wakeful babies are dealt with; in the next, the Freudian 'big three'—feeding problems, toilet training and sexuality. Then we look at the child's need for intellectual stimulation, the critical issue of whether mothers should go out to work or not, and how one copes with discipline. Finally, parenthood itself—what the

246

father's role should be, and why so many mothers get so depressed about bringing up children.

Sleep is a vital issue to the parent who has no nanny to rustle into the nursery and cope. The Aldrichs' discovery that the baby's developmental plan involved a sharply decreasing need for sleep was not greeted with enthusiasm. Dr Spock's first edition allowed that babies should be left to take the sleep they needed. Some, he warned, were unusually wakeful. Although most slept for a little after meals, others didn't. They could be encouraged by a little rocking, and an older child could take a cuddly toy to bed. 'In simpler societies, grown-ups and children go to sleep curled up together, so let him have his favourite toys.' If the child kept getting up, 'keep putting him back to bed . . . and don't lock the door'.

Florence Swanson, in her contribution to *Your Child Makes Sense*, remained studiously vague on exactly how much sleep children needed, but went into the question of sleep problems at around the age of two in some detail. Parents were told to try and understand what a child was trying to tell them when he insisted on coming into their room two or three times a night.

> It may be related to his fear that his parents are going to leave him, or that he will not wake up after going to sleep [references to separation anxiety and death wish]. This frightened feeling is not remedied by spanking the child and putting him back to bed, but rather by additional attempts at general composure in the household and secure relationships between the child and his parents.

Sleeping medicines were to be avoided—although if both mother and child became over tense about the problem, the 'cycle of tension' could be broken by giving them for a few nights.

More traditional manuals, however, reacted against these novel ideas by returning to the security of sleep tables and the old assumption that 'many hours of unbroken sleep are vitally necessary for the rapidly developing brain and nervous system' (*Good Housekeeping Baby Book*). Ruth Martin, in her brisk *Before the Baby and After* (1958) declared that 'in the early days, the baby does practically nothing but eat and sleep—which is as it should be'. Mothers could expect their babies to sleep for twenty-one to twenty-four hours a day (yes, twenty-four) for the first two months, nineteen to twenty for the second two, and perhaps sixteen hours a day at six months to a year.

Dorothy Hudson admitted that the average was more like twenty hours a day in the first months, and very variable. But she remained determined to train the baby properly, criticizing parents who woke their babies up, or over-stimulated them to show them off to visitors. 'Parents may so easily make this mistake, encouraging their baby to take notice and show off how forward he is, when he would be far better off sleeping. The result may be a too active mind, and a failure, after a while, to settle normally into the routine of sleep' (*Modern Parenthood*). She was in tune with Willis J. Potts, who poured scorn on the free-wheeling attitudes of 'misguided psychiatrists' who said: 'Don't frustrate the baby, let him develop his own schedule.' This was as much of a mistake as the rigid schedules imposed on babies in the 1920s. 'Such nonsense! Babies like routine. In fact they are much like old folks, who want to eat on time, then relax and take a snooze' (*Your Wonderful Baby*). Although healthy babies would instinctively get as much sleep as they required, it was still worth adjusting baby's sleeping schedule to suit family life. Even Spock had wheeled a little to the right in the conservative early 1960s—if baby was wakeful after meals, 'I'd try to change his mind.' A string net could be stretched over the top of the toddler's cot. The message was gentle coercion.

This realistic middle road was not to be followed for long. Dr Hugh Jolly, a London hospital doctor who continued the dogmatic approach of Bull and Watson, offered parents small hope for peace at night. 'I am often asked', he wrote wearily in *Book of Child Care*, 'how long a child should sleep at night. The answer is as long as he wants to, and not any fixed number of hours.' A child no more needed a fixed amount of sleep than a fixed amount of food; individual variation was enormous. On the whole it seemed to Dr Jolly that bright children needed less sleep than others, and often less than their parents. 'No harm comes to the child from this. If in fact he spends his time at night playing, instead of sleeping, he is opting to work overtime. His parents have problems, not himself.'

Although this revelation led dozens of dedicated mothers to shake their torpid babies awake in order to keep up with the Jollybabies, more recent research has questioned the existence of a correlation between intelligence and hours of sleep. But Dr Jolly did not envisage the nightly shift work between parents that his facts on sleep implied. The baby's attitude was to be 'influenced'. Details of method were few—the idea was to 'convey the impression from the start that you expect your baby to spend his nights sleeping, not because he needs so many hours sleep a night, but because parents need a rest from children'. If all other means of comforting had failed, then the baby would have to be left to cry.

Added to the 1980 edition of the *Book of Child Care* was a new option, typical of the anthropological bent in modern baby-care: the family bed. In developing countries, Dr Jolly pointed out, the infant usually sleeps with the mother, and this makes night feeds easier. Like Ribble, he believed that stories of the dangers of overlaying and suffocating were exaggerated—perhaps stemming from deliberate infanticide. Single beds and separate bedrooms were a social custom which grew up in the eighteenth century, and there was now 'a growing tendency to return to the family bed'. Putting the baby between mother and father in bed 'will bring him closer to you both'. New bonds would be created, and a distant father became closer, even if away all day. Those who shared a family bed 'say that sexual relations are not a problem', although 'other rooms may need to be used at times'. The spectre of Freud was still not scotched. Did the pre-eighteenth-century families that Jolly recommended imitating skulk downstairs to the sofa too? Nor, he added, was bedwetting 'the problem that might be imagined'. The age at which the child left the family bed varied—it might be at around two or three, or even later.

At least people were trying to go to sleep in Jolly's family bed. Penelope Leach returned to the Aldrichs' view that the parent's job was not to train the child to go to sleep, but to educate her to stay awake. Naps taken in a basically wakeful day replaced the old picture of foods and 'playtime' briefly interrupting sleep. In fact, it was quite possible for a 'night-waking pattern' to get established in a baby. To comfort parents who believed that this was due to their own failure, she declared that 'at least 50 per cent of all children between one and two make a fuss about being put to bed. Night after night, toddlers are rocked and sat with, cuddled, taken downstairs again, nursed to sleep on the parents' bed, slapped, scolded and fed again'.

Leach's answer was neither the defeat of bringing the baby downstairs again, nor the desertion of leaving her to cry it out. Quick attention, before the baby was thoroughly aroused, might settle her off. Otherwise one could pay five-minute visits until the crying stopped: 'get her to see that you are there always, but at this time of day you are completely boring.' Leach was also prepared to anchor the baby physically in her cot, but only by the discreet means of keeping her in a legless sleeping bag, even after she could walk, or by guilefully dropping the base of the cot within its frame a few inches if she seemed about to climb out.

Another common answer to the problem of persuading a baby that it needed sleep when there was no sign of it needing any, nor any support from the books for the idea that it needed it, was the use of sedatives. Chloral was the last resort of the Illingworths, and Phenergan or Vallergan for John Cobb in *Babyshock* ('a new style baby book, mother rather than child-centered'). For the first time, sedatives in a healthy baby's life were recommended rather than deplored. Arguably this was an admission of defeat. Having denied parents the comfort of a predictable bedtime routine, by suggesting they follow their baby's 'waking patterns', the experts made nights a purgatory of indecision solved only by the use of drugs.

A clear indication of the rejection of behaviourism was the concern expressed over the infant's crying. This was no longer something which it was taught not to do, but a worrying phenomenon which required detailed analysis. It implied a failure on the parents' part in meeting the emotional needs of their baby. The Aldrichs had introduced the idea that a baby crying inexplicably, when neither hungry nor wet, might be bored; the new insight provided by the psychoanalysts was that baby might also be lonely or fearful. Whatever the cause of crying, the infant had to be attended to immediately.

> Often an infant whose cry has not been answered will become enraged. An infant expresses rage almost from the moment of birth. He knows he is helpless. By ignoring his cries or making him wait and perhaps laughing at his impotent anger when you do go into his room, you only irritate him further and increase his feelings of helplessness ... Whatever emotional closeness you might have established will be strained to breaking point.

Dunbar's advice was somewhat cryptic in the context of a newborn baby: 'Answer his call right away, and if you find he is making unreasonable demands, tell him so in a way he can understand. Instead of punishing him, or making him wait or ignoring his cries, show him what he can do for himself without you' (*Your Child's Mind and Body*).

The Illingworths revealed that much so-called crying in new babies was 'just shouting' as there were no evident tears, but they agreed that the crying baby should be quickly attended to. Crying for exercise was over. Personality could affect crying: 'Some are happy placid babies from the first day. Others will lose no time in making it clear that if they disapprove of things they will not hesitate to say so, and they cry at the least thing.' Alternatively, with a hint of Adler, the baby's very first cry could be seen as 'an overwhelming sense of inferiority at thus suddenly being confronted by reality without ever having to deal with its problems'. The mother was warned against interpreting crying as due to hunger. A good test of the hunger cry was that it did not stop when the baby was picked up, or only for a minute or two. 'We have seen babies offered the breast every time they cried, whereas all they wanted was to be picked up and loved.'

Although some postwar manuals took wind very seriously, offering X-ray photographs of where it lay in the stomach, most experts agreed with the Illingworths that 'crying due to wind is in fact due to something else—hunger, boredom,

251

loneliness or colic'. Dr Spock continued to allow wind as a source of discomfort throughout all his editions, although he added plenty of alternatives. But Dr Jolly would have none of this. Having pointed out that air swallowing was as natural to adults as to babies, he wrote:

> For reasons that are not clear to me, people in the western countries have become obsessed by a need to get the wind out of their babies. Mothers in primitive tribes have never heard about 'the wind', and there are also some western countries where the fetish of 'bringing up the wind' does not exist.

Mothers in quest of burps were inclined to interrupt their baby's feeds unnecessarily, Jolly felt, or to ascribe crying through loneliness to a need to burp. Since Jollybabies spent very little time flat on their back or front, it is possible that they were less susceptible to wind. Wind was not a problem often considered by nineteenth-century manuals—it was a spin-off from the attempt to leave babies alone in their cots or prams for so much of the day.

Crying from boredom became the most popular single reason for mystery crying. Such babies, who might be exceptionally intelligent, were far happier when carried around, propped in a chair, or kicking freely on a rug, even in their first few weeks of life, than when swaddled up briskly and tucked up to sleep like the old-fashioned 'good' babies. Penelope Leach revived Hugh Downman's plea from the eighteenth century for 'communicated warmth', when she suggested that 'comfort contact', rather than boredom, might be what such crying really demanded. Rather than interpreting the baby as an artful little monkey who had her parents at her beck and call, she felt that 'she is not crying to make you pick her up, but because you put her down in the first place'.

Alternatively, as 'infant stim' became more and more *de rigueur*, crying could be caused by fatigue, or over-stimulation. There had been little danger of this in decades more careful of the developing 'nervous system' discovered at the turn of the century, but modern babies, encouraged to experience life to the full, could quite easily become overtired.

Fatigue as cause was first introduced by Dr Spock in 1968. Leach gave a careful explanation of how the varying temperaments of babies meant that they had different needs. Normally welcome activities—play, bathtime, nappy changes, and even feeds—could cause crying if 'mistimed'. A life without routine had its hazards.

There remained a dustbin for all inexplicable crying in newborns—three-month colic. Again a reason for crying relatively new to the manuals, but vaguely felt to be digestive, colic was a mystery. For Spock and Jolly the only answer was for the mother to get away from the baby occasionally, to give herself a break. Leach would have none of that. 'You are faced with a bad few weeks. Although you cannot cure your baby's attacks, you cannot leave her to suffer them alone either. She will need all your time and attention while they last, so concentrate on organizing your life to free yourself to cope with the least possible stress.' For other experts, it was back to the medicine chest—even Leach conceded a sedative occasionally. Dr Jolly suspected that this problem, like so many others encountered by mothers, was due to the mother's tension rather than innate in the baby. 'Your doctor may prescribe an anti-colic medicine,' he wrote, 'but if it works it is more likely to be due to your becoming relaxed than to any direct effect of the drug.'

Misery could now be acceptably appeased, however, by the use of a comforter, or, as it was now respectably rechristened, the 'transitional comfort object' (TCO). The philosophy behind allowing teddy bears, blankets, or dummies (long appreciated by babies) was that they served to bridge separation between mother and child in the first three years, and quite possibly until later on in childhood, if not throughout life. Watson had disallowed toys in bed, and the era of hygiene had found TCOs disgusting. Dorothy Canfield showed a profound appreciation of comforters in her account of three-year-old Stephen's agony over the threatened washing of his teddy-bear. His mother's friend displayed 'a hideous, pitiable, tragic wreck, which she had said was a washed teddy-bear'.

'It suddenly occurred to me, Mrs Knapp, that the amount

of dirt and microbes that creature had been accumulating for two years must be beyond words. Molly drags it around on the floor, as like as not . . .'

'Yes, just like Stephen with his Teddy,' Stephen's mother had said.

'And once I thought of it, it made me shudder. So I just put it into the tub and washed it. You see, it came out all right.'

She held up the dreadful remains by one limp, lumpy arm, and both mothers looked at it with interest and approval.

When Stephen eventually recovered his teddy, shut by mother in a bureau drawer until she had time to wash it,

He sat down on the floor, holding the bear tightly in his arms, wave after wave of relief washing over him in a warm, relaxing flood. All his life long, ever since he could remember, more than three years now, he had gone to sleep with his big Teddy in his arms. The sight of the faithful pointed face, like no other face, the friendly staring black eyes, the familiar feel of the dear, woolly body close to him—they were saturated with a thousand memories of peace, with a thousand associations of comfort and escape from trouble. (*The Homemaker*)

The TCO has had a long and respectable history in children's nurseries, but only acquired enough status to be mentioned by the manual writers after the publication of D. W. Winnicott's *The Child, the Family and the Outside World*. Winnicott saw comforters as a symbol of the mother's breast which the baby used for the transition between the physical presence of the mother and the mental picture of her that the baby could eventually conjure up to help him while she wasn't around. Other thinkers added the idea that the comforter's significance was due to it being under the baby's own control, or being an extension of the baby's own body.

Although the Illingworths recognized that 'from a year or so, sleep often becomes associated with a particular teddy, rag, or toy, so that when tired he looks for and hugs the teddy, and demands it before going to sleep', major thought does not seem to have been given to comforters until the late 1970s. Spock added a long section on their importance in his 1979 edition, tucked in front of an approving section on thumb-sucking. Following Winnicott, he saw them as fundamental to the child's peace of mind, easing 'the first sense of separateness', which was noted by Bowlby and others at about that age. However unhygienic, unprepossessing or cumbersome, the comfort object had to be thoughtfully toted around, and a holiday without it could be a disaster. In a passage which hints that equality for infants may soon slide into positive discrimination against parents, Spock wrote:

> The little girl (or boy) creates certain comforting assurances of her parents out of her cuddly toy and her thumb for example. BUT it's not a parent who can envelop her or control her, it's a parent *she* can control. (It's interesting to see how a young child will sometimes abuse or slap the object which is so precious to her.)

Leach said the same thing in less aggressive, more 'magic world of childhood' terms:

> A baby's cuddly takes on a very real importance for her. It is her familiar; the thing that spells safety and security, wards off evil and promises your return. She may simply hold it and finger it, or she may use it in all kinds of elaborate ways. A scarf, for example, may be wound round her head with one end looped around her face so that she can suck her thumb through it.

From being despatched as unhygienic, comforters have become something of a cult. A teddy-bear rally was held recently at Longleat; whole shops are devoted to them; they covered every inch of the cover of Hamley's Christmas 1981 catalogue. The *Reader's Digest Mothercare Book* encouraged comfort objects to 'keep a toddler happy and willing to enjoy and explore new situations when he might otherwise be anxious and miserable', and emphasized that children might be expected to retain their comforters for four years or more.

Spock even wondered whether children should be positively encouraged to have comforters to help them through their experience of separation.

The ancient gods of fresh air and exercise no longer commanded much respect. Babies were understood to have a built-in capacity to exercise themselves, given reasonable freedom of movement, and the frantic legpulls and mini-press-ups of the age of austerity faded away. Mothers no longer felt called upon to spend long hours of the day out of doors with their children, although many still felt faintly guilty that they did not. A walk with baby became a feature of the routine written into the BMA publications, but now as much for the mother's good—reducing her sense of isolation—as for the baby's.

With less need to stay out of doors for long periods, there was a reversion to early-nineteenth-century standards in handling babies and carrying them around. Attitudes to the pram changed. Some fresh-air enthusiasts still advised using one of the old, high, carriage prams as a day-bed outside, but portable cots became so easy to put up when required that even this use declined. The soft baby-carrier tied around the parent's back or front was increasingly recommended for the occasional promenade.

The seeds of doubt concerning prams was sown in the first edition of Ronald and Cynthia Illingworth's conservatively reliable *Babies and Young Children*. The Illingworths wrote paediatric textbooks which have been touchstones of references for GPs since the 1950s. Their books for parents, although revised frequently, shifted remarkably little from their original 'common-sense' approach, informed but not carried away by the vagaries of research. A clue to their fundamental divorce from Spock's tenderness towards children is given by the quality of the cartoons with which both books were illustrated. Spock's mischievous toddlers are cheerful imps—the Illingworths' children have a genuinely fiendish quality.

The Illingworths criticized misuse of prams in their first edition (1954). 'It is very common practice to leave a baby crying for hours on end in his pram outside the house, with nothing to do but a brick wall to see, when all he wants is something to watch.' A later edition elaborated: 'You cannot expect the year-old baby to learn much if he is left out in the pram all day, without any play stimulation, morning and afternoon, and just brought in for a meal, change of nappy and bedtime.' But they repeated the longstanding requirement that 'the lining of the pram should be dark, so that there is less reflection on sunny days, and less dazzle for baby'. Babies in carrycots and prams continued to be sunk in black or navy gloom.

Dr Jolly saw a pram as useful, but emphasized that a baby could spend too long in it, even if he appeared content to sit all day. 'He should be encouraged to enjoy himself more actively by having the chance to play elsewhere. Spending too long in the pram reduces the stimulus for learning other activities.' Promoting intelligence was allied to the collapse of sleep routines. The pram as convenient soporific was replaced by soft cloth baby chairs which could be stood on the table for eye-to-eye interaction with baby.

Using baby-carriers is easier in city life—for jumping in and out of cars, trains or buses—or for country walking. Perhaps most important of all, it recovers a lost contact between mother and father and baby. Ann Oakley, in *From Here to Maternity*, records fathers' objections to pushing prams, but acceptance of light pushchairs or slings. The flimsy design of modern prams reflects their decreasing use. They tend to be too light for anyone but a passive baby to ride in, liable to topple over if rocked by a determined two-year-old. The massively permanent, carriage-built prams that reached a peak of liveried perfection in the 1950s and early 1960s have all but disappeared.

Oral, Anal and Phallic Preoccupations

When feeding babies came under the scrutiny of the Freudians, three aspects assumed a new significance: dealing with biting the nipple, when to wean, and how to avoid the traumas involved in thus separating the baby from its mother. Biting the nipple—not an issue which had hit the

257

headlines in former times—now had to be handled very carefully. Buxbaum cited a problem four year old who had bitten his mother's breast as a baby. 'The mother flatly refused to let the baby have the breast ever again. This early frustration was followed by a complete rejection of the child by the mother, who placed him with foster parents when he was an infant. In spite of their efforts, the baby remained undernourished and unhappy.' Her prescription to restore his eating ability was 'to "spoil" such a child with food in every respect. He needs a great deal of affection, especially during feeding: every whim of his, as to what, when or how to eat should be followed', so that he would eventually get 'a friendlier outlook on life'.

Spock was conscious of the problem of biting, but by 1979 he was allowing mothers to discourage biting without feeling guilty—'a finger slipped inside her gum and a firm "no" surprises and usually inhibits her'. Jolly and Leach babies never bit—at least no index entry on the subject is given. But the question of biting the nipple remains a reasonably important one, as it is a real fear in the minds of many new mothers wavering between breast and bottle, a hangover from the Freudian caveats and kid-glove treatment.

The Freudians' attitude to breast-feeding tended to discourage it. America had never been seized with fervour by the Truby King crusade: it was proud of the sophisticated and convenient formula industry. When the Freudians advised that weaning should be postponed to the middle of the second year, as the satisfaction of oral impulses was vital to the development of a healthy little psyche, even the enthusiastic flagged. Moreover, the rage for demand-feeding and schedule-free eating, in a society where embarrassment was still caused by the sight of a breast bared for action, discouraged natural feeding. D. W. Winnicott's concept of the 'breast-feeding orgy' was attractive only to the most liberated.

So, although breast-feeding continued to be classed as preferable, bottle-feeding became increasingly acceptable. Writers were also conscious of the possibility of failure. Bending over backwards to reassure mothers who couldn't nurse, they effectively demoralized those who could. 'When in doubt, leave it out', was Flanders Dunbar's catchy little aphorism.

Most young mothers wonder whether or not they should nurse their babies. You do not *have* to nurse your child. Scientific evidence today indicates that children who have never been nursed are just as healthy, sometimes more healthy, both physically and emotionally, as children who are nursed. If you want to nurse your child, by all means do so, but allow your doctor to suggest from the very beginning additions to his breast diet such as orange juice, extra formula, or cereal. If you are reluctant to nurse your child, if it makes you tense and uncomfortable, or if you are too busy and are just doing it because you have an idea that it is your duty, do not attempt it. (*Your Child's Mind and Body*)

Although weaning was to be postponed until the second year, mothers were advised to give up breast-feeding once the teeth started to come through at six months (the spectre of biting again) and to put the baby on to a bottle. They could reasonably feel that it was hardly worth starting to breast-feed if it merely doubled the weaning traumas. Moreover, to breast-feed a second child could create severe sibling rivalry. Bottles, visible, transferable, neat and respectable, were the order of the day for those who could afford them.

In the 1970s fashion changed. Research emphasized the chemical as well as the emotional value of breast-feeding. The few organizations which had remained true to the idea of breast-feeding—the La Leche League in the United States, the National Childbirth Trust in Britain—suddenly found themselves besieged by mothers eager to feed naturally. Reacting against the clinical pessimism of the paediatricians, they offered nervous mothers the best possible support—that of other nursing mothers. Sylvia Close, Penny and Andrew Stanway, and other writers emphasize the importance and ease of breast-feeding, using an atmosphere of relaxed confidence and mutual support systems rather than the old exhortations to duty typical of the Plunket nurse. Flexibility is the watchword. Breast-feeding can be mixed with bottle-feeding, so that a mother can go out to work and still feed her baby. It can be started up even after months of bottle-feeding—for that matter it can even be established in a woman who has adopted a baby. These are specialist manuals, however. Interestingly, in the standard works, Spock, Leach, Jolly and the rest, breast-feeding is still approached with caution. This is aimed, thoughtfully, at the mothers who don't manage to nurse their baby, but unfortunately has the effect of increasing the likelihood of failure.

It is now the province of the well-informed middle-class Western woman to try to breast-feed her baby, having taken as her model the contented native women shown by the anthropologists with babies tied round them in enveloping shawls, happily suckling as the mood takes them. Ironically fewer and fewer of these women in developing countries are feeding their babies. Besieged by advertisements for powdered milks (as used in the West) they are demanding, for status reasons, artificial baby food which their economies can ill afford. Low standards of hygiene mean that abandoning breast-feeding increases infant mortality, all in the name of civilization.

Concern over the toddler's feeding problems reached a degree only possible in prosperous, postwar society. The fussy eater, so briskly dealt with in earlier decades, was endowed by the Freudians with a significance out of all proportion to his size. The child's mouth, parents were told, was not just for eating with, but for exploring his surroundings with. The distinction between clean and dirty did not exist for the baby. He tried to feel and eat everything he could pick up—faeces and urine included. Children only developed a feeling of disgust from the reaction of the people around them. Buxbaum, whose views on feeding were referred to earlier on, produced yet another anecdote to scare mothers of toddlers. A little boy wanted to try a taste of mustard. His mother, 'generally annoyed about the child's attitude of wanting everything', thought that this would be a good opportunity to break the child from this annoying habit, and decided to let him taste a spoonful of mustard. Not having read Glenn Doman, the boy was stunned by the bitter taste, spat out the mustard furiously, and cried bitterly.

From then on, he refused to take any new food, and also reacted by vomiting to any food that was forced upon him. The mother tried to cope with the difficulty ... on the advice of an old family doctor, she proceeded to make the baby take back the food he had just thrown-up. The results of this experience were disastrous for the child, not only as far as his relationship to food was concerned, but also in his relationship to his mother and people in general ... He became distrustful, suspicious, had no friends, while at the same time craved affection. The experience of the mustard incident became symbolic of his relationship with people. (*Your Child Makes Sense*)

This sort of anecdote, better suited to a book by R. D. Laing than a baby-care manual, was typical of the horror stories at the back of mothers' minds when they attempted, with understandable hesitancy, to introduce their babies to solid food. The art of persuasion reached its height in Spock's classic description of the child who would only swallow mouthfuls offered alternately by mother and grandmother while his father drove his car slowly to and fro past the kitchen window.

Another element which could interfere with the child's enjoyment of food was 'emotional contagion'. Even small children sensed other people's attitudes about food. One little girl aged four months, quoted by Dunbar, would not eat liver soup when her granny served it because she detected the distaste felt for it by granny. When offered it by her parents, enthusiasts themselves for liver and bacon, she ate it with great relish.

Table manners also took a hammering under the fun-food philosophy. The atmosphere of experiment and fun was not to be interfered with while the baby was little. Even when older, parents should rely on the child 'following the pattern of the group' while eating, and not create possible hostilities and frustrations by making them use a spoon, or later a knife and fork, correctly. To tell children not to touch their food with their fingers made them connect the food with other dirty or dangerous things which they were told not to touch. This made the food 'unfriendly', and 'the baby is therefore justified when he refuses to take into his mouth what he is not supposed to touch'. A tricky four year old was cured by being allowed to mess his food around in innumerable ways until 'he convinced himself that it was neither bad nor dangerous; he could therefore venture to put it inside himself'.

It is interesting to contrast this anxiety with the bracing attitude taken in ration-book Britain. The Illingworths saw food refusal as an attention-getting device, usually caused by over-anxiety that the child conform to the parents' estimates of what, how much, and how their child should eat. While conceding that some foods were disliked by some children, their cure for 'the commonest of behaviour problems' was simply to ignore what the child did with his food, keeping the pudding out of sight until the meat course had had a chance, and not worrying unduly about the child's weight. If he didn't eat at one meal, he was certainly not to be given anything to eat between meals.

The tensions over feeding created by Freud were potentially relaxed by the experiment carried out by Dr Clara Davis on self-selected feeding. Referred to by the Aldrichs as evidence of the baby's competence in following its own developmental plan, it was taken up by Spock and many other writers with enthusiasm as a way to make mothers relax their worries over the quality and quantity of the food their children ate. The worries had been raised by the ideal balanced diets that the manuals had set up themselves. I think it is worth describing Dr Davis's experiment in some detail, in order to establish the fact, somewhat skated over by the manual-writers who mention it, that it is a laboratory experiment, unlikely to be reproducible domestically.

A group of fifteen children (aged from six to eleven months) was observed for periods varying from six months to four and a half years. A large assortment of cooked, raw, uncombined, unseasoned food, commonly used by older children and adults, was served to them, finely cut or mashed. They were given three meals a day. No food was given to them between meals. Complete data of the food served, consumed, and the food remaining were recorded. In the dining-room each child had his own small table, and all the foods were placed in the trays before him, each in a separate dish. The children ate with spoons or fingers as they wished and the empty dishes were refilled. The attendants were trained to refrain from talking, commentating, or displaying any interest in what was eaten. All the children ate heartily with keen appetite, day in, day out. It was not unusual for some children to eat three or four bananas at one meal, or five to seven servings of potatoes. One child frequently drank a quart of milk at the noon meal besides other foods. Yet none was fat; all were solid, well-built, healthy and vigorous children. They presented no problems in behaviour ... From an analysis of the 36,400 meals eaten by these children, it was apparent that their food intake in calories, proteins, carbohydrates and fat conformed closely to generally accepted standards.

The Davis experiment, although unlikely to be accurately copied in the home, made respectable the major shift which has ended 'nursery cookery'. The isolated mother, with only one or two children to feed, is no longer told to create bland messes of balanced protein and vitamin intake for the baby. The ideal is again an anthropological one, of babies helping themselves to scraps from their parents' plates, possibly made mushy by chewing in the mother's mouth, more often processed in a blender to suit them. Chewing, as the enthusiasts point out, has the added effect of pre-digesting the food a little.

Commercial companies have not been slow to move in on the trend to give baby his version of grown-up food. They make it easy for mothers who, dieting perhaps or still underrating themselves, are not eating a meal themselves in the middle of the day. Instead little packets or tins of roast beef dinner, cheese 'n egg supper, or apricot and semolina dessert can be thrust down baby's throat. Contrast these with the unambitiously flavoured infant foods of earlier decades— it is clear that the baby is coming much closer to sharing adult life.

The second bonus emphasized by the manuals advocating

these artificial preparations is a psychological one. Mothers are warned that stress can arise between them and their baby if it rejects a special preparation which may have taken a long time to prepare. Instant foods can be instantly junked if found distasteful, and the blame put on the manufacturer not the mother. Except in books regarded as somewhat eccentric (Levy's *Natural Rearing of Children*, Adelle Davis' *Let's Have Healthy Children*), bought foods are given equal ratings with the homemade product. The 'stone that turns all things to gold' is still the little bottle of vitamin drops, an insurance policy which guarantees that however rotten the bulk of baby's diet, it is getting some elusive 'essential goodness'.

Strictness about eating between meals relaxed considerably; snacks were after all a logical extension of demand feeding. Spock limited them to fruit juice or fruit, but Penelope Leach accepted that they were likely to become the most attractive part of the small child's diet, and suggested coping with a picky eater by changing meals into snacks and snacks into meals. So chocolate and crisps could be served with meals, and snacks should consist of plain bread, meat, and other hated elements of a 'good diet'. Making the curious assumption that mothers would be choosing only between snack foods and 'manufactured foods', she wrote:

> Snack foods are said to be 'all rubbish, no goodness in them'. In fact, these foods are neither more nor less likely to be nutritionally valueless than any of the manufactured foods you serve at table. A hot dog, for instance, is a nicely balanced item of diet. Dairy ice-cream from a reputable manufacturer is an excellent food, and at least as good for your child as a homemade custard or milk pudding. Even the lowly potato crisp (too salty to be good for babies) is only potato, with the water removed, fried in vegetable oil. As such, it is a surprisingly good source of vegetable protein, and in no way worse for a child than a helping of french fries.

The emphasis, in modern advice on feeding, is on the emotional satisfaction that it gives. Mothers feel they can leave worries over nutrition to the makers of the foods, and concentrate on their smiles as they spoon it in. Research, still very incomplete, on food allergies may soon temper this optimism. Hyperactivity, widely misinterpreted as a sign of intelligence, has been shown to be connected in some cases with food colouring—the yellow of cornflakes and the pink of cough mixture or pink ice-cream. If the packet is to be believed, there is a great deal more in 'the lowly potato crisp' than potato and vegetable oil.

Coping with excretion reached as fantastically complex proportions as breast-feeding once the Freudians revealed the true meaning of the bowel movement to the baby. Sphincter control was part of Freud's second, 'anal' phase, or Erikson's more veiled 'autonomy versus doubt or shame'. The issue of toilet training was an important part of the toddler's struggle for independence. 'Muscle Control' was Buxbaum's extension of the subject, and her analysis of it was as 'the time when parents ask most questions like when to allow and when to forbid, when to make demands on the child, how to praise and when to punish, and most of all, how to make the child mind'. In more recent books, which assume a more enlightened approach to toilet training, it has become known as the 'terrible twos' or the 'no!no!no! stage'. Holding on to or letting go of the bowel movements has become transferred to holding on to or letting go of mother, and separation anxiety has seized the minds of theorists as the key problem of the period. Erikson had hinted at this when he conceded that in societies where the anal zone was not the centre of child-rearing efforts at this age, some other aspect of behaviour might become equally significant in the battle for self-establishment.

The Freudians had explained that the bowel movement was seen by the child as an extension of itself. So when a parent asked the child to give it up, it was asking for a sacrifice of some sort from the child. As Selma H. Fraiberg put it, 'he comes to regard this act in the same way that an older child regards a gift to a loved person'. To insensitively flush it down the toilet was 'a strange way to accept an offering of such value'. Moreover, the toilet itself created quite new, twentieth-century problems:

This vitreous monster with its yawning jaws does not invite friendship or confidence at this age. The most superficial observation will reveal that it swallows up objects with a mighty roar, causes them to disappear in its secret depths, then rises thirstily for its next victim which might be—just anyone. (*The Magic Years*)

Opinion on how one should actually deal with the vexed question of the bowel movement veered from one extreme to the other. Although a variety of advice was always available, there seems to have been a swing from enthusiasm to deadpan, and finally back to qualified excitement. Thus D. W. Winnicott, who set the whole matter 'within the love relationship that exists between the two of you', sketched an A. A. Milne-style scenario in which:

> the baby, lying over there in the cot, finds a way of letting you know that a motion has been passed; and soon you will even get an inkling that there is going to be a motion . . . It is as if he said, 'I think I am going to want to pass a motion; are you interested?' and you (without exactly saying so) answer 'Yes,' and you let him know that you are not interested because you are frightened that he will make a mess, or because you feel that you ought to be teaching him to be clean. If you are interested it is because you love your baby in the way that mothers do, and that whatever is important to the baby is important to you. (*The Child, the Family and the Outside World*)

Training had to wait, therefore, until the child would be pleased to please mother. 'One lucky day, the child tells us or signals us that he is having or about to have a b.m., we lead him to the potty chair, get his pants down, and to his great surprise and interest the b.m. goes into the pot. We are pleased, he is interested and pleased that we are pleased, and the first step in training has been completed.' Fraiberg added that the stool should perhaps be left in the pot while the child was in the bathroom, in case the child was baffled by praise for his gift being followed by flushing it down the toilet.

Good Housekeeping's Mothercraft (1959) emphasized that

'elimination is closely bound up with the emotions, and for that reason the mother should train a child slowly and patiently, keeping to his own pace, and not making too rigid demands, which he is not capable of meeting'. It gave no further details of the reasoning behind the new mode of toilet training. Thus the digest of the Freudians' message was that the abnormal could be commonplace unless extreme care was exercised. Mystified grannies protested that *they* had never had all this trouble—their daughters could quote back to them Powdermaker and Grimes's caveat that 'many a mother has the feeling ingrained into her from her own childhood training that anything to do with the lavatory is dirty, repulsive and degrading'. Or they could point to Irene Josselyn's claim: 'The compulsively neat woman is eager to toilet train her child. In many cases early toilet training is a wish to be able to point with pride to that achievement. It is a tangible evidence of the ability of the adult to master that child.' (*Psychosocial Development of Children*)

Spock, always an accurate monitor of changes in thinking, began by declaring: 'I think that the best method of toilet training is to leave bowel-training almost entirely up to your baby' (1945 edn). The most parents could do was to guide, not to train. An amusing cartoon was subtitled: 'Be friendly and easygoing about the bathroom'. Possible pride and poss-essiveness in the products was mentioned and parents were warned that they must avoid a pitched battle, or an unhealthy guilt might arise in the child's mind connected with dirt. Moreover, 'you can never really beat him in a battle . . . all you can work with is his willingness'. Every child would com-pletely train himself, sooner or later, 'if no struggle had taken place'.

The late 1960s edition of *Baby and Child Care* was less sanguine, more positive and persistent. 'By the time the child is eighteen months old, I think you should begin his training even if there is no sign of readiness.' Spock then apologized for the anxiety caused to parents, and 'the present increased difficulty in toilet training caused by parent educators like myself.' The amusing cartoon was dropped. This was the era of deadpan impassivity. A swing from pride and possessive-ness to aversion was to be encouraged, and 'habits of

267

Fig. 3 This sketch, encouraging free and easy potty training, was dropped from later editions of Spock's *Baby and Child Care* when a demand for discipline returned

cleanliness resurrected'. Even if the toddler balked, training was to continue. Neither too much nor too little comment was to be offered. 'A few words of praise are appropriate,' offered Willis J. Potts, and 'grunting conveys an idea to the child's mind'. If pants were soiled within minutes of an unsuccessful session on the pot, 'curb the natural tendency to be cross . . . Total indifference will come to the rescue.'

Toilet training in the 1970s was seen as a power struggle rather than a basis for neurosis. Rudolf Dreikurs in *Happy Children* ignored the old Freudian fears and concentrated on training as a theatre for battle. Both he and Jolly felt that the solution was to play it cool—the child should be put back into nappies if it reacted against the pot. 'By this means [the mother] is removing the circumstances causing the child to do battle with her, so preventing bowel actions from becoming an area of conflict between herself and her child' (*Common Sense about Babies and Children*).

But Spock was following a new star, and abandoning the battlefield metaphor that had haunted bathrooms for so long. Fired by enthusiasm for Brazelton's guaranteed successful method of potty training, he swung back to his original theory that training should take place entirely in the toddler's own time, even if not until it was three, and that it should be accompanied with a good deal of smiling orchestration. Step-by-step detail of the technique was offered; special potty chairs, practice with nappies on, acceptance of the offering. That parents continued to find it impossible to be casual about potty training—perhaps because it led to such side-effects as the stool in father's hat that Dreikurs instanced—was reflected both by this lengthy and detailed section, and in the rash of specialist books devoted entirely to toilet training which came on the market in the late 1970s. All were confident of success, be it in a day, a week or a decade, and profusely illustrated. One thoughtfully showed mothers how to pull their toddlers' pants down. The general effect of psychology's analysis of the implications of toilet training has been for more attention to be directed to it than ever before. Wistfully Spock looked back to the simplicity of the old days, when he himself had grown up. His final statement on the matter was to emphasize its importance as a symbol of 'a life-long preference for unsticky hands, clean clothes, for a neat home, for an orderly way of doing business'.

A muddled time for parents and advisers alike also followed general acceptance of Freud's opinion that sexuality lay at the root of many childhood personality disorders. Bending over backwards to be frank and open, parents nevertheless mentally ticked off any mention of the genitals, or manipulation as masturbation was now known, as proof of Freud's theories. It remains true that an odd smirk appears on parents' faces when the subject arises, and the smirk is quickly transferred to the face of the child. Officially, sex is at the deadpan stage that toilet training once went through, though there are schools of thought that feel it ought to be included under the heading of fun.

In the 1950s C. W. Valentine stated a plausible case for sexual interest being merely an aspect of general curiosity. He pointed out that children who regularly saw each other naked and going to the toilet were totally matter of fact about it. One child certainly showed a great curiosity over her own navel, but there was no hint of penis envy among the girls or castration complex in the boys. He ridiculed Dr Susan Isaacs's tendency to interpret children's behaviour as symbolic, and quoted her report of a mother bathing a baby:

> At bathtime he got his duck and put it into the bath near the plughole, saying, 'Duck want a wee. Duck wee in hole. Duck have penis.' I asked him which was the duck's penis and he pointed to a place on its underside and said, 'Penis dere', but there was nothing like a penis there. (Quoted in *The Normal Child*)

Isaacs interpreted this as 'denial of castration anxiety', to Valentine's amusement. The story also revealed, he might have added, the obsessive interest the parent showed in extending the conversation about the penis which the child had introduced in a quite natural way. Valentine inclined to the escapist school which thought masturbation was caused by tight knickers, and pointed out how rarely parents reported observing it. Even his hated Susan Isaacs, 'in spite of her predilection for finding sex phenomena', could only find one instance of masturbation in her three years' observation of children at her Malting House School in Cambridge. 'Momentary touching' could and should be ignored, and he agreed with her that if a persistent case did occur, then 'the child is in need of skilled therapeutic help, *not* whippings or leg splints'.

Fraiberg's chapter on sex education (entitled 'Education for Love') criticized the 'agricultural analogy' of 'the daddy plants a seed' which 'at least two generations of parents have been grateful for'. But the truth, she added, tended to be effectively denied by small children who refused to believe, or to forget, as soon as they heard it. One six year old was quoted as saying loyally: 'Well, maybe some parents do that, but not mine.' Genuine sex education, thought Fraiberg, should be extended beyond the facts of life to the satisfactory establishment of male and female roles. Anxieties about the details of procreation usually reflected a personal uncertainty in the child which clear identification with the appropriate parent could solve. Lessons in the feminine arts of cooking, house-keeping, and good grooming had been moved out of the orbit of the family into school or Girl Scouts. Thus they were 'devitalized' and 'lost their vital connections with love, intimacy and the deeper motives that bring forth feminine identification'. In order for the tomboy to accept her fem-ininity, she had to be 'loved for herself as a little girl and loved for her feminine qualities'.

Spock juggled the confusing and contradictory advice on how to deal with sex in the under-fives with his customary dexterity. Again, one can track changing moods through his alterations. The first edition's advice to the mother who happened on some group sex play was to 'check your impulse to be shocked or angry. Usually nothing has to be said, because children turn to something else when in-terrupted in this way. If not, the mother can cheerfully suggest some other game.' By 1968, he decided that:

> you'll probably be at least a little bit surprised or shocked. In expressing your disapproval it's better to be fairly matter-of-fact rather than very shocked or angry. You want him to know that you don't want him to do it, but you don't want him to feel that he's a criminal. You can say, for instance, 'Mother doesn't want you to do that again', or 'that isn't polite' and shoo the children away on some other activity.

Parents didn't have to ignore masturbation and other sex play: 'We were all brought up to be disturbed by it, and we can never unlearn that. We can't be comfortable with our children if they are doing things we dislike.'

Commenting on the full swing in half a century from excessive modesty to full nudity, Spock found modern views 'healthier and more wholesome' but also warned that there was evidence that children could be upset by the overwhelm-ing sight of naked parents. They might make 'snatching gestures' which could be disconcerting for fathers. His final recommendation was for parents to keep 'reasonably covered, and have some privacy in the bathroom and toilet'.

Dr Jolly reflected on parents' 'probably inadequate knowledge of sex', and warned them not to give their small children too much information in an effort to shift responsibility fast. Freud's latent period might not be 'quite as free of sexual interest as some would believe it to be', so parents could no longer breathe a sigh of relief as their child turned six. He disagreed with Valentine over the rarity of masturbation—it was 'an almost universal practice in both sexes'. Any uneasiness that parents felt over it was due to their own sexual guilt. It was best for parents to avoid comment, although if a child insisted on working himself up in front of a great aunt, it could be explained that it was essentially a private activity, like nose-picking.

An aspect of sex education which had interested thinkers like Selma Fraiberg was the establishment of male and female rolès in childhood. But her emphasis on the importance of definite sexual identification became thoroughly confused in the 1970s by the Women's Movement's campaign to end sex discrimination. Writers who recommended dolls for girls and trains for boys were then criticized, as was the almost universal use of the masculine pronoun in books of advice. Response varied from Martin Richards's tepid footnote that he was loath to confuse babies and their mothers, so would retain 'he', through Spock's balancing trick, 'Your baby (let's say that she's a girl)', to Leach's wholehearted 'she'. Spock also added profuse apologies in his most recent edition for his bad old ways, but failed to add more than a veneer of egalitarianism in his first chapter. Jolly has remained unrepentant—as *Spare Rib* pointed out (Oct 1981): 'Fathers are advised to buy their sons Action Man if they want to play with dolls; and in his brief section on one-parent families he states, "a father has to provide a mother-substitute to run the home while he is out at work"!'

Certainly in their hints on sex education the manuals reflect the loosening up of inhibitions; coldness and brutality in response to natural sexuality have disappeared for good. The problem that remains is due to the uncertainty over what women think they or their daughters should be in the sexual context—and that is a matter that extends far beyond books

on baby-care. Probably the best book to face up to the subject
is Nancy Friday's *My Mother, Myself*.

Play, Day Care and Discipline

The intensity with which children's playtime was approached by all postwar writers on baby-care derived from its
dual importance, its implications for both emotional and
intellectual development. The psychoanalyst, long accustomed to play therapy, which allowed the child to reveal
hidden problems by 'playing them out', saw its function as
emotional expression. It was the means by which the child
showed what it really thought about itself and its family, and
by which it was relieved of guilt feelings, aggressions,
jealousies and other neuroses. The developmental psychologist, on the other hand, was interested in play as an aid to
cognition. Toys were crutches through which to grasp new
facts about the nature of the outside world. The same toy
could fulfil both approaches. For Spock a set of stacking
beakers provided useful practice in holding and letting go,
and putting things into things, and indicated emotional
readiness for toilet training. Pulaski, on the other hand,
pointed to their use in developing seriation, a cognitive
operation which underlay the concept of number. 'Logical
understanding of serial relationships grows out of years of
concrete experience of putting things in order, thus con-
structing the notion that sizes progress from small to big, or
from short to tall. That is why stacking toys graded in size are
important for baby.'
Meals, newly established as a funtime, were similarly
doubly instructive. Buxbaum, as we have seen, found mess-
ing about with food good therapy for children too frightened
of dirt. On the other hand, Piaget watched his son Laurent
with delight as he pulled bits of bread to bits and dropped
them systematically around his high chair.

Like a young Galileo, the boy was watching with absorbed
interest to see where the bread would land. If he dropped it

273

in front of him, the bread landed in front; if from the left side, the bread landed on the left side. This may seem unnecessarily messy experimentation to the parent with years of experience of the law of gravity, but for the child it can be a fascinating discovery. (Pulaski, *Your Baby's Mind*)

A photograph in Richards's *Infancy* shows a mother pulling a dramatic grimace for baby's benefit as he eats, and the caption runs: ' "Rub a dub dub . . . thanks for the grub . . . yeah, yeah, yeah!" Emotional rituals of this kind are important for both baby and parent.'

Erikson's essay, later lengthened to a book, *Toys and Reasons*, provided a basic text for the psychoanalytical interpretation of play. It was built around two themes—play as 'ego-synthesis' and play as identity builder. In the effort to establish his ego, the child moved from the 'autocosmos' (play centring upon his own body) to the 'microsphere' (his own little world of toys), and then to the 'macrosphere' (the world shared with others). Disappointment in the microsphere—the parent summarily clearing away an important construction or confiscating a valued possession—led to retreat into the autocosmos: daydreaming, thumbsucking, masturbating. Equally the microsphere was 'an indispensable harbour for the overhauling of shattered emotions after periods of rough going in the social seas'. The fact that in such solitary play the child could be counted upon to bring in whatever aspect of his ego had been ruffled the most was the fundamental condition for play therapy.

Erikson placed a high value on children playing alone, free from interference from other children or adults. It reflected child-rearing practice at the time, when for practical reasons children were left to play while their mothers occupied themselves domestically. Erikson's second contribution to playtime was his concept of play as training for life, as identity-builder. Thus the Indian boys' bows and arrows were applied first to birds, then rabbits, and finally to buffalo. As a matter of course, children were assigned tasks within their competence, and were expected, without undue praise, to perform them. To define play as we did in our culture, as 'not work', was to 'exclude our children from an early source of a sense of identity'. Because of the complexity of our civilization, children could not master more than a small part of it. Childhood tended to become 'a separate segment of life, with its own folklore and literature', instead of a preliminary to an adult role.

So although life had to be fun, play was 'a serious business'. Spock pointed out that 'a child loves his play not because it is easy but because it is hard'. The parent had to provide the child with toys suited to its stage in life. 'If all mothers and fathers thought more about the suitability of toys, there would possibly be fewer children in desperate need of skilled help in our psychological clinics today, and the problem child would cease to exist,' claimed Hilary Page (*Playtime in the First Five Years*, 1953). Charlotte Buhler explained how definite harm could come from allowing the small child to use older children's toys: 'Immature manipulation may result in damage and breakage, creating a sense of disappointment and frustration. This, if continual, is likely to cause some form of maladjustment to his material surroundings.' If too many toys were provided, 'decisions become increasingly difficult, and possibilities are bypassed in the ensuing mental confusion'. How, mused the intelligent parent, can I remove that inappropriately complex toy from my child without shattering her microsphere and sending her back into her autocosmos?

The digestion of play theory by the manuals led to a compromise. Powdermaker and Grimes wrote:

On as many occasions as possible, [the child] may be allowed to help, and he derives great pleasure both from doing the thing and from the feeling of responsibility and importance that it gives him. There are other times, obviously, when it is difficult and impractical for the child to take part in adult's work. Ordinarily a child of four cannot be allowed to use the kitchen stove for fear of burning himself; he cannot use the washtubs because they are too high; and he cannot set the table without close supervision because he might break the plates.

Instead, he could be given toy versions of these domestic activities, and exercise his imagination by pretending they were real. His concentration span was inadequate for any real use to be made of his assistance. If these fantasy adventures were not enough to give him the necessary sense of identity with the real world, then he could be taken out on trips to building sites, railway stations and small centres of production where it was hoped that he would grasp what it was all about.

Concern over ego-synthesis was replaced by the followers of Piaget with an emphasis on the role of play in cognitive development. Play was not just a serious business, it was a stimulus to intelligence. Moreover, an adult presence—preferably the mother—was an essential. Dr Jolly claimed that, although 'development cannot be hastened', it 'can be discouraged by lack of love or interest'. Plenty of attention, mothers inferred, could turn their babies into cleverer children. From about eighteen months to three years, 'a toddler expects to have the undivided attention of his mother ... This is such an important learning period that you should be involved in his play even though at times your role is to sit quietly observing. But that does not mean that you can read your book. The intelligent toddler will soon complain about that.' There were 'certain quite short periods when the child is particularly ready to develop in particular fields', and 'you must be ready to respond to cues from your baby'.

Leach expected similar devotion from the mother. The baby of three to six months 'has ... a full programme of activities mapped out for these months. But very few of them are activities which he can start alone, or conduct without help for more than two minutes.' Rapidly substituting toy for rattle for tactile object was not enough. The baby often wanted social play, 'to interact with his mother ... Without fairly constant help and attention and plenty of freely given social play, he gets bored; when he is bored, he gets cross.' Imagine, she suggested, that you were paralysed, unable to speak and explain what you wanted—exceptionally responsive and thoughtful nursing care would be needed to make you comfortable. Similarly, your baby's needs should be considered, predicted and catered to . Admittedly, how completely you could do this depended on how rich you were.

> Simply in terms of time, the mother who can do a week's shopping in the family car and store it in a large fridge, pop the day's washing in an automatic machine and call running a vacuum cleaner over carpeted floors 'housework' has an enormous advantage over the mother who must push the pram daily to distant shops, queue in a launderette, and wash linoleum. Somehow these simple facts are too often ignored in research into child-rearing. (*Baby and Child*)

Before lower-income groups dropped Leach into their inadequate pedal-bins, she offered them a few crumbs of comfort by revealing that although child developmentalists paid lip-service to the idea that early experiences were important to later development, 'the proposition was notoriously difficult to prove . . . In fact many people have now reached the conclusion that it is the "general atmosphere" which surrounds the child, rather than specific practice which is important.' Ready response to crying was the only practice which researchers had discovered to have a correlation with a degree of attachment to mother. Nevertheless, she concluded, 'highly attentive, responsive, socializing mothers were the ones who had the infants who were well advanced in all fields and strongly attached to them'. Slam went the dustbin lids.

Leach, Pulaski, Richards and earlier theorists like Valentine made the point, either in their prefaces or throughout their books, that they based much of their advice on experiences with their own children. The impression given by their books is that a mother has little to do except bring up her children. Erikson's play as an apprenticeship for life is not possible in a world especially tailored to the child's needs—unless the life to be lived is that of a developmental psychologist.

Despite received ideas on the importance of the mother to the small child, manuals had to cope with the undeniable social fact that more and more mothers were going out to work. Dramatic increases in the numbers of working women took place during the 1950s, and the trend has steadily continued. Manuals began to recognize the problem of adjustment for women who left jobs to become mothers, instead of assuming, as romantic fiction continues to do, that wedding bells and a baby was what life was all about. 'Putting the jam on the bread,' rather than acute financial need, was quoted as the most common motive for working mothers in Yudkin and Holme's 1963 survey. But allied to this was 'the dual motive of boredom and loneliness'.

It took some time for manuals which had absorbed Bowlby to accept the possibility of a mother not spending all her time with her baby. The Illingworths and Spock discouraged it in their earlier editions, except in cases of acute financial need. 'It would save money in the end', Spock argued, 'if government paid a comfortable allowance to all mothers of young children who would otherwise be compelled to work ... Useful, well-adjusted citizens are the most valuable possessions a country has, and good mother care during early childhood is the surest way to produce them.' He generously allowed 'a few mothers—particularly those with professional training' to work, because 'they wouldn't feel happy otherwise ... after all, an unhappy mother can't bring up very happy children'. There was none of Thomas Wentworth Higginson's 1882 plea not to exchange present goods for prospective and merely possible ones. If mothers had to go to work, then they should provide individual care for their children until about the age of two, and by the 1958 edition this had risen to the even more conservative age of three.

In the 1970s a remarkable volte-face took place in many manuals. Research by psychologist Jerome Kagan in a specially constructed day-care centre in Boston led him to the conclusion that such care affected neither attachment to mother nor rate of cognitive development, 'the two critical concerns of American parents'. His studies suggested that the dreaded 'separation anxiety' was a normal stage of development, a 'maturing of the cognitive competence' which emerged at seven months, peaked at eighteen months and then declined in most children. It was not an abnormal feature, caused by a mother's mishandling of her child. Kagan had his critics as well as his supporters, but a debate had at

278

least been initiated. The guiltily unhappy new mother, distorting her natural inclination into a lap with an encouraging smile on top, could see a light at the end of the tunnel of togetherness.

The Illingworths qualified their original caveat, 'we feel very strongly that it is undesirable for a mother to go out to work when her child is under three years of age', to the more objective 'many people feel . . .'. They admitted that 'extensive research has not shown that children suffer from their mother being at work, provided that suitable arrangements are made for them', and that 'research has shown that a mother who works is less likely to have psychiatric problems than the one who stays at home'.

Dr Spock jumped on to the new bandwagon with an agility remarkable for a man of his age. His previous skimpy section on working mothers, sandwiched between premature babies and handicapped children in a group of miscellaneous problems at the end of the book, was totally overhauled and refitted into the first chapter. He faced up squarely and generously to the case for women's liberation and equality of job opportunity. Parents could perhaps both cut down to part-time work, or arrange that their work dovetailed, so that they could care for the baby between them. Men should explain at work that they had responsibility for the care of their children in order to inspire others to do the same. But before all free women rush out to buy Spock, they should read the small print. The work that mothers yearned for was cunningly undermined, described as rarely satisfying, far more often merely a means to the twin ends of status and money. Nevertheless, he conceded kindly, women 'quite fairly ask to enjoy the same status as men, and there is no reason why they shouldn't go out to work if they feel limited or frustrated by home life'. They were, after all, he might have added, the children of the 1950s, brought up never to be limited or frustrated at all.

In discussing day-care, Spock made it clear that it would be very difficult for the mother to leave her child in fact. He pointed out that children in day-care didn't have 'the daily stimulation from loving parents' that the child at home received.

They read to her, show her pictures. These are the attitudes that foster emotional depth and a keen intelligence ... Whether the children will grow up to be lifelong optimists or pessimists, whether warmly loving or cool, whether trustful or suspicious, will depend to a considerable extent on the attitudes of the individuals who take care of their first two years.

Bowlby's attachment and loss spectre was reinforced by the threat of the IQ, of not attaining 'full intellectual potential'.

The caretaker envisaged by Spock for the mother who asserted her right to work was an archaic figure. In a passage descended directly from the ancient advice books on the qualities to be sought in a nurse, he wrote:

Most likely it will be a woman. Towards the children she should be affectionate, understanding, comfortable, sensible, and self confident. She should love and enjoy them without smothering them with affection. She should be able to control them without nagging or severity ... Avoid a person who is cross, reproving, fussy, humourless or full of theories ... Cleanliness and carefulness are more important than experience ... Some people focus on the education of a nurse or childminder, but I think it's unimportant compared with the other qualities, especially for young children.

For Jolly, nannies had two major drawbacks. One was that they might fill the mother's role in the child's life. The second was the 'danger that particularly the old-school nanny will not agree with your basic premise of fun rather than perfection'. Notice how smoothly the mother is told what her basic premise is. Jolly also criticized the traditional resort of the working mother, the use of granny as caretaker. The point has already been made that one of the reasons mothers looked to books rather than their mothers for advice on baby-care after the Second World War was that so much radical new thinking, and new styles of life, made granny seem a little dated. Every mother knows the feeling of uncertainty which encounters with grannies can produce. However, the uncertainty is as likely to be caused by distance. If she is a rare visitor, granny's lack of knowledge of her grandchild conflicts with her own assumption—traditionally correct—that her wisdom in such matters could be passed on to her daughter. Jolly doubted whether a mother's mother could be of use to her, and instead made her a positively risky person to leave the baby with. It was 'taken for granted', he wrote, that the new mother 'will have the advice of experts and will not have to rely on the advice of her own mother. The previous generation of mothers may not necessarily be the best advisers of the present generation.' After reading his book: 'I hope that you will be able to make decisions from your own instincts . . . and you will be less influenced by the rigid rules laid down for the upbringing of previous generations of children.' Ultimately, 'you are likely to be happier if you take a short-term view of life for a while after your baby is born, regarding his care as your present job and letting your future career look after itself'.

Experts who felt that mothers shouldn't leave their small babies cloaked their (quite reasonable) position with the crumb of comfort that motherhood ought to be seen as a job. The young Spock had called for a wage for mothers, and this idea continued to have a following. Leach, whose approach to motherhood was such a total one, repeatedly put it into a job context, and with deafening silence made no reference whatever to the debate over working mothers and quality of caretakers which raged around her. The unfitness of the analogy was apparent when she wrote:

> Being a mother is probably the most exhausting job which exists in Western society. Hours on duty and on call add up to twenty-four per day. There are no overtime payments, time off in lieu, money for unsocial hours. No weekend or holiday breaks are provided, and you only get a tea break if you make the tea yourself. The pay is usually atrocious. No union would stand for it.

By this stage it should be clear that motherhood is not a job, any more than childhood, adolescence or senility is. Cat-egorizing it as a job put mothers on completely the wrong tack, and ensured dissatisfaction with the appalling 'conditions of service' which Leach outlined. Leach's own justification for the 24-hour-a-day devoted attention which she felt the baby deserved from its mother was that having a baby was a choice (just like a job). 'Unrealistic though this view of dedicated parenthood may be, I make no apology for it,' she wrote. 'In these days of good contraception and world over-population, there is a moral obligation to rear as well as we can the children we have.'

Alternately, some parents are trying to stop the exclusion of the child and the isolation of the mother by taking babies out into the real world. This has a certain logic to it, particularly since the dangerous factory conditions which led to their legal exclusion from working life in the mid-nineteenth century have largely disappeared. It would require a major shift from child-centred life for parents: children would have to be brought up to fit in in a way they do not at present. We would have to reconsider Watson's ideal of 'a child who is willing to be around adults without fighting incessantly for notice'. The popular anthropological parallels accommodate the idea comfortably: mothers bend over the rice fields with babies slung across their backs. Perhaps the hot-house nursery years are coming to an end.

The question of discipline—of making the child conform to certain requirements—was redefined by the new approaches to baby-care as a problem of coexistence. With no long-term aim but that of having fun, the spectre of discipline only arose when the parents reached the limits of their tolerance.

At first, the existence of those limits was skated over. Full of the importance of baby's right to follow his developmental plan, to explore and discover just as his inner drives directed him, the Aldrichs, Ribble and young Spock denied any possibility of 'spoiling'. The infant had to be free to eat, sleep and play as he pleased. Earlier descriptions of managing these issues have made it clear that coercion or punishment was not to be considered. Drugs were more acceptable than desertion.

A little later in the baby's life, Fraiberg explained:

all the clever stratagems, the household recipes for obtaining the co-operation of a child in the control of impulse boil down to one essential point: the child co-operates in his training because he wants parental love and approval and he feels parental disapproval as a temporary withdrawal of affection and esteem. (*The Magic Years*)

Loss of self-esteem in this manner produced 'the feeling we call "guilt" '. Guilt was a concept which had to be handled with kid gloves, since psychoanalysis had established it as the basis for countless neuroses. Enough guilt had to be felt to inhibit wrong behaviour, but not so much that the child ended up 'feeling like a potential murderer'. The child was not to feel rejected for his misdoings. 'If our reaction is of such strength that the child feels worthless and despised for his offense, then we have abused our powers as parents, and have created the possibility that exaggerated guilt feelings and self-hatred will play a part in this child's personality development.'

In practical terms this meant that if a child bit his mother, 'the only thing you can do to keep from being bitten again is to draw back when he gets that gleam in his eye' (Spock, 1945). To understand everything is to forgive everything, and biting was simply a stage in the child's assertion of his individuality. Sibling rivalry was another occasion on which tolerance was demanded. Having a second baby was compared to bringing home a second husband. The second child should be neglected as much as possible in favour of the first child, suggested Spock. Nappies and feeds should be dealt with as far as possible while the older child was out of the house. Father should be primed not to inquire after the newborn's well-being when he returned from work, and the older child should never be compelled to share toys with the baby. Apparent affection from the older child should be regarded with suspicion as it probably veiled fierce jealousy.

Limiting discipline to psychological warfare meant that any form of corporal punishment was out. Elinor Smith summarized as well as ridiculed the new position:

Spanking, hitting with old sneakers, throwing andirons, locking the child in a dungeon with nothing but bread and water for a week, slapping, pinching, biting, kicking, using the stocks or pillory are frowned on by the modern psychologists. And by modern parents too. (Frowned upon for the parents, that is. These things are simply the signs of a healthy, outgoing personality on the part of the child.) (*Complete Book of Absolutely Perfect Baby and Child Care*)

Instead the ideal was calm discussion with the child about the rights and wrongs of the position. The Parent Effectiveness Training movement was Dr Thomas Gordon's attempt to bridge the generation gap with improved communication, family councils and the 'no-lose' method for resolving conflict. 'Parent and child are in a situation in which their needs conflict. The parent asks the child to join him in trying to find a solution acceptable to them both. One or both offer possible solutions. They evaluate them, finally choosing one acceptable to both' (*How to be an Effective Parent*). Maureen Freely's novel, *Mother's Helper*, parodied this system of child-rearing with black accuracy, revealing its reliance on parental casuistry and evasion.

Child-centred discipline was not slow to fall into disrepute in a social context. Spock's third edition (1968) showed new thinking. Spoiling, even in the first few weeks, 'clearly is possible'. Although harm done at this stage could usually be undone in a few days, by three months 'you can be a little more suspicious'. As a result of three-month colic, a baby could well have been walked and amused for long periods. 'Naturally they want their company anyway. Now it's time to turn a little less tender-hearted. I don't mean you should turn severe all of a sudden. But when it's bedtime you can tell your baby cheerfully but firmly that he has to sleep and that you have to go, even if he cries for a few minutes.'

Other causes of spoiling were 'a parent who's too eager to amuse ... parents who submit too easily ... parents who have waited for a long time for a baby, or adopted one'. Whatever the underlying factors, 'these parents are a little too willing to sacrifice their own comforts and their own rights, too anxious to give their babies everything they ask for'. Babies needed firm guidance from their parents, and would be made uneasy by such shillyshallying. Other books in the 1960s took this 'firm line' approach, and a new interest in behaviourism as a psychological disciplining technique developed. Permissiveness became a dirty word, widely blamed upon the Freudians' theories, although the Freudians could and did argue that when their theories did lead to excessive permissiveness, it was generally because they were misinterpreted.

To return to practical terms, parents did not just have to draw back to avoid being bitten, they could also 'show quite clearly that they don't like it, and won't let it happen again' (Spock, 1958). Second children stood a much better chance of survival now that parents were told to 'let their love of the new baby be evident', and not just to pretend to hug the older child who advanced on the baby with a grim look and a weapon, but to 'jump and grab him and tell him that he can't hurt the baby'.

Sibling rivalry was a key concern in discipline, as it tended to be the first serious arena of confrontation between toddler and parent once meals and pots were conceded without a fight. Spock clearly felt profoundly guilty about the whole affair.

Jealous quarrelling between brothers and sisters has recently been tolerated MUCH MORE than it was in the previous generation. The psychological reasoning has been that jealousy is normal; if it is inhibited too severely, by making a child feel excessively guilty it can cause various disorders of the personality. Parents shouldn't be badgering their children over *every little* thing, anyway. There is considerable truth in these concepts. But when parents have followed them too exclusively, without consideration for the rights of the family or the ethics of society, the jealous child has been allowed to be much too mean to the younger one, has kept the family in an uproar and ended up with a guilty conscience anyway, because of the cruelty he has got away with. (1968 edn)

Sibling rivalry remained a standard entry in indexes of children's problems. Few writers had the courage of Mrs Frankenburg, who maintained (in the 1954 edition of *Common Sense in the Nursery*) that the opinion of consultant psychologists, 'who only see maladjusted children', was mistaken. 'They are prone to think that the exception is the rule. Most of them, for instance, take it for granted that jealousy when a new baby arrives is a normal reaction, whereas it is nothing of the kind.' Although 'the dowager baby' had to be looked to, jealousy did not have to be assumed. Today jealousy is now so accepted that most children are swift to fulfil their parent's expectations of it.

Attempts at promoting firmer handling of babies in the 1960s were countered by research. Frank Donovan suggested that:

> a child's developing sense of initiative may be discouraged because many of the projects dreamed up are of a kind that cannot be permitted and the child feels he is faced by a universal NO . . . It is very important, therefore, for healthy personality development that much leeway and encourage-ment be given to the child's show of enterprise and imagination and that punishment be kept at a minimum. (*Raising Your Children*)

These 'noes' should not be resented by the parent. They are 'the only tool which the two-year-old has at his command to express his unwillingness to do as we wish him to'. Requests to the child 'should be couched in the form of "Let's do this, shall we?" implying a willingness to meet him half way'.

Opinions on discipline remain very different; the lap theorist and the Olympian continue side by side. Advice on temper tantrums is a good illustration of this. The approach favoured by iron men and women is described in an article on 'The Elimination of Tantrum Behavior by Extinction Pro-cedures', which is quoted in detail by Frank Donovan. Like the wash-stand approach (p. 151), it involved firm action, 'consistent with the learning principle that, in general, behavior that is not reinforced will be extinguished'.

> A parent put S. to bed in a leisurely and relaxed fashion. After bedtime pleasantries, the parent left the bedroom and closed the door. S. screamed and raged, but the parent did not enter the room.

On the first night S. screamed for forty-five minutes. On the second night she did not cry at all, probably because she was too exhausted from the performance of the first night. On subsequent nights the tantrum was of shorter duration until, finally, by the tenth occasion S. no longer whimpered, fussed or cried when the parent left the room. Rather, she smiled as they left.

Leaving that rather macabre smile aside, consider Penelope Leach's method. She saw the tantrum as an expression of extreme frustration, 'an emotional blown fuse'. It was 'most usual in active, energetic, determined children', and was 'not within the toddler's control at all'. The mother's main task was to make sure the child didn't hurt himself or anyone else, because to recover to proof that he was dangerous would be traumatic for him.

So it may be best for his mother to hold him, on the floor, secure in her arms. As he calms down he finds himself close to her. He finds, often with touching amazement, that everything is quite unchanged by the storm. Slowly he relaxes, the screams subside into sobs; the furious monster reverts to a pathetic baby who has frightened himself silly.

To avoid temper tantrums, mothers should be as patient and tactful as possible. 'Very few issues are worth a direct clash ... The mother needs to ask herself, "Why can't he? Do I really mind if he does?" The mother's mouth may be open to say no when just in time she realises that the issue doesn't really matter'—at least not to a doormat.

The final modern word on the subject deserves to go to Brazelton, who reflects recent interest in the mother rather than the child. Referring to Anna Freud's perception of the 'disintegration of the baby or child's ego at the end of a day', he added, 'it appears to me that the mother's ego disintegrates simultaneously'. On the subject of discipline he interested himself in the establishment of 'limits'. In the eighth month, 'when the baby begins to tease for attention and also begins to understand "no", it is time for parents to begin to think about setting limits'. These limits were not just for the good of the child, giving him a sense of security, but for the preservation of his parents' sanity. So

> bedtime is largely a parents' decision, it should be handled firmly, and with an understanding of the fact that few children ever want to give up at night ... No mother can tolerate night demands over a long period, especially with other children who need her ... I am sure that children, in some way, understand and appreciate our need for independence at night. They may not like it, but in our culture we expect them to develop such independence.

If the Aldrichs discovered in 1939 that babies were human beings, Brazelton revealed in 1974 that parents were as well— tired, fallible human beings, needing reassurance as much as their children did. In his books at last we can read about real babies and real parents.

Busy Fathers, Worried Mothers

One solution to the mother's quandary was to share parenting, to allow and enable fathers to take on infant care. Traditionally, the baby had not been the father's province; most of the references to fathers in the manuals left him in the background. Lacking breasts and being out to work all day were potent disadvantages. But with effective substitutes for mother's milk, and part-time or flexitime work, the situation could change. Psychoanalysts approved of an increased fatherly presence, pointing out that his absence too often left little boys without a point of reference for imitation.

In America the matter was encouraged by a fear of matriarchy which emerged openly after the Second World War. Edward A. Strecher examined what he called 'An American Problem' in *Their Mothers' Sons*, a book inspired by the 'cold, hard facts that 1,825,000 men were rejected for military service because of psychiatric disorders, that almost another 600,000 were discharged from the Army for neuropsychiatric reasons or their equivalent, and that fully 500,000 more attempted to evade the draft'. These men had the common failing, Strecher asserted, of immaturity. 'Maturity is not an inborn trait; it is not hereditary. It is the result of early background, environment, training, and unselfish parental love . . . In the vast majority of case histories, a "mom" is at fault.' Strecher's 'moms' were the overpossessive, dominant mothers who failed to loosen the psychological apronstrings that bound their children to them.

Phyllis Hostler's *Child's World* showed opinion moving along the road to shared parenting, although she described the father as 'the first intruder' into the 'magic circle' of mother and child. Nevertheless, 'in these enlightened days' he was allowed 'more privileges to bring a dry nappy from the airer, or supply extra pocket money, or take charge of the Sunday walk'. While the child was still in arms, Hostler warned that 'he may show a marked lack of appreciation for his parent. He realizes he has a special interest in the mother and a particular claim to her attention . . . the baby will sometimes push him away as he bends to kiss the mother' (so much for the argument that using the masculine pronoun for baby makes for clarity). Without reflecting that such behaviour was due to traditional handling rather than being natural to the baby, Hostler decided to offer the father a participatory role only later on in childhood. Even then, it was via the mother's mediation. She had to prime the child with the right attitude towards the absent threat. Instead of: 'Be quiet! Daddy's resting! You wait until I tell Daddy of this! Daddy will be cross when he gets home!', the mother was to reveal 'other and truer aspects of fatherhood: "Let's save it for Daddy. Now we must stop and get Daddy's tea. He'll be hungry when he gets home. Let's ask Daddy to mend it. We'll ask Daddy what we'd better do. He'll know." A consistent attitude of this kind will allay the child's anxiety before it gets too strong, and make him eager to find a place for his father in the family circle.' She added the caveat that unless he did accept his father, 'with all his rights', he would 'carry with him to the end of his life the tags of this infantile jealousy and fear. Freud indeed went so far as to see in such a failure (which he termed the Oedipus complex) a central feature in all neurosis'.

Warming to her theme in later editions, Hostler advised fathers to take part in the physical handling of the baby from the very beginning, so he was promoted from laundry-boy to 'a second being whose stronger hands bathe and change baby occasionally, and whose deeper voice soothes him'. Her model family remained, however, the traditional one of neat and tidy mum at home, and strong clever father ranging freely at home and abroad. Consider this advice:

> He will develop a whole series of special games, of hunting and fighting and rough and tumble, peculiar to him and which satisfy the need of the child to be aggressive just as the quieter games he plays with his mother satisfy his other needs. He will enlist his aid in the delightful messy jobs which fall his lot, watering the garden, washing the car, clearing out the woodshed, and in these activities experience the constant companionship the mother knows so well when the child follows her about the house.
>
> Later, father and children can go off alone on expeditions that only daddies can deal with competently, visits to the science museum, the railway station, or the new building site.

Hostler's advice was a defence against Freud. More modern writers—inspired by sociologists who recommended 'a three-person model, including two adults of the opposite sex' as 'more efficient for socialization than the two-person mother-child model' (Bronfenbrenner), as well as by the women's movement—have been far more thorough-going in their attitudes. Brazelton included single fathers as well as single mothers among his categories of parent in *Toddlers and Parents*, although his earlier book remained *Infants and Mothers*. The Consumers' Guide *Caring for Your Child* shows fathers changing nappies, women doctors and girls in baseball suits in its attempt to correct a sexist bias. Too often, however, the easy way out—a family togetherness picture on the cover of the *Reader's Digest Mothercare Book*, for example—cloaked an unchanged Hostler-like attitude to family life. Leach unrepentantly ignored fathers, leaving them out of the index of *Babyhood*, and without a reference on the 'developmental map' of infancy. Her mother and baby existed in a hall of mirrors.

The shift in emphasis from Freud to Piaget has made it easier for fathers to enjoy parenting. Threats of murder from a small son can be reinterpreted as the magical world of the two year old rather than as being in deadly earnest. They need no longer feel alarmed and guilty if they admire the charming line of their tiny daughter's naked hips. Instead, they can read about and promote her cognitive growth with all the enthusiasm of the turn-of-the-century 'scientific educators'. Just as anal fixations are acquiring the cachet of the rare breed because of relaxed approaches to potty training, so Oedipus and Electra can fade away as fathers return to the nest.

Worrying about one's baby did not start in 1950. Mrs Panton analysed 'that blue feeling' very accurately back in 1896; autobiographies and novels clearly described the shock that responsibility could bring to the less confident parent. In an earlier age of uncertainty, the nanny provided a convenient method of solving the problem until it solved itself. She was also a crucial companion for the mother. In Elizabeth Cambridge's pre-war novel, *Hostages to Fortune*, the heroine grows to appreciate her unwanted daughter through the competent offices of the nurse who handles 'sossy pusskins' with such confidence. Formal routines allowed no time for guilt and anxiety. Earlier manuals did not examine the concept of the depressed mother at all. Perhaps they were insensitive to her—perhaps she was less depressed.

From the 1950s onwards a definite difference in the degree and quality of anxiety took place. 'Four-day blues' were invented, and glibly set down to hormonal changes—although according to Martin Richards they do not seem to be suffered in many non-industrial countries. They are much more common among mothers who have their babies in the strange institutional world of the hospital. By junking grannies and trusting to the experts, as Jolly recommends, mothers have lost an essential sheet anchor to their cultural traditions. The queues of clinically depressed mothers in doctors' surgeries testify to the failure of book-learnt motherhood.

Spock, for example, assumed self-doubt from the start. 'You know more than you think you do,' was his opening sentence, and shortly afterwards he added 'parental doubts are normal'. His sections dealing with depression in mothers have lengthened with every new edition. 'Nagging anxieties can undermine parents' enjoyment of their babies,' warned Brazelton. 'Baby books tell her how to be the perfect mother ... The different advice she receives may conflict so thoroughly that she is left in a serious quandary. When she cannot follow this advice, she feels confused and guilty.'

Not only does the wide range of advice at any one time confuse parents, but they also have the uneasy feeling that the next edition of an important maternal crutch like Spock or Jolly will be 'completely revised in the light of new research' and reveal that everything they have done so far has been wrong. New books on baby-care, in order to be really new, leapfrog over each other in a race to be different, to give new interpretations of old behaviour, to classify once and for all the normal. Parents quake on the brink of a huge quagmire of research, wondering what 'new facts' will explode the current theories.

The reasons offered for post-natal depression (not the immediate blues after birth, but the more or less serious form identified in mothers during their children's babyhood) are very diverse. Lack of adjustment after leaving a job, isolation from the community, physical fatigue due to broken nights, the 'helplessly complicated guilt feelings' of working mothers, poor mothering in one's own childhood, are all pointed to in turn. The huge sales of books of advice on baby-care reflect these anxieties, although few manuals succeed in alleviating them. Many arguably add to them.

Standard advice given to the depressed mother is to take a break from the baby for a while. Local authorities often put babies into care to alleviate a fraught mother–child situation, because they have to consider the safety of the child. Baby-battering is a subject which has left pathology and entered the indexes of Spock, Jolly and the rest. It is carefully 'understood'; if not acceptable, it is forgivable. 'You probably need a break from the baby,' declared the Illingworths in their 1977 edition—professional help should be sought. Jolly explained that the first few weeks were often 'filled with despair and exhaustion rather than the contented elation mothers, and fathers, are supposed to feel'. This was because the mother was expecting too much of herself and her baby—she had to accept that life had changed, that she 'can't do as much looking after of husband and home and other interests'. Her best hope was to give in and devote herself to the baby. A depressed mother should go right away from the baby—if she felt like hitting it she should put it into its cot, make a cup of tea, and go out of the house more often.

The manuals struggle ineffectually to deal with maternal depression. Attempts at explanation cannot be cures, and the occasional night out is hardly likely to be adequate for a mother who feels the whole shape of her culture is wrong. The most useful offering on the subject is the type of comment made by Richards in *Infancy*. This is not really a manual of advice; it is a record of the present conclusions of research into child development, and is careful to emphasize the tentative nature of its 'facts'. He criticizes the 'Madonna and Child idealization' which conventional approaches to motherhood have encouraged (only since the Second World War, one might add). His advice to the depressed parent is to talk about it with 'their co-parent or anyone else they trust'. The Boston Women's Collective has a similar point-of-view, and the effect of books like Ann Oakley's *From Here to Maternity* is the reassuring one of seeming to be sitting across a room listening to the experiences of other mothers.

It felt right to end this survey of how mothers have been told to bring up their babies by considering post-natal depression, since the mood of modern mothers is as accurately reflected by depression as that of their eighteenth-century counterparts was by the optimism of Rousseau's 'We know not what nature allows us to be.' Hundreds of experts are now at great pains to tell us exactly what nature allows us to be, and the prospect is bleak.

It would be unfair not to admit that there are healthy signs of a reaction away from doctrine. *Miriam Stoppard's Book of Baby Care*, Leach's *Baby and Child* and Brazelton's *Infants and Mothers*, and *Toddlers and Parents* try to approach the subject differently, to describe rather than proscribe. Leach claims: 'I am not laying down rules, I am not telling you what to do. I am passing on to you a complex and to me entrancing folklore of babyhood which, once upon a time, you might have had from your own extended family.' Nevertheless a close examination of her folklore reduces it to a peculiarly modern collection of approaches. If Brazelton emphasizes the differences rather than the similarities among the families that he uses to push his points home, he still has some very definite views of the rights and wrongs of family life.

Parents probably can't do without baby-care manuals of one sort or another – if only to look up the symptoms of measles in. But I hope that reading about the enormous range of advice and opinion which has been offered to parents in the last two centuries will scotch a few myths. Firstly, techniques of handling children do not seem to have made the steady progress towards improvement that historians of childhood suggest. Nor does there seem to be any agreement on what constitutes ideal children. Is it the independent, problem-solving child of the behaviourists, the sensitive intellectual wrapped up in its mother favoured by the more modern developmental psychologists, or the sling-bound uncomplaining baby spectating with interest on the adult world around it? Finally, the manuals are clearly by no means infallible authorities. We must keep them where they belong – as tools, not tyrants, symptoms of the indecisiveness of our age, not certainties. No one has yet produced the elusive blueprint for a perfect child. Confident in this, perhaps we can bring up our children in the way that feels right, that fits in with our own life-style and values, instead of 'by the book'.

Bibliography

I have tried to make this bibliography as useful as possible to people interested in reading more about the history of baby-care by including my background reading, as well as books specifically referred to in the text. Other books which contain good bibliographies are Lloyd de Mause, *History of Childhood*, Daniel Beekman, *The Mechanical Baby* and Bernard Wishy, *The Child and the Republic*.

Abbott, Jacob, *Gentle Measures in the Management and Training of the Young*, Harper, New York, 1872.
—— *Rollo at Work, Rollo at Play*, 1840; Dent Everyman edn, London, 1909.
Abbott, J. S. C., *The Mother at Home, or the Principles of Maternal Duty*, Religious Text Society, London, 1830.
Abt, Isaac Arthur, *The Baby's Food*, Saunders, Phil., 1917.
Acland, Mrs Arthur, *Child Training*, Sidgwick & Jackson, London, 1914.
Acland, Eleanor, *Goodbye for the Present, the Story of Two Childhoods: Milly, 1878, and Ellen, 1913–24*, Hodder & Stoughton, London, 1935.
Adams, Grace, *Your Child is Normal: the Psychology of Young Childhood*, Covici, Friede, New York, 1935.
Adler, Alfred, *The Education of Children*, trans. E. and F. Jensen, Allen & Unwin, London and New York, 1930.
—— *Guiding the Child on the Principles of Individual Psychology*, trans. B. Ginzberg, Allen & Unwin, London and New York, 1930.
—— *The Neurotic Constitution*, trans. B. Ghreck, Kegan Paul, London, 1921.
—— *What Life Should Mean to You*, Allen & Unwin, London and New York, 1932.
Adler, Felix, *The Moral Instruction of Children*, Appleton, New York; Arnold, London, 1892.
Alcott, Amos Bronson, *Observations on the Principles and Methods of Infant Instruction*, Carter & Hendree, Boston, 1830.

Bibliography

Alcott, William Andrus, *The Young Mother*, G. W. Light, Boston, 1836.

Aldrich, Charles Anderson, and Mary M., *Babies Are Human Beings*, Macmillan, New York, 1938; English edn, *Understand Your Baby*, Black, London, 1939.

Allbutt, Henry Arthur, *Every Mother's Handbook*, Simpkins, London, 1897.

—— *The Wife's Handbook, with Hints on the Management of Babies*, 2nd edn, Ramsey, London, 1886.

Ambron, Susann Robinson, *Child Development*, Holt Rinehart, New York, 1975.

Ansell, C., *On the Rates of Mortality at Early Periods of Life, and Other Statistics of Families in the Upper and Professional Classes*, National Life Assurance Company, London, 1874.

Arbuthnot, John, *An Essay Concerning the Nature of Ailments*, Jonson, London, 1731.

Aries, Philippe, *Centuries of Childhood*, trans. R. Baldick, Cape, London, 1962.

Armstrong, George, *An Account of the Diseases Most Incident to Children*, T. Caddell, London, 1767.

—— *A General Account of the Dispensary for the Relief of the Infant Poor, Instituted by Dr George Armstrong*, London, 1772.

Armstrong, John, *Young Woman's Guide to Virtue, Economy and Happiness*, 6th edn, Mackenzie & Dent, Newcastle upon Tyne, 1825.

Ashby, Henry, *Health in the Nursery*, Longman, London, 1898; new edn, 1912.

Asquith, Cynthia, *The Child at Home*, Nisbet, London, 1923. Plagiarizes Mrs Frankenburg severely.

Astruc, Jean, *General and Complete Treatise on all Diseases Incident to Children from Birth to Age 15, with Particular Instructions to Tender Mothers, Prudent Midwives and Careful Nurses*, English edn, Nourse, London, 1746.

Babies and How to Take Care of Them, anon., Ward Lock, London, 1879. Cambridge University Library.

Badinter, Elisabeth, *The Myth of Motherhood*, trans. Roger Legris, Souvenir Press, London; Centaur, New York, 1982. Limited historically, but some good insights.

Baldwin, Bird T., and Strecker, Lorle I., *Psychology of the Pre-School Child*, Appleton, New York and London, 1925.

Bibliography

Balint, Alice, *Psychoanalysis of the Nursery*, trans. from Hungarian, Routledge, London, 1953.

Ballexserd, Jacques, *Dissertation sur l'éducation physique des enfants, depuis leur naissance jusqu'à l'âge de puberté*, Paris, 1762.

Ballin, Ada, *From Cradle to School, a Book for Mothers*, Constable, London, 1902.

Banks, John, *A Rebuke to Unfaithful Parents and a Rod for Stubborn Children*, 2nd edn, T. Soule, London, 1749.

Banks, Joseph Ambrose, *Prosperity and Parenthood: a Study of Family Planning among the Victorian Middle Classes*, Routledge, London, 1954.

—— and Olive, *Feminism and Family Planning*, Liverpool University Press, 1964.

Barnett, Thomas Ratcliffe, *The Finest Baby in the World: Letters from a Man to Himself about His Child*, Oliphant, London, 1904.

Baruch, Dorothy, *New Ways in Discipline: You and Your Child Today*, Whittleston, New York, 1949.

—— *You, Your Children and War*, Appleton, New York, 1942.

Barwell, Louisa Mary, *Infant Treatment under Two Years of Age*, Chambers, Edinburgh, 1840; Gihon, Phil., 1850.

—— *Nursery Government: Hints Addressed to Mothers and Nursery-maids on the Management of Young Children*, Chapman & Hall, London, 1836.

Batten, L. W., *The Single-handed Mother*, Allen & Unwin, London, 1939.

Bauer, William Waldo, *Stop Annoying Your Children*, Bobbs Merrill, Indianapolis, 1947.

Beecher, Catherine Esther, *Woman's Profession as Mother and Educator, with Views in Opposition to Women's Suffrage*, Maclean, Phil. and Boston, 1872.

—— and Stowe, Harriet Elizabeth Beecher, *The American Woman's Home*, Ford, New York, 1869.

Beekman, Daniel, *The Mechanical Baby*, Dobson, London, 1979. A useful pioneer work in the history of baby-care manuals, with a good bibliography.

Beeton, Isabella, *Household Management*, Ward Lock, London, successive edns from 1861 to 1960.

Behn, Aphra, *Ten Pleasures of Marriage*, 1682; ed. Job Harvey, Navarre Society, London, 1922.

Bibliography

Bell, Robert, *Our Children, and How to Keep Them Well and Treat Them when They are Ill*, Bryce, Glasgow, 1887.

Bennett, Victoria, and Isaacs, Susan, *Health and Education in the Nursery*, Routledge, London, 1931.

Benson, Arthur Christopher, and Viscount Esher, *The Letters of Queen Victoria, 1831–64*, vol. 1, John Murray, London, 1907.

Bettelheim, Bruno, *Children of the Dream*, Thames & Hudson, London, 1969.

Biedert, Philippe, *Die Kindermahrung im sanglingsalter*, Stuttgart, 1880.

Blackwell, Elizabeth, *Counsel to Parents on the Moral Education of Children*, Hirst Simyth, London, 1878.

—— *How to Keep a Household in Health*, Ladies' Sanitary Association, London, 1870.

Boas, George, *The Cult of Childhood*, Warburg Institute, London, 1966. An art historian's approach through portraits and literature.

Bodin, Margaret A., *Piaget*, Harvester, London, 1979.

Boston Women's Collective, *Our Bodies, Ourselves*, Simon & Schuster, New York, 1976.

—— *Ourselves and Our Children*, Simon & Schuster, New York, 1978.

Bottome, Phyllis, *Alfred Adler, Apostle of Freedom*, Faber, London, 1939.

Bowdich, E. W., *Confidential Chats with Mothers on the Healthy Rearing of Children*, Baillière, London, 1890.

Bowlby, John, *Child Care and the Growth of Love*, Penguin, Harmondsworth, 1953.

—— *Maternal Care and Mental Health*, WHO, Geneva, 1952.

Bowley, Agatha Hilliam, *Natural Development of the Child*, Livingstone, Edinburgh, 1942.

Boyd, William, *The History of Western Education*, Black, London, 1921.

Brady, Margaret, *Child's Health and Happiness*, Health for All, London, 1948.

Braidwood, Peter Murray, *The Domestic Management of Children*, Smith Elder, London, 1874.

Branca, Patricia, *Silent Sisterhood*, Croom Helm, London, 1975.

—— *Women in Europe since 1750*, Croom Helm, London, 1978.

Bibliography

Brazelton, T. Berry, *Infants and Mothers: Differences in Development*, Delacorte, New York, 1969.

—— *Toddlers and Parents*, Delacorte, New York, 1974.

Bremner, Robert Hamlett (ed.), *Childhood and Youth in America, a Documentary History*, 5 vols, Harvard Press, Cambridge, Mass., 1970 on.

Brereton, Ethel C., *The Happy Nursery*, Williams & Norgate, London, 1927.

Bretherton, Ralph Harold, *The Child Mind*, a novel, John Lane, London, 1903.

Briffault, Robert, *The Mothers*, 1927; abr. G. R. Taylor, Allen & Unwin, London, 1959.

Briggs, Dorothy Corkhill, *Your Child's Self-esteem: the Key to His Life*, Doubleday, New York, 1970.

Brigham, Amariah, *Remarks on the Influence of Mental Cultivation and Mental Excitement on Health*, 2nd edn, Marsh, Capen & Lyon, Boston, 1833.

Brockbank, Edward Mansfield, *Children, Their Care and Management*, Hodder & Stoughton, London, 1912.

Bronfenbrenner, Urie, *Two Worlds of Childhood, US and USSR*, Russell Sage Foundation, New York, 1970.

Broom, Beatrice Mary, *Happy Infant Management*, Hutchinson, London, 1944.

Brouzet, N., *Essai sur l'éducation médicinale des enfants, et sur leurs maladies*, 2 vols, Paris, 1754; English trans., 1755.

Buchan, William, *Advice to Mothers on the Subject of their own Health and on the Means of Promoting the Health, Strength and Beauty of their Offspring*, Cadell & Davis, London, 1803; US edn, 1812.

—— *Domestic Medicine*, Balfour, Auld & Smellie, Edinburgh, 1769; 26th edn, 1830; trans. French, 1788.

—— *Offices and Duties of a Mother*, London, 1800.

Budin, P., *The Nursling*, trans. W. J. Maloney, Caxton, London, 1907.

Buffon, Le Clerc, Georges Louis, Comte de, *Histoire naturelle, générale et particulière*, 15 tomes, Paris, 1749–67; added to, until 44 vols by 1803.

Bull, Thomas, *Hints to Mothers*, Longman, London, 1837; 14th edn, 1877.

—— *Maternal Management of Children in Health and Disease*, Longman, London, 1840; 8th edn, 1877.

Burger, Lisbeth, *Other People's Babies: Leaves from a Midwife's Diary*, Constable, London, 1934.

Burke, Coralie Evelyn, *Child Study and Education*, Browne & Nolan, Dublin, 1908.

Burns, Jabez, *Mothers of the Wise and Good, with Select Essays on Maternal Duties and Influence*, Houlston & Stoneman, London, 1846.

Burrell, Kathleen Joan (pseudonym of Margaret Alleyne), *The Little Foxes*, London, c. 1900.

Bushnell, Horace, *Views on Christian Nurture*, Edwin Hunt, Hartford, Conn., 1848.

Buxbaum, Edith, *Your Child Makes Sense, a Guidebook for Parents*, foreword by Anna Freud, English edn, Allen & Unwin, London, 1951.

Cable, Mary, *The Little Darlings, a History of Childrearing in the US*, Scribner, New York, 1975.

Cadogan, William, *Essay on the Nursing and Management of Children*, John Knapton, London, 1748.

Caird, Mona, *Fortnightly Review*, 1890 (quoted in Banks, J. A. and O., q.v.).

Calhoun, A. W., *Social History of the American Family*, 3 vols, A. H. Clark, Cleveland, US, 1917–19.

Calverton, Victor-Francis, and Schmalhausen, Samuel Daniel (eds), *New Generation: the Intimate Problems of Parents and Their Children*, Allen & Unwin, London and New York, 1930.

Cambridge, Elizabeth, *Hostages to Fortune*, Cape, London, 1933.

Cameron, Hector Charles, *The Nervous Child*, 4th edn, Oxford University Press, 1930.

Campbell, Helen, *Practical Motherhood*, Longman, London, 1910.

Canfield, Dorothy, *The Homemaker*, a novel, Cape, London, 1924.

—— (Fisher) *A Montessori Mother*, Holt, NY, 1913.

—— *Mothers and Children*, Constable, London, 1915.

Cassell's Book of the Household, Cassell, London, 1890.

Cautley, Edmund, *Natural and Artificial Methods of Feeding Infants and Young Children*, J. and A. Churchill, London, 1897.

Chaloner, Leonore Maude (Len), *Enjoy Your Baby*, Ward Lock, London, 1957.

—— *Modern Babies and Nurseries*, Oxford University Press, 1929.

Bibliography

—— *Mothers' Encyclopaedia*, Allen & Unwin, London and New York, 1936.

Chavasse, Pye Henry, *Advice to Mothers*, Longman, London, 1839; 21st edn, much revised, 1939; 1st US edn, 1862; last edn, 1948.

—— *Counsel to Mothers*, Churchill, London, 1869; 6th edn, 1890.

Cheadle, W. B., *On the Principles and Exact Conditions to be Observed in the Artificial Feeding of Infants*, Smith & Elder, London, 1887; 6th edn, 1906.

Child, Lydia Maria, *The Mother's Book*, 2nd edn, Carter & Hendree, Boston, 1831.

Child, Mrs, *The Family Nurse*, Rich, Bentley, London, 1837.

Child's Best Instructor in Spelling and Reading, anon., pub. Edward Duly, 1757. Cambridge University Library.

Child's Grammar, Designed to Enable Ladies Who May not Have Attended to the Subject Themselves to Instruct their Children, London, 1799. Cambridge University Library.

Church, Joseph, *Understanding Your Child from Birth to Three*, Random House, New York, 1973.

Cleveland, Elizabeth, *Training the Toddler*, Lippincott, Phil., 1925.

Close, Sylvia, *The Knowhow of Breast Feeding*, J. Wright, Bristol, 1972.

Cobb, John, *Babyshock, a Mother's First Five Years*, Hutchinson, London, 1980.

Cobbett, William, *Advice to Young Men and Incidentally Young Women ... on How To Be a Father*, published by the author, Andover, 1829.

Cohen, David, *J. B. Watson, The Founder of Behaviourism*, Routledge & Kegan Paul, London, 1979.

Collins, R., *A Practical Treatise on Midwifery*, Longman, London, 1835.

Combe, Andrew, *Principles of Physiology Applied to the Preservation of Health, and to the Improvement of Physical and Mental Education*, Black, Edinburgh, 1834.

—— *Treatise on the Physiological and Moral Management of Infancy*, Maclachlan, Edinburgh, 1840; Philadelphia, 1840; 11th edn, 1890.

Combe, George, *The Constitution of Man*, Anderson, Edinburgh, 1828.

—— *Life and Correspondence of Andrew Combe M.D.*, McLachlan & Stewart, Edinburgh, 1850.

301

Complete Servant, c. 1820. London Library.

Conquest, Dr John Ticker, *Letters to a Mother on the Management of Herself and Her Children in Health and Disease ... with Remarks upon Chloroform*, new edn, Longman, London, 1848.

Conyers, Richard, *Disputatio Medica Inauguralis de Morbis Infantum*, Lugduni Batavorum, 1729.

Coveney, Peter, *Poor Monkey: the Child in Literature*, Rockcliff, London, 1957. Freud-ridden, but illuminating.

Cox, Catherine, *Early Mental Traits of 300 Geniuses*, Stanford University Press, US; Harrap, London, 1926.

Crellin, John Keith, *Medical Ceramics*, Wellcome Institute, London, 1969.

Crump, Lucy, *Nursery Life 300 Years Ago: the Story of a Dauphin of France, 1601–10*, Routledge, London, 1929.

Cunnington, Cecil Willett, *Feminine Attitudes in the Nineteenth Century*, Heinemann, London and Toronto, 1935.

—— *Nursery Notes for Mothers*, Baillière, London, 1913.

Cunnington, Phyllis, and Buck, Anne Mary, *Children's Costume in England, Fourteenth to Nineteenth Century*, Black, London, 1965.

Cuthbert, Anne, *Housewife's Baby Book*, Hulton, London, 1948.

Darton, Frederick Joseph Harvey (ed.), *Life and Times of Mrs Sherwood*, Wells Gardner, London, 1910.

Darwall, John, *Plain Instructions for the Management of Infants, with Practical Observations on the Disorders of Children*, Whittaker, London, 1830.

Darwin, Charles Robert, 'Biographical Sketch of an Infant', *Mind*, no. 7, 1877.

Davidson, Hugh Stevenson, *Marriage and Motherhood*, Jack, London, 1912.

Davies, John Dunn, *Phrenology, Fad and Science*, Yale University Press, 1955.

Davies, Margaret Llewellyn (ed.), *Maternity, Letters from Working Women*, L. and V. Woolf, London, 1915; reprinted Virago, London, 1978.

Davin, Anna, 'Imperialism and Motherhood', *History Workshop*, 5, Spring 1978.

Davis, Adelle, *Let's Have Healthy Children*, Harcourt Brace, New York, 1951.

Davis, Clara, 'Self-selected Feeding', *Ohio State Medical Journal*, vol. 34, no. 8, Aug 1938.

Day, Thomas, *The History of Sandford and Merton, a Work*

Bibliography

Intended for the Use of Children, Stockday, London, 1783–9.

Defoe, Daniel, *The Family Instructor*, Eman Mathews, London, 1715.

Dendy, Walter C., *Book of the Nursery*, Whittaker, London, 1833.

Dobson, James C., *Dare to Discipline*, Tynedale House, Ill., 1970.

Dodson, Fitzhugh, *How to Parent*, Nash, Los Angeles, 1970.

Doman, Glenn, *Teach Your Baby Maths*, Cape, London, 1979.

—— *Teach Your Baby to Read*, Cape, London, 1965.

Donaldson, Margaret, *Children's Minds*, Collins, Glasgow, 1978. Post-Piaget thinking for the up to date.

Donovan, Frank, *Raising Your Children: What Behaviourist Scientists Have Discovered*, Crowell, New York, 1968.

Downman, Hugh, *Infancy, or the Management of Children: A Didactic Poem*, 1774–6; 7th edn, London, 1809.

Drake, T. G. H., 'American Infant Feeding Bottles as Disclosed by U.S. Patent Specifications, 1841–1946', *Journal of the History of Medicine and Allied Sciences*, III, no. 2, 507–24.

—— 'Infant Feeding in England and France from 1750 to 1800', *American Journal of Diseases of Childhood*, 39, 1930.

—— 'Pap and Panada', *Annals of Medical History*, new ser., 3/209, 1931.

—— 'The Wet Nurse in Eighteenth-century France', *Bulletin of the History of Medicine*, 1940.

Dreikurs, Rudolf, and Soltz, Vicki, *Children, the Challenge*, Duell, New York, 1964; English title, *Happy Children*, Fontana, London, 1972.

Drever, James, and Drummond, Margaret, *Psychology of the Preschool Child*, Partridge, London, 1929.

Drummond, Margaret, *The Dawn of Mind, an Introduction to Child Psychology*, Arnold, London, 1918.

Drummond, William B., *The Child: His Nature and Nurture*, Dent, London, 1901.

—— *Introduction to Child Study*, Arnold, London, 1907.

Dunbar, Flanders, *Your Child's Mind and Body*, Random House, New York, 1949.

Dunn, Courtenay, *Natural History of the Child*, Sampson Low, Edinburgh, 1919.

Dwight, Theodore, *The Father's Book*, Springfield, Mass., 1834.

Earle, A. M., *Child Life in Early Colonial Days*, Macmillan, New York, 1899.

Bibliography

Earle, John, *Micro-cosmographie*, Stansby, London, 1628.

Eberle, John, *Treatise on the Diseases and Physical Education of Children*, 3rd edn, Phil., 1841.

Edge, Patricia, *Training the Toddler*, Faber, London, 1944.

Edgeworth, Maria, *Moral Tales for Young People*, Johnson, London, 1801.

—— and Richard Lovell, *Essays on Practical Education*, Johnson, London, 1789; 2nd US edn, 1815.

Elias, E., *Enjoy Your Baby*, Faber, London, 1945.

Eliot, Martha, *Infant Care*, US Dept of Labour, Children's Bureau, Washington D.C., 1929.

Ellis, Florence M. Hatton, *Record of a Child's Life*, Simpkin, Marshall & Co., London, 1902.

Ellis, Sarah, *The Mothers of England, Their Influence and Responsibility*, London, 1843.

Elwes, Hervey, *The Modern Child: an Anthology in Verse and Prose*, Foulis, Edinburgh and London, 1908.

Encyclopaedia Britannica, 1st edn, 'Nursing'.

English Matron, (anon.), London, 1846.

Erasmus, Desiderius, *Christian Marriage*, 1526.

Erikson, Erik, *Childhood and Society*, Norton, New York, 1950.

—— *Toys and Reasons*, Norton, New York, 1977.

Ettmuller, M., *Etmullerus Abridged*, 2nd edn, London, 1703.

Eysenck, Hans Jurgen, *Uses and Abuses of Psychology*, Penguin, Harmondsworth, 1953.

Faegre, Marion, *Infant Care*, US Dept of Labour, Children's Bureau, Washington D.C., 1951.

Farjeon, Eleanor, *Nursery in the Nineties*, Gollancz, London, 1935.

Female Instructor and Young Wife's Companion (anon.—Hugh Smith?), Fisher, Liverpool, 1811.

Fennings, Alfred, *Every Mother's Book, or the Child's Best Doctor*, London, 1856. Cambridge University Library.

Fielding, Sarah, *The Governess, or Little Female Academy*, 1749; Oxford University Press reprint, 1968.

Foley, Winifred, *Child in the Forest*, BBC, London, 1974.

Forbush, William Byron, *Character Training of Children*, Funk & Wagnalls, New York and London, 1911.

Forsyth, D., 'History of Infant Feeding from Elizabethan Times', *Proceedings of the Royal Society of Medicine*, 4, 1911.

Fraiberg, Selma, *The Magic Years: Understanding and Handling the Problems of Early Childhood*, Scribner, New York, 1959.

Bibliography

Frankenburg, Charis Ursula, *Common Sense in the Nursery*, Cape, London, 1922; later edns 1934, 1954.

—— *Not Old, Madam, Vintage*, autobiography, Galaxy, Lavenham, 1975.

Freely, Maureen, *Mother's Helper*, Cape, London, 1980.

Fremantle, Anne (ed.), *The Wynne Diaries: Harriet Wynne, 1789–1828*, Oxford University Press, 1940.

Freud, Anna, *Psychoanalysis for Teachers and Parents*, Emerson, New York, 1935.

Freud, Sigmund, *Standard Works*, ed. James Strachey, vol. 7, *Infant Sexuality*, vol. 10, *Little Hans*, Hogarth, London, 1953–5.

Friday, Nancy, *My Mother, Myself, the Daughter's Search for Identity*, Delacorte, New York, 1977. To sort out any remaining hang-ups with granny.

Froebel, Friedrich Wilhelm August, *Education of Man*, 1826; reprinted Appleton, New York, 1891.

Fyfe, Hamilton, 'About Toys', *Good Words*, Dec. 1862.

Gairdner, D., 'Fate of the Foreskin', *British Medical Journal*, I, 1949. Circumcision—swings in fashion for and against.

Galton, Francis, *Eugenics, Its Definition, Scope and Aims*, Sociological Society of London, 1905.

—— *Hereditary Genius*, London, 1869.

—— *Inquiries into the Human Faculty*, Macmillan, London, 1883.

Gardner, Mary, *Nursery Management*, Eveleigh Nash, London, 1914.

Garrison, F. H., 'History of Pediatrics', in Isaac A. Abt (ed.), *Pediatrics*, vol. I, Saunders, Phil. and London, 1923.

Gaskell, Elizabeth Cleghorn, *My Diary*, privately printed, 1923. Fifty pages of day-to-day motherhood—exceptionally good reading.

Gathorne-Hardy, Jonathan, *Rise and Fall of the British Nanny*, Hodder, London, 1972.

Genlis, Stephanie Felicité Brulart de, *Adele and Theodore, Letters on Education*, Paris, 1782; Cadell, London, 1783.

Gentleman's Magazine, 'Some Causes of Infant Mortality in Children under Two', probably by W. Cadogan, 1765.

Gesell, Arnold, *The Guidance of Mental Growth in Infant and Child*, Macmillan, New York, 1930.

——, Ames, Louise, and Ilg, Frances, *The Child from Five to Ten*, Harper, New York, 1946.

—— and Ilg, Frances, *Infant and Child in the Culture of Today*,

Bibliography

Hamish Hamilton, London and New York, 1943.

—— et al, *The First Five Years of Life*, Harper, New York, 1940.

Gibbens, John, *Care of Young Babies*, Churchill, London, 1940.

Gibbs, Mary, *Years of the Nannies*, Hutchinson, London, 1960.

Gillis, John R., *Youth and History: Tradition and Change in European Age Relations, 1770 to the Present*, Academy Press, New York, 1974.

Gilman, Charlotte Perkins, *The Home, its Work and Influence*, McClure, New York; Heinemann, London, 1904.

Glaxo Baby Book, The, Joseph Nathan, London, 1908, 14th edn, 1921.

Glover, E., *Freud or Jung*, Allen & Unwin, London, 1950.

Godfrey, Elizabeth, *English Children in the Olden Times*, Methuen, London, 1907.

Godfrey, F. M., *Child Portraiture from Bellini to Cézanne*, Studio, London and New York, 1956.

Godwin, William, *The Enquirer: Reflections on Education, Manners and Literature*, London, 1797.

Goldblom, Alton, 'Evolution of the Concepts of Infant Feeding', *Archives of the Diseases of Childhood*, May 1954.

Good Housekeeping Baby Book, National Magazine Company, London, 1944–56.

Good Housekeeping's Mothercraft, Waverley, London, 1959.

Goodeve, H. H., *Hints on the General Management of Children in India*, Thacker, London, and Calcutta, 1844.

Goodrich, S. G., *Fireside Education*, Colman, New York, 1838; London, 1839.

Gordon, H. L., *The Modern Mother: a Guide to Girlhood, Motherhood and Infancy*, T. Werner Laurie, London, 1909.

Gordon, Thomas B., *Parent Effectiveness Training*, Wyden, New York, 1970; British title, *How To Be an Effective Parent*, Collins, London, 1973.

Graham, Harvery (pseudonym of I. H. Flack), *Eternal Eve*, Hutchinson, London, 1960.

Grant, Elizabeth, *Memoirs of a Highland Lady, 1797–1827*, Murray, London, 1898.

Green, J. A. (ed.), *Educational Ideas of Pestalozzi*, University Tutorial Press, London, 1905.

Greven, Philip J., Jr (ed.), *Child-rearing Concepts, 1628–1861*, Peacock, Itasca, Ill., 1973.

Grossmith, George and Weedon, *Diary of a Nobody*, Simpkin, London, 1892.

Guillemeaux, J., *De la Nourriture et gouvernement des enfants dès le commencement de leur naissance*, Buon, Paris, 1609.

Gull, Katherine Fernandes, *From Two to Seven*, University of London Press, 1948.

Hadfield, J. A., *Childhood and Adolescence*, Penguin, Harmondsworth, 1962, 1967.

Haight, Gordon S., *Mrs Sigourney, the Sweet Singer of Hartford*, Yale University Press, 1930.

Hall, Granville Stanley, *Aspects of Child Life and Education*, Ginn & Co., Boston, 1907.

Ham, Elizabeth, *Elizabeth Ham, by Herself, 1783–1820*, ed. Eric Gillett, Faber, London, 1945.

Hampshire, Jack, *Prams, Mailcarts and Bassinets*, Midas, Tonbridge, 1980.

Handlin, Oscar and Mary, *Facing Life: Youth and the Family in American History*, Little, Brown & Co., Boston, 1971.

Hannas, Linda, *The English Jigsaw Puzzle, 1760–1890*, Weyland, London, 1972.

Hanway, Jonas, *Earnest Appeal for Mercy to the Children of the Poor*, London, 1766.

Hardy, E. J., *Five Talents of Women*, London, 1888.

Hare, E. H., 'Masturbational Insanity: the History of an Ideal', *Journal of Mental Science*, 108, 1962.

Harker, Lizzie Allen, *A Romance of the Nursery*, John Lane, London and New York, 1903.

Harland, Marion, *Common Sense in the Nursery*, Morison, Glasgow, 1886.

Harrison, Elizabeth, *Study of Child Nature*, Kindergarten Training School, Chicago, 1891.

Hart, Beatrix Tudor and Landau, Ergy, *Play and Toys in the Nursery Years*, Country Life, 1938; Routledge, London, and Viking, New York, 1945.

Hartley, C. Gasquoine, *Mother and Son*, Eveleigh Nash & Co., London, 1923.

Hearth and Home, by a Quiet Woman, London, 1875.

Bibliography

Hearth and Home, or Men as They Are and Women as They Ought To Be, London, 1862.

Heberden, W., *Epitome of Infantile Diseases*, Lackinton, London, 1805.

Herbert, Martin, *Problems of Childhood*, Pan, London, 1975.

Hewer, Annie, M. *Baby of Today*, J. Wright, Bristol, 1921; 8th edn, 1945.

—— *Our Baby*, J. Wright, Bristol, 1891; 23rd edn, 1941.

Hewitt, Margaret, *Wives and Mothers in Victorian Industry*, Rockcliff, London, 1958.

—— and Pinchbeck, Ivy, *Children in English Society*, 2 vols, Routledge, London, 1969–73.

Higginson, Thomas Wentworth, *Common Sense about Women*, Bell, London, 1882.

Himes, Norman Edwin, *The National History of Contraception*, National Committee on Maternal Health, US, 1936.

Hoare, Louisa, *Hints for Improvement of Early Education and Nursery Discipline*, Salem, Mass., reprint of 5th London edn, 1829.

Hodgson, Helen, *Mrs Blossom on Babies*, Scientific Press, London, 1909.

Hogan, Louise, *Study of a Child*, New York, 1898.

Holt, Luther Emmett, *Care and Feeding of Children*, Appleton, New York, 1894; 24th edn, 1943.

—— *Diseases of Infancy and Childhood*, Appleton, New York, 1900; 6th edn, 1911.

—— *The Happy Baby*, Dodd, New York, 1924.

Holt, Luther Emmett, Jr, *Good Housekeeping Book of Baby and Child Care*, Appleton Century, New York, 1954.

—— and Duffus, Robert, *Luther Emmett Holt, Pioneer of a Children's Century*, Appleton Century, New York, 1940.

Holyoake, Austin, *Large or Small Families: On Which Side Lies the Balance of Comfort?*, London, 1870.

Home Discipline, by a Mother, Bath, 1841.

Horney, Karen, *Self-analysis*, Kegan Paul, London, 1942. For mothers who want to get to know themselves.

Hostler, Phyllis, *The Child's World*, Benn, London, 1953, 1965.

Hudson, Dorothy B., *Modern Parenthood*, Pearson, London, 1959.

Hughes, Mary Vivian, *A London Family, 1870–1900*, Oxford University Press, 1950.

Bibliography

Humphrey, Heman, *Domestic Education*, Amherst Adams, New York, 1840.

—— 'Restraining and Governing Children's Appetites and Passions', *Mothers' Magazine*, VIII, 6, 121–30.

Hunt, David, *Parents and Children in History: the Psychology of Family Life in Early Modern France*, Basic Books, New York, 1970.

Hurlock, Elizabeth B., *Child Growth and Development*, McGraw-Hill, New York, 1949, 1956.

Hurlock, Joseph, *Treatise on the Breeding of Teeth in Children*, Rivington, London, 1742.

Hutchison, Alice M., *The Child and His Problems*, Williams Norgate, London, 1925.

Hyde, Mary, *The Thrales of Streatham Park*, Harvard University Press, 1977. Hester Thrale's *Family Book*, full of personality and guilt-free maternity.

Ideas and Beliefs of the Victorians, Sylvan Press, London, 1949. Symposium of radio talks.

Illich, Ivan, *Medical Nemesis: the Expropriation of Health*, Calder/Boyars, London, 1975. For those who want to continue the theme of state interference.

Illingworth, Ronald Stanley and Cynthia Mary, *Babies and Young Children*, Churchill, London, 1954, and later edns.

—— *Lessons from Childhood: Some Aspects of the Early Life of Unusual Men and Women*, Livingstone, Edinburgh and London, 1966.

Isaacs, Susan, *The Behaviour of Young Children*, 2 vols, Routledge, London, 1930, 1933.

—— *The First Two Years*, University of London education pamphlet, 1937.

—— *The Nursery Years: the Mind of the Child from Birth to Six*, Routledge, London, 1929.

Jacobi, Abraham, 'Address', *American Medicine*, VIII, 1904, 795–805.

—— *Infant Hygiene*, Gerhardt, New York, 1877.

Jaeger, Gustav, *Rational Clothing Reform for Men, Women and Children*, Waterlow, London, 1889.

Jex-Blake, Sophia, *The Care of Infants, a Manual for Mothers and Nurses*, Macmillan, London, 1884.

Johnson, Walter, *Domestic Management of Children in Health and*

Bibliography

Disease on Hydropathic and Homeopathic Principles, London, 1857.

Jolly, Hugh, *Common Sense about Babies and Children*, Times, London, 1973.

—— *Book of Child Care*, Allen & Unwin, London, 1975, and subsequent edns.

Josselyn, Irene, *Psychosocial Development of Children*, Family Service Assoc. of America, New York, 1948.

Jung, Carl Gustav, 'Experiences Concerning the Psychic Life of the Child', in *Collected Papers on Analytical Psychology*, Baillière, London, 1916.

Kagan, Jerome, and others, *Infancy, and its Place in Human Development*, Harvard University Press, Cambridge, Mass., and London, 1978.

Kennedy, D. A., *The Child from Two to Five*, Faber, London, 1946.

Key, Ellen Karolina Sofia, *Century of the Child*, Putnam, New York and London, 1909.

—— *Renaissance of Motherhood*, Putnam, New York and London, 1914.

Kiefer, Monica, *American Children through Their Books, 1700–1835*, University of Pennsylvania Press; Oxford University Press, 1948.

King, Sir Frederick Truby, *The Expectant Mother, and Baby's First Months*, New Zealand, 1921; Macmillan, London, 1924.

—— *Feeding and Care of Baby*, New Zealand, 1913; later edns to 1945.

King, Lester S., *The Medical World of the Eighteenth Century*, Chicago, 1958.

King, Mary Truby, *Mothercraft*, Whitcomb & Tombs, Melbourne, 1934; 7th edn, 1939.

—— *Truby King, the Man: a Biography*, Allen & Unwin, London, 1948.

King-Hall, Magdalen, *Story of the Nursery*, Routledge, London, 1958.

Kitzinger, Sheila, *Experience of Childbirth*, Gollancz, London, 1962; Penguin, Harmondsworth, 1967.

Kok, Winifred de, *You and Your Child*, Cassell, London, 1955.

Kugelmass, I. Newton, *Growing Superior Children*, Appleton, New York, 1935.

Kuhn, Anne L., *Mother's Role in Childhood Education: New*

310

England Concepts, 1830–60, Yale, 1947. An excellent book, of more general interest than its title suggests.

Ladourie, Emmanuel Le Roy, *Montaillou*, trans. Barbara Bray, Scolar Press, London, 1978. For a twelfth-century angle: with plenty of caring in evidence.

Laing, R. D., *Conversations with Children*, Penguin, Harmondsworth, 1978.

—— and Esterson, A., *Sanity, Madness and the Family*, Tavistock, London, 1964.

Langer, W. L., 'Infanticide', *History of Childhood Quarterly*, I, 1974.

Laslett, Peter, and Wall, Richard, *Household and Family in Past Time*, Cambridge University Press, 1972.

Leach, Penelope, *Baby and Child*, Michael Joseph, London, 1977.

—— *Babyhood*, Penguin, Harmondsworth, 1974.

Levy, Juliette de Baïracli, *Natural Rearing of Children*, Faber & Faber, London, 1970.

Lewis, Min, and Haskell, Arnold, *Infantilia, Archaeology of the Nursery*, Dobson, London, 1971.

Liddiard, Mabel, *Mothercraft Manual*, Churchill, London, 1924; 6th edn, 1954.

Linton, E. L., *'The Girl of the Period', and Other Social Essays Reprinted from the 'Saturday Review'*, Bentley, London, 1883.

Lochhead, Marion Cleland, *Their First Ten Years—Victorian Childhood*, Murray, London, 1956.

Locke, John, *Essay Concerning Human Understanding*, Basset, London, 1690.

—— *Some Thoughts Concerning Education*, Churchill, London, 1693.

Lynd, Robert Staughton, and Merrell, Helen, *Middletown: a Study in Contemporary American Culture*, Harcourt Brace, New York, 1929.

Lynd, Sylvia, *English Children*, Collins, Glasgow, 1942.

McCleary, G. F., *The Maternity and Child Welfare Movement*, King, London, 1935.

McCoy, Raymond F., *A Critical Examination of the Ladies' Library and Inquiry into its Authorship*, University of Cincinnati MA thesis, 1935.

Macmillan, Margaret, *Early Childhood*, Sonnenschein, London, 1900.

Mahler, Margaret S., Pine, Fred, and Bergman, Anni, *The Psychological Birth of the Human Infant: Symbiosis and Individuation*, Hutchinson, London, 1975.

Maier, Henry W., *Three Theories of Child Development: Erikson, Piaget and Sears*, Harper, New York, 1965.

Mann, Mrs Horace, *Christianity in the Kitchen, a Physiological Cookbook*, Boston, 1861.

—— *Moral Culture of Infancy and Kindergarten Guide*, Boston, 1863.

March, Norah H., *Towards Racial Health: a Handbook on the Training of Boys and Girls*, Routledge, London, 1915.

Mare, Walter de la, *Early One Morning: Anthology of Early Memories*, Faber, London, 1949.

Marenholtz-Bulow, Baroness, *The Child and Child-nature*, Swann-Sonnenschein, London, 1893.

Martin, Ruth, *Before the Baby and After*, Hurst Blackett, London, 1958.

Martineau, Harriet, *Feats on the Fjords*, 1841; Everyman edn, Dent, London, 1910.

—— *Household Education*, London and New York, 1849.

—— *Society in America*, Saunders & Otley, New York and London, 1837.

Masefield, John, *The Street Today*, Dent, London, 1911.

Mason, Charlotte, *Home Education*, Kegan Paul & Trench, London, 1886; rev. edn, 1905.

Mause, Lloyd de, *History of Childhood*, Souvenir, London, 1978. A collection of papers by different authors—many useful bibliographies.

Maynard, Edith, *Baby: Useful Hints for Busy Mothers*, Wright, Bristol, 1906.

Mayor, Flora MacDonald, *The Third Mrs Symons*, Sidgwick & Jackson, London, 1913.

Mead, Margaret, *Coming of Age in Samoa*, Cape, London, 1929; Penguin reprint, 1943.

—— and Wolfenstein, Martha, *Childhood in Contemporary Cultures*, University of Chicago Press, 1955.

Mears, Martha, *Pupil of Nature; or Candid Advice to the Fair Sex on the Subjects of Pregnancy and Childbirth*, London, 1797.

Medley, Anne, *Your First Baby*, Faber, London, 1943.

Meynell, Alice, *The Children*, John Lane, London and New York, 1897. Beautiful thoughts on babies.

Bibliography

Miller, H. Crichton, *The New Psychology and the Parent*, Jarrolds, London, 1922.

Millet Robinet, Cora Elizabeth, *Conseil aux jeunes femmes sur leur condition et leurs devoirs de mère*, 2 vols, Paris, 1862.

Mintern, L., and Lambert, W., *Mothers of Six Cultures*, Wiley, New York, 1964.

Mitchell, B. R., and Deane, Phyllis, *Abstract of British Historical Statistics*, Cambridge University Press, 1971, and suppts.

Mitchison, Naomi, *Small Talk: Memoirs of an Edwardian Childhood*, Bodley Head, London, 1973.

Montaigne, Michel de, *Essays*, vol. II, no. 8, trans. Florio, 1603; Dent, London, 1928.

Montessori, Maria, *The Montessori Method*, trans. A. George, Stokes, New York, 1912.

—— *Secret of Childhood*, trans. B. B. Carter, Longman, London, 1936.

Montgomery, Fanny, *Early Influences*, Rivington, London, 1883.

Moore, George, *Training of Young Children on Christian and Natural Principles*, London, 1872.

More, Hannah, *Coelebs in Search of a Wife: Comprehending Observations on Domestic Habits and Manners, Religion and Morals*, Cadell, London, 1808–9.

—— *Hints towards Forming the Character of a Young Princess*, Cadell, London, 1805.

Morten, Honnor, *Child Nurture*, Mills & Boon, London, 1911.

—— *The Nursery Nurse's Companion*, Mills & Boon, London, 1910.

Moss, William, *Essay on the Management of Children*, London, 1781.

Motherhood Book, The, Amalgamated Press, London, 1934.

Mother's Oracle for the Health and Proper Rearing of Infants, London, 1833.

Muffet, Thomas, *Health's Improvement*, 1584; London, 1655.

Mulock, Diana Maria, *A Woman's Thoughts about Women*, Bungay, London, 1858.

Murphy, Sir Shirley Foster, *Our Homes, and How to Make Them Healthy*, Cassell, London, 1883.

Murray, F. B. (ed.), *Impact of Piagetian Theory*, Park Press, New York, 1979.

Musgrove, F., 'Decline of the Educative Family', *Universities' Quarterly*, 14, 377–404.

—— *Youth and the Social Order*, Routledge, London, 1965.

Bibliography

Neff, Wanda Fraiken, *Victorian Working Women, 1832–50*, Allen & Unwin, London, 1929.

Neill, Alexander Sutherland, *The Problem Child*, Jenkins, London, 1926.

—— *The Problem Parent*, Jenkins, London, 1932.

Nelson, James, *Essay on the Government of Children under Three Heads, viz, Health, Manners and Education*, Dodsley, London, 1753.

New System of Practical Domestic Economy, anon., London, 1824. Cambridge University Library.

Newman, G., *Infant Mortality, a Social Problem*, New Library of Medicine, London, 1906.

—— *Special Report on an Infant Milk Depot Established in Finsbury*, Finsbury Borough Council, London, 1905.

Newsom, John and Elizabeth, *Infant Care in an Urban Community*, Allen & Unwin, London, 1963.

Noyes, Anne B., *How I Kept My Baby Well*, Warrick & York, Baltimore, 1913.

Nurse's Guide, anon., 1729. Cambridge University Library.

Oakley, Ann, *From Here to Maternity*, Allen Lane, Harmondsworth, 1974.

Oates, R. K., 'Infant Feeding Practices', *British Medical Journal*, 2, 1973, 762–4.

Odenwald, Robert P., *Your Child's World: Practical Guidance for Catholic Parents*, Hale, London, 1958.

Our Children—How to Train and Rear Them, anon., London, 1874. Cambridge University Library.

Page, Hilary, *Playtime in the First Five Years*, Allen & Unwin, London, 1953.

Pantin, Evelyn, *Motherhood Book*, Thomson, London, 1932.

Panton, Jane Ellen, *From Kitchen to Garret*, 4th edn, Ward Downey, London, 1888.

—— *The Way They Should Go*, Ward Downey, London, 1896.

Parkes, Mrs William, *Domestic Duties—Instructions to Young Married Ladies*, Longman, London, 1825.

Pascal, Jacques, *Règlement pour les enfants*, Appendix to the Institutes of Port Royal, Paris, 1721.

Pechey, John, *General Treatise on the Diseases of Infants*, R. Wellington, London, 1697.

Pelagius Porcupinious, *Scandalizade*, London, 1750.

Bibliography

Pepler, Hilary Douglas Clark, *His Majesty: a Pamphlet on the Treatment of Children in Infancy*, Headley Bros, London, 1906.

Pepper, W., 'The Medical Side of Benjamin Franklin', *University of Pennsylvania Medical Bulletin*, 23, 1910.

Perez, Bernard, *The First Three Years of Childhood*, trans. from French by A. M. Christie, Sonnenschein & Co., London, 1885.

Pestalozzi, J. H., *How Gertrude Teaches her Children*, 1801, trans. Lucy Holland and Frances Turner, Swann-Sonnenschein, London, 1900.

Phelps, Almira, 'Observations on an Infant', 1833 (appendix to Saussure, q.v.).

Philp, Robert Kemp, *Practical Housewife*, London, 1855.

Piaget, Jean, *The Child's Construction of Reality*, trans. Margaret Cook, Routledge Kegan Paul, London, 1955.

—— *The Moral Judgement of the Child*, trans. Marjorie Gabain, Kegan Paul, London, 1932.

—— *The Origin of Intelligence*, trans. Margaret Cook, Routledge Kegan Paul, London, 1953.

Pink, Cyril V., *Foundations of Motherhood*, Cassell, London, 1930. My mother's bible.

Plaisted, Laura L., *Early Education of Children*, Oxford University Press, 1909.

Playfair, William Smoult, *Treatise on the Science and Practice of Midwifery*, Smith Elder, London, 1876.

Plumb, J. H., 'New World of Children in Eighteenth-century England', *Past and Present*, 67, 1975, 64–95.

—— 'The Great Change in Children', *Horizon*, XIII, Winter 1971.

Post, Emily, *Children are People and Ideal Parents are Comrades*, Funk & Wagnalls, New York, 1947.

Potts, Willis John, *Your Wonderful Baby*, Rand McNally, New York, 1966.

Powdermaker, Florence, and Grimes, Louise Ireland, *The Intelligent Parents' Manual* (US title: *Children in the Family*), Allen Lane, London and New York, 1944.

Preyer, Wilhelm, *The Mind of the Child*, trans. from German by H. W. Brown, Appleton, New York, 1893.

Pringle, Mia Kellmer, *The Needs of Children*, Hutchinson, London, 1975.

Pritchard, Eric Law, *Infant Education*, Marylebone Health Society, London, 1907.

Bibliography

—— *Physiological Feeding of Infants: a Practical Handbook and Key to the Physiological Nursery Chart*, 2nd edn, Kimpton, London, 1904.

Pryor, Karen, *Nursing Your Baby*, Harper & Row, New York, 1963.

Pulaski, Mary Ann, *Your Baby's Mind and How it Grows: Piaget for Parents*, Harper & Row, New York, 1978; Cassell, London, 1979.

Quillet, Claude, *Callipaediae*, trans. anon., John Morphen, London, 1710.

Raverat, Gwendolen, *Period Piece: a Cambridge Childhood*, Faber, London, 1952.

Read, Mary, *Mothercraft Manual*, Little, Brown, Boston, 1916.

Reader's Digest Mothercare Book, London, 1978.

Rendle-Short, John, 'Infant Management in the Eighteenth Century with Special Reference to the Work of William Cadogan', *Bulletin of the History of Medicine*, vol. XXXIV, no. 2, March/April 1960.

Rendle-Short, Morwenna and John, *Father of Childcare: Life of William Cadogan, and Facsimile Edition of the 1748 Essay on Nursing*, Bristol, 1966.

Reynolds, M. M., *Children from Seed to Saplings*, McGraw-Hill, New York and London, 1939.

Ribble, Margaret, *Rights of Infants*, Oxford University Press, 1943.

Richards, Martin, *Infancy: World of the Newborn*, Harper & Row, New York, 1980.

Richmond, Ennis, *Mind of a Child*, Longman, London and Cambridge, Mass., 1901.

Richter, Jean-Paul Friedrich, *Levana, or the Doctrine of Education*, 1814; trans. from German, Longman, London, 1848; and, by S. Wood, Swann-Sonnenschein, London, 1887.

Rodgers, Betsy, *Cloak of Charity: Studies in Eighteenth-century Philanthropy*, Methuen, London, 1949.

Roe, Frederic Gordon, *The Georgian Child*, Phoenix, London, 1961.

Ronge, Johann and Bertha, *Practical Guide to the English Kindergarten . . . an Exposition of Froebel's System of Infant Training*, 5th edn, Swann-Sonnenschein, London, 1873.

Rosenstein, Nicolas Rosen von, *The Diseases of Children and Their Remedies*, 1752; trans. from Swedish by A. Sparrman, London, 1776.

Rousseau, Jean Jacques, *Emile, ou l'éducation*, Amsterdam, 1762; trans. into English, pub. T. Bechet, London, 1762.

Routh, Charles Henry Felix, *Infant Feeding and Its Influence on Life*, Churchill, London, 1860.

Ruhrah, John, *Pediatrics of the Past*, Hoebner, New York, 1925.

Rusk, Robert Robinson, *History of Infant Education*, London University Press, 1933.

Ruskin, John, *Praeterita: Outlines of Scenes and Thoughts Perhaps Worthy of Memory in My Past Life*, Allen, Orpington, 1885.

Russell, Bertrand Arthur William, *On Education, Especially in Early Childhood*, Allen & Unwin, London, 1926.

Sadler, S. H., *The Bothers of Married Life*, Swann-Sonnenschein, London, 1903.

—— *Infant Feeding by Artificial Means*, Scientific Press, London, 1896. Riveting engravings of goats and asses feeding babies.

—— *Suggestions to Mothers*, London, c. 1890.

St Aubyn, Gwen, *Family Book*, intro. by Harold Nicolson, Barker, London, 1935.

St Pierre, Jacques Bernardin Henri de, *Paul et Virginie*, Lausanne, 1788; trans. H. M. Williams, Bailey, London, 1800.

Sainte Marthe, Scevole de, *Paedotrophia, a Didactic Poem*, c. 1585; trans. H. Tytler, Nichols, London, 1797.

Saleeby, Caleb, *Parenthood and Race Culture*, Cassell, London, 1909.

—— *Woman and Womanhood*, Heinemann, London, 1912.

Salk, Lee, *What Every Child Would Like His Parent to Know*, McKay, New York, 1972.

—— and Kramer, Rita, *How to Raise a Human Being*, Random House, New York, 1969.

Saussure, Albertine Necker de, *L'Education progressive, ou étude du cours de la vie*, Paris, 1828–32.

—— *Progressive Education, with Notes, Appendix and Translation by Emma Willard and Almira Phelps*, Tichnor, Boston, 1835. The Phelps appendix is a good example of a child-study mother in action.

Sayers, Dorothy, *Even the Parrot: Exemplary Conversations for Enlightened Children*, Gollanz, London, 1944. Not very relevant to the story, but very good fun.

Scharlatt, Elisabeth (ed.), *Kids, Day In, Day Out*, Fireside, New York, 1979.

Scharlieb, Mary, *Health and Sickness in the Nursery*, Williams & Norgate, London, 1926.

Bibliography

—— *Hopes of the Future: the Management of Childhood in Health and Disease*, Chapman & Hall, London, 1916.

—— *Maternity and Infancy*, Williams & Norgate, London, 1926.

—— *Psychology of Childhood*, Constable, London, 1927.

Schirsch, Anita, *Images of Childhood*, Main Street, New York, 1979.

Schweinitz, K. de, *How a Baby is Born: What Every Child Should Know*, Routledge, London, 1931; 14th edn, 1956.

Sears, Robert Richardson, Macoby, Eleanor, and Levin, Hans, *Patterns of Childrearing*, Row Peterson, Evanston, Ill., 1957.

Sévigné, Marie, Marchioness de, *Letters to Her Daughter*, 1726; trans. from French, London, 1727.

Sewell, Samuel J., 'The History of the Perambulator', *Journal of Royal Society of Arts*, Sept 1923.

Sharp, Jane, *The Midwives' Book: Directing Childbearing Women How to Behave Themselves in Their Conception, Breeding . . . and Nursing of Children*, with plates, London, 1671.

Sherbon, Florence Brown, *The Child: His Origin, Development and Care*, McGraw-Hill euthenics series, New York and London, 1934.

Sherwood, Mrs, *History of the Fairchild Family, or the Child's Manual: Being a Collection of Stories Calculated to Show the Importance and Effects of a Religious Education*, Hatchard, London, 1818–47.

Shinn, Millicent Washburn, 'Notes on the Development of a Child', *University of California Studies*, vol. 1, Berkeley, 1893; reprinted 1909.

Shorter, Edward, *Making of the Modern Family*, Basic Books, New York, 1975; Fontana, London, 1977.

Sigourney, Lydia H., *Letters to Mothers*, Hudson & Skinner, Hartford, Conn., 1838.

Simon, Rosemary, *Your Child and You*, Sphere, London, 1969.

Sinclair, Catherine, *Holiday House*, 1839; Hamish Hamilton, London, 1972.

Sitwell, Osbert, *Left Hand, Right Hand*, Little Brown Co., Boston, 1944.

Skinner, Burrhus Frederic, *Walden Two*, Macmillan, New York, 1948.

Smellie, William, *A Treatise on the Theory and Practice of Midwifery*, D. Wilson, London, 1752.

Smiles, Samuel, *Character*, John Murray, London, 1871.

——*Physical Education, or the Nurture and Management of Children*, Edinburgh, 1838.

Smith, Elinor Goulding, *The Complete Book of Absolutely Perfect Baby and Child Care*, Harcourt, Brace, New York, 1957. Excellent spoof of contemporary theory.

Smith, Hugh, *Letters to Married Women*, London, 1767; six English edns, and trans. into French and Dutch.

Smyth, Charles, 'The Evangelicals at Home', in *Ideas and Beliefs* (q.v.).

Spencer, Herbert, *Education, Intellectual, Moral and Physical*, London, 1861.

Spock, Benjamin, *Common Sense Book of Baby and Child Care*, Duell Sloan, New York, 1946; rev. edns 1957, 1968, 1979; London, 1956, 1969.

——*Problems of Parents*, Houghton Mifflin, Boston, 1962.

——*Raising Children in a Difficult Time*, Norton, New York, 1974.

Spon's Household Manual, Spon, London, 1887.

Stanway, Penny and Andrew, *Breast is Best*, Pan, London, 1978.

Stendler, C. B., 'Sixty Years of Child Training Practices', *Journal of Pediatrics*, 36, 122–36.

Stern, Bernard Joseph (ed.), *The Family, Past and Present*, Washington Progressive Education Assocn, New York and London, 1938.

Sterne, Laurence, *Tristram Shandy*, Dodley, London, 1760–67. Eighteenth-century babyhood briefly sketched in the early chapters of the novel.

Stewart, William A. C., and MacCann, William P., *The Educational Innovators*, Macmillan, London; St Martin's Press, New York, 1967.

Still, G. F., *History of Pediatrics*, Milford, London, 1931.

Stone, Lawrence, *Family, Sex and Marriage in England*, Cambridge University Press, 1977.

Stopes, Marie Charlotte Carmichael, *Your Baby's First Year*, Putnam, London, 1939.

Stoppard, Miriam, *Miriam Stoppard's Book of Baby Care*, Weidenfeld & Nicolson, London, 1977.

Strecher, Edward A., *Their Mothers' Sons*, Lippincott, New York, 1946.

Struve, Charles Augustus, *A Familiar Treatise on the Physical Education of Children*, trans. A. F. M. Willich, Murray & Highley, London, 1701.

Sully, James, *Studies of Childhood*, Longman, London, 1895.

Sylvia's Family Management, a Book of Thrift and Cottage Economy, Ward Lock, London, 1886.

Tansillo, Luigi, *The Nurse, a Poem*, 1550; trans. from Italian W. Roscoe, London, 1798.

Taylor, Ann and Jane, *Original Poems*, London, 1805.

—— *Practical Hints to a Young Female on the Duties of a Wife, a Mother and the Mistress of a Family*, London, 1815.

Taylor, Gordon Rattray, *The Angel-makers: Psychological Origins of Historical Change, 1750–1850*, Heinemann, London, 1958. Stimulating, perhaps far-fetched, Freudian interpretation of the subjugation of women.

Taylor, Isaac, *Home Education*, London, 1838.

Thom, Douglas, *Everyday Problems of the Everyday Child*, Appleton, New York, 1927.

Thrale, Hester: see Hyde, Mary.

Tissot, Samuel, *Advice to People in General with Regard to Their Health*, trans. from French, London, 1765; 7th edn, 1801, with preface by John Wesley.

Townsend, John Roe, *Written for Children: an Outline of English Language Children's Literature*, Kestrel, London, 1974.

Trench, Melasina, *Thoughts of a Parent on Education*, London, 1837.

Tytler, Sarah, *Childhood a Hundred Years Ago*, London, 1876.

Underwood, Michael, *Treatise on the Diseases of Children*, London, 1789; 77 edns (probably small ones) by 1819; US edn, 1793, 4th edn, 1842; trans. into French and German.

Unwin, Eileen, *Child Care*, Macmillan, London, 1952, 1973. A handbook for students.

Valentine, Charles Wilfred, *The Normal Child, and Some of His Abnormalities*, Penguin, Harmondsworth, 1956.

—— *Parents and Children*, Methuen, London, 1953.

Vicinus, Martha, *Suffer and Be Still: Women in the Victorian Age*, Indiana University Press, Bloomington, 1972; Methuen, London, 1980.

Vincent, E. E., 'Trends in Infant Care Ideas', *Child Development*, 22, 199–209.

Vincent, Ralph, *Nutrition of the Infant*, Baillière, London, 1904.

Bibliography

Wallace, Marjorie, 'Making a Baby a Genius', *Sunday Times,* colour suppt, 10 May 1981. Article on Glenn Doman's Better Baby Institute in Philadelphia.

Walsh, John Henry, *Manual of Domestic Economy,* Routledge, London, 1857, 1873.

Ward and Lock's Home Book, Ward Lock, London, c. 1880.

Warne's Model Housekeeper, Frederick Warne & Co., London, 1873, 1879.

Warren, Eliza, *How I Managed My Children from Infancy to Marriage,* London, 1865.

—— *How I Managed my Home on £200 a Year,* London, 1864.

Watson, John Broadus, *Behaviourism,* Norton, New York, 1925.

—— *Psychological Care of the Infant and Child,* Allen & Unwin, London and New York, 1928.

Watts, Isaac, *Divine and Moral Songs for the Use of Children,* London, 1715.

Weatherley, Lionel Alexander, *Young Wife's Own Book,* Griffith & Farrer, London, 1882.

Webster, Augusta, *A Housewife's Opinions,* London, 1879. Webster was also a translator of Aeschylus, and parliamentary critic.

West, Mrs Max, *Infant Care,* US Dept of Labour Children's Bureau, Washington DC, 1914.

Wharton, Edith, *The Children,* Appleton, New York, 1928. An excellent novel of the child-study movement in practice.

Whipple, Dorothy, *Our American Babies,* Barrows, New York, 1944.

—— and Crane, Marion, *Infant Care,* US Dept of Labour Children's Bureau, Washington DC, 1942.

White, Charlotte, *Women's Magazines 1693–1968,* Michae. Joseph, London, 1970.

White, Sheldon, and Notkin, Barbara, *Childhood: Pathways of Discovery,* Harper & Row, New York, 1980.

Whiting, Beatrice Blyth (ed.), *Six Cultures: Studies in Child-rearing,* Wiley, New York and London, 1963.

Wickes, Ian G. 'History of Infant Feeding', *Archives of the Diseases of Children,* 28, BMA, London, 1953. The most detailed and useful account of the subject.

Wiggin, Kate Douglas, *Children's Rights, a Book of Nursery Logic,* Houghton, Boston, 1892.

Wilderspin, Samuel, *Early Discipline Illustrated, or the Infant System Progressing and Successful,* London, 1832.

—— *The Infant System, for Developing the Intellectual and Moral Powers of All Children from One to Seven Years of Age*, London, 1834.

Williams, David, *Lectures on Education*, 3 vols, London, 1789.

Winnicott, D. W., *The Child and the Family*, Tavistock, London, 1957.

—— *The Child and the Outside World*, Tavistock, London, 1957.

—— *The Child, the Family and the Outside World*, Penguin, Harmondsworth, 1964.

Winterburn, Florence Hull, *Nursery Ethics*, Merriam, New York, 1895.

Wishy, Bernard, *The Child and the Republic: the Dawn of the Modern American Child Nurture*, University of Pennsylvania Press, 1968. Good nineteenth-century analysis.

Wohl, Antony (ed.), *The Victorian Family: Stresses and Structures*, Croom Helm, London, 1978.

Wolfenstein, Martha: see Mead, Margaret.

Wollstonecraft, Mary, *A Vindication of the Rights of Women*, 1792; Everyman edn, Dent, London, 1932.

Wood, Robert William, *Children, 1770–1890*, Evans, London, 1968.

Wright, Julia McNair, *The Complete Home*, Bradley, Phil., 1879.

Wrigley, E. A., *The Population History of England, 1541–1871: a Reconstruction*, Arnold, London, 1981.

Wrinch, Muriel, *Mothers and Babies*, Jack, London, 1924.

Yonge, Charlotte Mary, *The Daisy Chain, or Aspirations: a Family Chronicle*, Parker, London, 1856.

—— *Womankind*, London, 1876.

Yudkin, Simon, and Holme, Anthea, *Working Mothers and their Children*, Michael Joseph, London, 1963.

Selected Periodicals

Babyland, Baby's Pictorial, British Medical Journal, British Mother Magazine, British Mothers' Journal, Childlife Quarterly, Children's Dressmaker, Englishwoman's Domestic Magazine, Family Economiser, Family Magazine, Gentleman's Magazine, Girl's Own Annual, Girl's Own Paper, History of Childhood Quarterly (later

Journal of Psychohistory), *House and Home, The Household, Journal of Domestic Appliances, Ladies' Home Journal, Ladies' Pictorial, Ladies' Treasury, Lady's Weekly Paper, Lancet, Magazine of Domestic Economy, Medical Times, Mother, Mother and Child, Mother and Home, Mother's Assistant, Mother's Companion, Mother's Friend, Mother's Help and Little Dressmaker, Mother's Magazine, Mother's Medical Adviser, Mother's Treasury, Nineteenth Century, Nursery World, Parents' Magazine, Pedagogical Seminary, Penny Scrap Book, People's Journal, Perambulator Gazette and Nursery Trader, Saturday Review, Sewing Machine and Pram Gazette, Woman and Home, Woman's Home Companion, Woman's Home Journal, Woman's Journal, Woman's Own, Woman's World.*

Index